Playing
Tennis

Win More Matches, Have More Fun,

and Gain a Mental Advantage!

by David Ranney

1208 Newton Street
Bellingham, WA 98229
david@maxtennis.com
www.pureperformancesports.com
www.innerbasketball.com
www.innerbaseball.com
www.maxtennis.com

Also by David Ranney

Playing Zen-Sational Baseball

Becoming a Zen-Sational Basketball Shooter

Tennis: Play the Mental Game

Playing Zen-Sational Tennis

ISBN-13: 978-1490504551

ISBN-10: 1490504559

Cover design by: Roderick C Burton, Bellingham, Wash.
Christopher Burkhardt, Fountain Valley, Calif.

Edited by: Christopher Burkhardt

3

Praise

"After only a few days of owning your book, my tennis game has improved dramatically! I never thought I could experience this big a jump and unlike changing grips, switching racquets, or whatever, this is the kind of change that will be permanent...Although it's kind of nerve wracking to just follow the ball with your eyes all the way to the racquet and just hit it, regardless of whether it goes in or out, this is letting me hit the ball so much deeper and harder than before. Thanks very much."

John

"David's principles will make you a believer in the paradox that by "letting go" you achieve more. Wait until you experience a mind and body that has "let go", is calm, and relaxed; it feels unbelievably fun! You will achieve greater focus, concentration and results on the tennis court."

Carla Lyons, Bellingham, WA

"I love improvement and your ideas have been terrific to that end. I have another disciple in "the fold" as I let him read your book. He has been practicing both "core" foundations; breathing and watching. He has improved also. He is a 50 year old 4.5 player. His wife noticed him mumbling his mantra while studying the "core" and promptly took it away from him and now she is in "the fold" as well. We may have started a groundswell. I even have another friend studying it and his initial reaction was "I'm too old to learn new tricks!" Au contraire!

I am where I can see the ball actually slow after it lands allowing my feeble mind time to relax and execute the shot as opposed to reacting to the initial rate of pace during its' flight. That is interesting to watch. The BIGGEST benefit of all is just keeping all the other SPAM debris or conscious thought from interfering with actual play. It is such a relaxing way to play; mindless."

George Kraft, Seattle, WA

"Working with David and the concepts he sets forth in his book simply made tennis more fun. Like many tennis players, I spent all of my energy working to obtain the perfect stroke. Each time the ball came over the net, I was concerned with having the perfect backswing, the perfect contact point, a strong follow-through. My fixation on the physical aspects of the game always resulted in a negative experience; every time I swung the racket, something went wrong.

When I started working with David, he changed my entire focus. Instead of worrying about the physical details, he taught me to focus my mind in a manner that allows my body to hit the shots I know I have. His teachings provided me the tools necessary to quit worrying about the details of each stroke, and to focus upon the ball and relaxation. David, through his book, teaches to not judge your swing or your shot. Instead, ask what happened and let your body make its own corrections. For me, the immediate positive result is that I was no longer criticizing each and every one of my shots. This made the game more fun.

Playing Zen-Sational Tennis

His teachings are surprisingly simple yet effective -- focus your mind away from the physical production of a stroke so that your body is relaxed and hits the stroke you've learned. His book sets forth very simple and straightforward tools to make sure that your mind stays on task, and stays out of the way of your body.

Yes my game has gotten much better. I'm able to stay in points much longer, stay relaxed in tight matches, and stay focused on the game and not the details of the stroke. But like most of us, that is only part of the goal. I play tennis for fun. After working with David, I've had more fun playing tennis in the last three years that I did in the previous 30.

I would recommend anyone who wants to have fun with tennis (and get better) to read the book and stick with the tools that he provides."

Doug Robertson, owner, Bellingham Tennis Club.
Doug's been playing since age 9 and is now on the other side of 40.

"Thanks Dave!!!! I've put what you taught me into practice and it's made an incredible difference for me. I think it's the biggest revelation I've ever experienced in my 20 some odd years of trying to get better at this game."

Alisa Hashimoto, Seattle, WA

Playing Zen-Sational Tennis

"DAAAAAAAAAAAAAAAAAAAAAAAAAAAAAVE!!!!!

hehe man I love you!!

I played Malta open semi final today and lost first set 6-2. I had your book with me on the court and read about choking and seeing the ball, then BAM! 6-4 6-1 :) Dude I am so happy thank you soooo soooo much.

I have final on Sunday @ 5pm!!!

THANKSSSSSSSSSSSSS ONCE AGAIN!!! YOUR BOOK REALLY HELPED!!!"

Matija Pecotic, Malta

"Let me tell you how pleased I am with your book, I have been working on breathing and watching the spin of the ball and just those two things have cut my unforced errors in half. (I am the queen of errors)."

Phyllis, Sedona, AZ

"I am really enjoying your book and making an attempt to integrate it into my game. I'll let you know how it goes. Thanks for your inspiration."

Joe, Philadelphia, PA

Playing Zen-Sational Tennis

"I own a lot of tennis books, and your book is excellent. I have read some other mental tennis books, but I have a hard time finishing them because of all the boring Psychology terms which make me fall asleep. I love your book because it is written by a tennis player. It is easy understand, and apply.

Thank you."

P.T

"I've really enjoyed reading your book. I have learned so much from you. It definitely shows in my game. I've talked to many of my tennis friends about your concepts and am always recommending your book."

Jennifer

"After much skepticism I purchased your book. Because it is not very expensive, I could afford to take a chance to read about what you teach. As a tennis instructor I am always curious as to what else is going on in the tennis industry to try to keep up with what is going on out there.

I have to say, your book has helped my game immensely. I have never felt IN MY ENTIRE LIFE I have ever played up to my potential. I played one year of college tennis at Lamar University in Beaumont, TX in 1987 - 1988. I got burned out (just very frustrated) and swore I was never going to play again. Long story short, I ended up teaching lessons in 1993 and have been ever since. Now, this is my first experience in teaching tennis and we sometimes would play doubles in our spare time when it was slow. Let me tell you how intimidating that was. I played to other's expectations and have never played up to my potential ever.

After reading your e-book (and I am not done yet) my game has elevated immensely. I have to tell you that I am starting to hit shots that I know that I can make. I should say, I am allowing my body to make the shots that I know it can make. Other people can actually see what I know that my body is capable of doing. I am also not getting angry and letting my conscious mind interfere with my other subconscious mind. I haven't finished your book yet, because I am having so much fun focusing and concentrating on the spin of the ball to the blur of my racket and breathing through the bounce and the hit during rallies and from the serve through the return during those shots as well.

To avoid rambling even more, I am going to simply say, "Thank you!" I am really getting in tune with my body and letting it do what it can do. I also want to say that I have caught myself telling others. bits and pieces of what I have learned from you and making the mistake of telling them that I am finally playing up to my potential. When in fact, I don't know if I have actually reached my potential but I know that I am hitting the ball cleaner and more consistently than I ever have. I may not even know my own potential. I am ptimistically thinking that it is higher than I even thought (and I am not trying to be or sound egotistical). I just don't want to sell myself short.

Thanks again."

Mike Alcott, USPTA Head Tennis Professional, The Briar Club Houston, TX 77027

Playing Zen-Sational Tennis

"It has been almost one year since I met you at the National Indoor's in Seattle last year and took "the little test" with you and bought your book. I have worked continuously for months on the Mental Game and the Core Principles. As you have stated many times - it does take time. And work. And perseverance. However, it's starting to pay off. In June I played in the Intermountain Sectionals and had the "best loss" I can ever remember. Three sets, tie breakers, service breaks back and forth, etc. I lost 7-5 in the third. But I was mentally there all the way. The other guy played a little better that day. A few weeks ago I played down in a 55's tournament in Washington, D.C. and won the tournament. It was all about the mental game. I will go re-read your book again."

David

"I don't know if you remember but I sent a note saying I was ordering your book for my husband for his birthday - well he has read about 6 pages so far and I have been traveling and busy but I have read through lesson 4 so far and have even put your ideas into play and it is so great the way they are working for me!

My husband usually gives me the alleys when we play but last week, I didn't take the alleys and I won 3 out of the 6 games - he commented I was playing great - - - I owe it all to you!!! I used the relaxation method - and breathing - and I am working on seeing the ball - - I have to read the bounce and hit and get that working too - I am so excited! I am going to re-read what I already read plus continue on in the book. I just love it.

Thank you so much - for sharing your wealth of knowledge!"

Dottie

"I am still reading The Inner Game of Tennis by Timothy Gallwey, based on your suggestion. It is very informative as you call it the "Bible of mental tennis".

Just to let you know that I bought 6 mental tennis books at the same time I bought your book, and I found yours is the best among all the others. (I did not pick Timothy's book in the first round.)

Also, I wish to let you know that in the last 40 years, I went through many tennis teachers and books. Even though I have never met you (I appreciate that I did have a chance to talk to you), I regard you as the best teach I have ever known in my life.

Thank you in advance."

Constant

Playing Zen-Sational Tennis

Table of Contents

Foreword 22

Introduction to the Mental Game 24

About David Ranney And The Best Lesson I Ever Received 25

How to Make These Lessons Work for You 29

What You Will Learn When You Read These Lessons 32

Your Psychic Reading 33

Why You Should Play the Mental Game 34

Lesson No. 1: A Discussion Of What The Mental Game Is 35

    What Is The Mental Game Anyway? 36

    My Definition Of The Mental Game 37

    Why I Don't Want You To Try To Win & The Ultimate Goal 39

Lesson No. 2: A Huge Issue That Is Damaging Your Game 42

Lesson No. 3: The Core Principles Of The Mental Game 44

    The Principle of Focus 45

    The Principle of Relaxation 46

    The Principle of Playing Without Judgment 46

    The Mental Game Core Principle Statements 47

Playing Zen-Sational Tennis

The Core Principles 48

Lesson No. 4: You Need To Drill And How To Do It ... 50

Lesson No. 5: How To Drill When No One Will Drill With You 53

Lesson No. 6: See The Ball! Do You Really Know What That Means? 55

The Bounce-Hit Game 62

Lesson No. 7: Drills For Seeing The Ball 64

Drill No. 1: Seeing The Ball 64

Drill No. 12: The Spinning Game 66

Drill No. 11: The Second Generation Bounce-Hit Game 67

Drill No. 13: The Trajectory Drill 70

Lesson No. 8: An Unknown But Powerful Technique When Hitting: Breathing 71

Lesson No. 9: Drills For Working On Your Breathing .. 78

Drill No. 2: Paying Attention To Your Breathing 79

Drill No. 3: Combining Seeing The Ball And Breathing 81

Lesson No. 10: What Is So Important About Relaxation? 81

Lesson No. 11: You Must Play The Short Game 88

Lesson No. 12: The Second Generation Short Game 90

Practicing Ground Strokes 90

13

Practicing Volleys And Half Volleys 92

Lesson No. 13: A Missing Piece Of The Puzzle 95

Lesson No 14: Work On Seeing The Ball In A New Way
.... 98

Lesson No. 15: The Process For Learning Anything
And/Or Fixing Your Errors 101

Lesson No. 16: Classic Tim Gallwey: Body Awareness
Is Very Important 105

Drill No. 4: Feeling And Relaxing Your Strokes ... 105

Lesson No. 17: A Short Review Of What To Do When
You Play Games Or A Match 109

Lesson No. 18: Playing By Instinct 111

Lesson No. 19: How To Know If You Are Playing The
Mental Game Properly 115

Lesson No. 20: The Mother Of All Tips 118

Lesson No. 21: Finish The Follow-through, No Matter
What 122

Lesson No. 22: Focus Your Awareness In Segments
.... 125

Lesson No. 23: Do You Ever Listen To The Ball? 128

Lesson No. 24: Important Things To Do When
Practicing 130

Lesson No. 25: Give Yourself A Lesson Every Time
You Play 132

Lesson No. 26: Secrets Of Winning The Mental Game
And The Steps You Need To Take 135

Playing Zen-Sational Tennis

Lesson No. 27: Stop Getting Nervous Before A Tournament Or Important Match.............................139

Lesson No. 28: Ground Stokes: A Check List Of Things To Practice...141

Lesson No. 29: How To Stop Getting Angry With Yourself..143

Lesson No. 30: Why "Slow" Or "Easy" Balls Are Not Easy..145

Lesson No. 31: Volleys: A Checklist Of Things To Practice..147

Lesson No. 32: What To Do To Prevent Choking.....148

Lesson No. 33: The Power Of Active Visualization...152

Lesson No. 34: Consistency: The First And Last Resort 154

Drill No. 5: A Consistency Drill.............................155

Lesson No. 35: What To Do When You Are Ahead In A Game Or Set..158

Lesson No. 36: Why Pumping Your Fist May Not Work 161

Lesson No. 37: More On Fist Pumping.................164

Lesson No. 38: You Must Change Your Unproductive Thoughts...166

Lesson No. 39: Cause And Results: What Is This All About? 168

Lesson No. 40: When You Don't Play Well.............170

Lesson No. 41: The Three Major Weaknesses And How You Can Exploit Them 171

Lesson No. 42: A Basic Singles Strategy 174

Lesson No. 43: Singles Strategy For Everyone, Including Younger Players 178

Lesson No. 44: The Value Of Playing Tournaments 180

Lesson No. 45: What To Do When You Play A Tiebreaker 182

Lesson No. 46: How Well Are You Doing The Core Principles? 185

Lesson No. 47: What You Might Be Missing When You "See The Ball" 186

Lesson No. 48: Are You Still Working On Your Breathing? 187

Lesson No. 49: What To Do When There Are Visual And/Or Noise Distractions 190

Lesson No. 50: What To Do When You Play Better In Your Warm-Up Than You Do When The Game Starts 191

Lesson No. 51: What To Do When You Miss Shots And How To Fix Them 194

What To Do When The Shot Goes Long 195

What To Do When The Shot Goes Into The Net.. 198

What To Do When The Shot Goes Wide 199

Lesson No. 52: What To Do When Your Whole Game Starts To Go Badly: The One Minute Method 200

Lesson No 53: Why Preprogramming Is As Important As Reprogramming 202

Lesson No. 54: What Do You Do And/Or Think About In Between Points? 206

Lesson No. 55: What To Do When You Hit The Ball Off Center 209

Lesson No. 56: How To Help Your Body Learn To Hit Accurately 211

Lesson No. 57: How To Decide And Then Hit The Ball Where You Want It To Go 214

Lesson No. 58: Why You Should Hit All Serve Returns Cross-court 216

The Return Of Serve When Playing Singles 216

The Return Of Serve When Playing Doubles 220

Lesson No. 59: How To Hit The Return Of Serve Into The Court 222

Practice Your Returns: Method No. 1 223

Practice Your Returns: Method No. 2 224

Hitting A More Consistent Return 225

Lesson No. 60: How To Warm Up For A Match 228

Lesson No. 61: How To Aim The Serve 231

Lesson No. 62: A Checklist If You Are Missing Your Serve 238

Lesson No. 63: Warm Up Your Serve and Return Of Serve This Way 240

Lesson No. 64: Do Not Hit Winners 242

Lesson No. 65: Why You Should Hit Your Overheads As Hard As You Can... 245

Lesson No. 66: How To Hit Running Balls 247

Lesson No. 67: Two Running Drills......................... 249

    Drill No. 6: Running Drill No. 1 250

    Drill No. 7: Running Drill No. 2 251

Lesson No. 68: How To Think About And Deal With Your Weaknesses... 253

Lesson No. 69: How To Determine If Your Opponent's Forehand Or Backhand Is Weaker......................... 255

Lesson No. 70: How To Play At The Top Of Your Game Every Time.. 256

Lesson No. 71: A Basic Doubles Strategy, Version No. 1.. 258

    When You Are At Net 260

    Where To Stand And What To Do When You Are At Net And Your Partner Is Serving......................... 261

    Where To Stand And What To Do When You Are At Net And Your Partner Is Receiving The Serve..... 262

    Where To Stand And What To Do When You Are Serving In The Deuce Court 263

    Where To Stand And What To Do When You Are Serving In The Ad Court 264

    Where To Stand And What To Do When You Are Receiving The Serve In The Deuce Court 264

Playing Zen-Sational Tennis

Where To Stand And What To Do When You Are Receiving In The Ad Court.....................................265

The Basic Rule On Where To Be Positioned When At Net...265

The Three Basic Rules 266

Lesson No. 72: A Basic Doubles Strategy, Version No. 2...267

General Rules For When You Are At Net 271

Lesson No. 73: Breathing Patterns When You Play Doubles...274

Lesson No. 74: Playing In Front Of Crowds..............277

Lesson No. 75: The Difference Between Those Who Play The Mental Game And Those Who Don't? 280

Lesson No. 76: What Is EFT ? 283

Lesson No. 77: What Is A Foundational Place Anyway? 285

Lesson No. 78: Why Losing Is Good 288

Lesson No. 79: What To Do When You Have A Question And Don't Know The Answer....................290

Lesson No. 80: Where To Hit Your Lob And How To Practice It...291

Where To Hit Your Lob 291

How To Practice Your Lob 292

Lesson No. 81: If You Get A Short Ball....................293

Lesson No. 82: Three Special Additions To The Core Principles 295

Lesson No. 83: The Final Bounce 297

Lesson No. 84: Relaxing Between Hits 299

Lesson No. 85: Help! My Conscious Mind Won't Stop Interfering 301

Lesson No. 86: When You Serve A Let Ball On Your First Serve 304

Lesson No. 87: Watch Out For Your Ego Mind 305

Lesson No. 88: Books And Articles To Read 307

About Ron Waite 307

About David Smith 308

Lesson No. 89: A Before and After Match Analysis . 309

Lesson No. 90: Five Things You Absolutely Have To Work On When You Drill 317

Lesson No. 91: This Lesson Is The Last One That You Will Get 321

Mental Game Core Principles Drills 321

Drill No. 1: Seeing The Ball 322

Drill No. 2: Paying Attention To Your Breathing ... 324

Drill No. 3: Combining Seeing The Ball And Breathing 326

Drill No. 4: Feeling And Relaxing Your Strokes ... 326

Drill No. 5: A Consistency Drill 329

Drill No. 6: Running Drill No. 1 331

Drill No. 7: Running Drill No. 2 333

Drill No. 8: Volley Drills 335

Drills for Specific Shots and Other Little Games 336

Drill No. 9: The Return Of Serve Drill....................336

Drill No. 10: The Lob And Overhead Drill.............338

Drill No. 11: The Second Generation Bounce-Hit
Game..340

Drill No. 12: The Spinning Game 343

Drill No. 13: The Trajectory Drill...........................343

Drill No. 14: The Listening Game..........................344

Two Fun Quizzes If You Are Feeling Smart..............345

A Little Quiz 345

Answers to the Little Quiz 347

A Big Quiz..350

Answers to the Big Quiz 351

Foreword

If you are reading this, two things are certain: You are likely serious about your tennis and you believe there is something out there that is going to make you a better tennis player.

This book is it!

During my tennis teaching days, I was often asked; "Ken, can you teach me a forehand, backhand, overhead smash, footwork, etc." I always answered in the affirmative and followed it with, "Oh yeah, I can also teach you how to play tennis because they (your strokes) are not much related to playing the game."

Rarely, if ever, do you have the opportunity to read something that has been written firsthand. This book will make you a better tennis player because the information in it is tried, tested and true. And it comes from a great tennis player in his own right: David Ranney. Dave's experience speaks for itself, and his advice in this book is solid. Here are some questions you can ask yourself to determine the value of the content in this book.

Who has a better forehand, Roger Federer or Andre Agassi?

Who has a better backhand, Lindsay Davenport or Serena Williams?

Who was a better player, Pete Sampras or Rod Laver?

The answer to each of these questions is that it is essentially indistinguishable. The logical conclusion is then that if "strokes" don't make the difference among all these greats then what does? EXACTLY!

It is the mental part of the game that each of these people is commonly great at. You too can become a much, much better player without changing your strokes. The great coach Robert Van't Hof once said; "If you do the right thing at the right time in tennis you are likely going to win." The catch is how do you get there? This book will give you a path to follow. Use it and you'll be miles ahead of people you are equal with now.

You need only to look back at how many countless hours you have put into the development of your strokes. Now you have to spend the same dedication on the mental part of your game. Dave Ranney will guide you through the steps you need to practice to become a much better tennis player.

Ken Stuart, Owner of Palisades Tennis Club, Newport Beach and former world-class player

Introduction to the Mental Game

Hi, my name is David Ranney. Welcome to the exciting world of using your mind to help you play great tennis.

The simple fact is what you are doing now isn't working so well and you are searching for a better way. Am I right?

Are you ready to change? Are you ready to remake your game and become a phenomenal player? If you will do the things you read in these lessons, you will have to improve. Guaranteed. Not only will your tennis game improve but, guess what? You'll probably enjoy playing even more!

So, what is this Zen stuff all about? The word *Zen* is from the Japanese pronunciation of the Chinese word **Chán** which can be approximately translated as "meditation" or "meditative state."

No, you don't have to go to India, Japan or China and sit in a cave to learn to meditate because I will give you everything you need to do and know in this book.

Plus, these lessons will be in simple terms, they will be easy to understand, and for the most part the lessons are very short.

I know a person who is a Zen Buddhist. One day I asked him how he practiced being one. He said he did a lot of meditations and I asked him to give me an example. He said that he would just meditate and listen to all the sounds around him with no thoughts or judgments, but just being aware of them.

Well, guess what? This is what I have you do in many of my lessons, except we are being aware of what is happening not only on the tennis court but also what is going on inside of us that may be interfering with us playing our very best or what is helping us play our very best. And, of course, this is all happening without judgments.

In order to really play the game of tennis to its highest level, we must figure out how to attain a meditative state of mind. In this book, I will give you many things to focus (meditate) on and many ideas as to how you can achieve your goal of playing the best that you are capable of.

This is a process that will never end, but I can promise you that if you will learn to play the way I lay out for you in this book, you will find playing ever so much more fun and rewarding. Not to mention playing much better.

Before I get into these lessons, let me tell you a little about me and how I got started teaching the Mental Game and the best lesson I ever received.

About David Ranney And The Best Lesson I Ever Received

Here is my story about how I got into playing and teaching the Mental Game

- I started playing tournaments when I was 10 years old.

- When I was about 13 I started taking lessons from a teaching pro named Dick Skeen. Dick was a very renowned pro and his big claim to fame was teaching Jack Kramer and my mom who was No. 1 in Orange County for a number of years. Shortly after I started learning from Dick I started to win more matches and tournaments.
- I was ranked No. 2 in Southern California in the 15 & Under. I was ranked No. 2 in Southern California in the 18 & Under.
- I was nationally ranked No. 6 in Singles as a Junior
- I was nationally ranked No. 3 in Doubles as a Junior
- I had the honor of representing the U.S. at Junior Wimbledon where I got to the Semi-finals. I lost to the Russian, which was the last person I wanted to lose to. Can you guess why I maybe didn't play very well? If you don't know, you will know after reading this book. To give you a little hint, it was because I tried way too hard to win.
- I played on the Junior Davis Cup team
- I played on the USC tennis team with Dennis Ralston, Stan Smith and Bob Lutz to name a few and the three years I lettered varsity we were National Champions.

As you can see I was a pretty good player, but not a great one.

But, I had a big problem. My attitude stunk and I was very negative. I used to yell and scream on the tennis court because I would get so incredibly frustrated. I thought that if I could only stroke the ball perfectly I would never miss. But of course, I couldn't do that every time.

Playing Zen-Sational Tennis

My attitude was also horrible. I hated myself for getting so angry and frustrated, but I couldn't stop. I had no idea why I played badly at times or why I played well sometimes, and I didn't have a clue as to how to turn my game around when I wasn't playing well. I never beat players who were just a little better than I was. Remember I told you that I was ranked No. 2 in Southern California in the 15 and 18 and under? Well, a player named Jerry Cromwell was the one who was ranked No. 1 and I never ever beat him, and you can imagine how many times I played him.

After college, I began teaching tennis the traditional way until my conversion to teaching the Inner Game of Tennis when I was in my 30s. What happened was one day I was reading the *LA Magazine* about an instructor who was teaching the *Inner Game of Tennis*. His name was Tim Gallwey.

I knew I had to have a lesson from this man, and I was determined to go to the ends of the earth to find him. As it turned out, he was right there in my hometown of Los Angeles.

To make a long story longer, I took two lessons from Tim, and he completely changed my life. In the first 10 minutes of the first lesson, I felt that the weight of the world was taken off my back. He taught me to relax to the extent that I never got angry or yelled again – an amazing accomplishment since I had already spent all of my tennis life getting upset with my play.

It was the best lesson I ever received and it changed my life forever.

All of a sudden my tennis game was more consistent, and overnight my endurance increased and I wasn't as tense. This shift kept my energy focused on mastering the Mental Game. For the first time, I was beating people I could never beat before. I was winning close matches and striking the ball better than any other time in my life.

My weekly doubles partner, Keith Nielson, said I wasn't as much fun to play anymore because he couldn't get me angry. To sum it all up, I felt like a completely new person when I was on the court.

After just two lessons with Tim Gallwey, he not only completely changed my own tennis game but also gave me a whole new way of teaching. I asked Tim to come to the Jack Kramer Tennis Club, where I was an assistant teaching pro under Robert Lansdorp, so he could give clinics to all of my students. There I watched Tim in action. As a result, I adapted his ideas and modified them slightly to fit my own way of teaching.

I will be forever grateful to Tim Gallwey for showing me how to make this change. His book has been my "Tennis Bible" and is truly one of the best books ever written on the mental aspects of the game. You can find his book in most bookstores.

In the 25-plus years since then, I have been studying the Mental Game so that I could achieve the state of mind that would allow my body to play at its very best. I wanted to know how to play "out of my mind" every time I played. The concepts I will present to you here will show you how to do this.

These concepts, as you will see, are easy to talk about, but it will take a lot of work and practice for you to get there. Or, maybe not.

I knew that these ideas worked for me, but I wasn't sure if they would work for anybody else. Over the years, I have worked with many beginners, average players and good tournament players to see if these techniques could help any player.

I discovered that not only do they work for all ability levels, but you can use them for the rest of your tennis life. I am at an age where my game is supposed to be "over the hill" but my tennis game is actually getting better. Maybe I can't run as well, but if I can get to the ball and hit it, I just don't miss very often.

How to Make These Lessons Work for You

To maximize the benefits of this book, first familiarize yourself with, and if possible, memorize the Mental Game Core Principles (Lesson No. 3). These principles will give you the foundation for every tip, idea, and instruction in this book. I suggest that you keep a copy of these Core Principles with you so that you can read them every time before you play. **Using these Core Principles is an absolute must for tournament play.**

The Lessons in this book are listed in a deliberate order. Even though these lessons are in order of how I believe you should learn them, I would like to encourage you to read through the entire book first.

Reading through the entire book first is extremely important because there are so many important lessons that you will want to know right now. It is also the only way for you to know everything there is to know about playing the Mental Game and give you an idea as to what is in store for you.

29

Then go back and start with Lesson No. 1. It has been suggested that you read and work on about 5 lessons at a time each week. That way you will have gotten through all the lessons in 16 weeks.

Another suggestion is that you read and work with one lesson at a time spending as much time on each lesson for as long as you like until you feel the need to move on.

However, you have my permission to skip to any lesson at any time if you are having a particular problem. Aren't you glad I gave you permission? ☺

Even though you are working through each lesson one or 5 at a time, I would suggest that you re-read the entire book again after 3 months, 6 months, 9 months, and then after 1 year. After 1 year, you should have been able to work through all the lessons. Then I would suggest that you re-read the book once a year.

As you'll see throughout this book, I have bolded some words, phrases, or sentences. Please pay particular attention to these words as they will be critical to your improvement.

I have had many e-mails from people who have read my first book *Tennis: Play the Mental Game* who have said that each time they read through my book, they discover new things they had missed or they have discovered a deeper understanding of what I am saying about playing the Mental Game.

All this being said, you may approach using these lessons any way that feels right for you. The only really important thing is that you read the lessons, implement them into your play and keep working on your Mental Game for as long as you continue playing tennis.

I would suggest that you put this book on your Kindle, Nook, or iPad and that you keep it with you when you go to play.

You can download for free the PDF file of this book if you go to **www.maxtennis.com/new_book_download.php**. Or you can always get the e-book on Amazon.com or at Barnes & Noble for a price.

It would be good to read the lesson you want to work on at home and then again just before you get on the court. That way you will really know and understand the lessons you are working on when you go to play.

In order to really make these lessons work, you must have them pretty much memorized. You can't say to your opponent, "Hold on a minute while I look at the lesson on ….."

There is another thing that you will find when you read through the lessons. I will be repeating myself over and over and over again about the three main concepts that absolutely must be worked on in order to make everything work.

These are seeing the ball, breathing, and relaxing. Please don't get tired of hearing me talk about them. It has been my experience that most of my students do not take these things as seriously as they really are, as they must be done every time you play – and on every shot in order to play the way you want.

These students finally "get it" after constant reminders, and when they do they see how much better they play. I am hoping that you are not one of these and that you not only get it the first time, but are actually able to put these concepts into practice immediately.

One last comment before you get to the lessons. **AS YOU READ LESSON NO. 6 ON SEEING THE BALL, YOU ABSOLUTELY MUST GET THE ANSWER TO MY TEST WHICH TELLS YOU EXACTLY HOW TO SEE THE BALL.** The answer can **ONLY** be found on my website and the web address is ONLY found in Lesson No. 6 on seeing the ball.

What You Will Learn When You Read These Lessons

These series of lessons will spell out very precisely what playing the Mental Game looks like and how you will know if you are doing it right. You are going to learn some very helpful concepts about how to practice your strokes and practice the Mental Game that you won't find anywhere else. These concepts are the result of over 25 years of studying, practicing, and teaching the inner game of tennis.

After you read these lessons one by one and put these principles into play, you will be entering a whole different way of playing that will speed up your learning and help you enjoy the game more.

However, there is a catch. You still have to read each lesson more than once. You also will have to be willing to change the way you think and allow yourself to believe in playing this way. You have to practice it and truly play it. If you only read the lessons, you will not get the improvements you want. You have to apply these techniques as soon as you learn and understand them.

Playing Zen-Sational Tennis

In this book, I won't get into the whole philosophy behind the Mental Game. You can get this information from reading Timothy Gallwey's *The Inner Game of Tennis*. In fact, Gallwey's book is really required reading, as it will give you the background to what I am trying to teach you. In my opinion, the other present-day books on sports psychology pretty much rehash what Tim Gallwey wrote over 30 years ago, only not as eloquently.

But the mental part always comes first, because mastering the mental part of the game so you can play in the zone remains the ultimate goal. However, you also need to work on your strokes, strategies, and drills, in addition to the mental side.

Your Psychic Reading

Did you know I am also a psychic? Well, I am and I am going to give you a reading right now concerning your tennis life.

I am now looking into my crystal ball which will tell all about your tennis game. Just give me a few seconds to get into my trance. Omm-m-m.

I see that you love the game of tennis, but you feel that you are just not playing the best you can. At times (maybe most of the time), you are not enjoying yourself because you are getting more and more frustrated and you just don't know why you are missing so many balls. You are trying so hard to stroke the ball correctly, trying so hard to play well, and trying so hard to win, and you just can't seem to make it happen. You want more from tennis, and so you are searching for a different or better way of playing.

So, how did I do? Do you now believe I am psychic? Please check your mailbox in a couple of days for my $125 invoice for this reading.

Why You Should Play the Mental Game

Here is a list of the reasons why you may want to play the Mental Game. How many do you think apply to you?

- Do you want to win more matches? We will talk about winning in a moment.
- What about so that you can play better?
- What about so that you will play more consistently?
- How about so that you will enjoy playing more?
- Maybe you want to know why you missed a shot and be able to fix things on the spot.
- Maybe you want some real solutions that work so that you won't get angry or frustrated anymore.
- What about improving your strokes much more quickly?

These are some pretty good reasons, don't you think?

Which of these reasons do you think I hear most often once my students start playing the Mental Game? If you guessed "Enjoyment of the game more" you would be correct.

34

I had a friend who I was coaching and she was ready to give up tennis. She was a very good player and was good enough to be ranked nationally in her age division. But she rediscovered her love for the game because she changed the way she thought and the way she played.

I also have some husband and wife students who now sometimes talk for hours about tennis and what is going on with them when they play. Well, maybe not for hours, but they do talk a lot more and are really enjoying their conversations.

Lesson No. 1: A Discussion Of What The Mental Game Is

Welcome and congratulations for taking the first step in mastering the Mental Game of tennis by buying this book! You are about to learn some concepts and techniques that will absolutely improve your tennis bigtime. That is, if you read these lessons and then work on the ideas and skills presented.

OK, it may take some time and nothing substitutes for hitting lots of balls, but you will learn faster and achieve a higher level of skill than using the traditional methods only.

As you may know, I do not get into the actual mechanics of how to stroke the ball. There are so many great coaches out there that can teach you that. Here I will be giving you mental concepts and techniques only. (Some of which will help you stroke the ball better.)

I also want you to know what you can do to "fix" things when you start missing too many shots. You want to be able to make these fixes right now and not wait for the next game or the next 5 games to get back "your groove."

Think of these lessons like you were taking a college course and you had to have a textbook. Then your instructor would have you go through it one lesson at a time and have you actually learn it and do it.

By reading these lessons, I will be guiding you through in the order that I believe makes the most sense. There are no time issues unless you are in a hurry to improve. Just read and do the lessons at your own pace.

Before I get into the actual techniques, I need you to understand exactly what the Mental Game really is and how thinking (or not thinking) about winning fits into the picture.

So you will get two lessons here. One on the Mental Game and one about winning.

Please be sure to read both.

What Is The Mental Game Anyway?

The first order of business is to know what the Mental Game really is. Most people don't really know what it is or how to work on it so to get started I have three questions that you need to ask yourself.

Don't worry if you can't answer all the questions correctly. By the time you finish reading this, you will know all.

- What percentage of the game do you think is mental?
- What percentage of the time that you play and practice do you work on your Mental Game?
- If you were going to work on your Mental Game, what is it and how would you work on it?

Most people say that the Mental Game is anywhere from 75 to 100% and most people answer that even though they feel that the game is this percentage, they don't practice it anywhere close to it if at all.

On the last question, most people don't have a clue or they give me some vague answer about what the Mental Game is.

This last question is the really important one because if you don't know what the Mental Game is, how can you even begin to practice it?

My Definition Of The Mental Game

The Mental Game is the relationship between your "Conscious Mind," your "Other-Than-Conscious Mind," and your body. It is your Conscious Mind which sets the goals then it gets out of the way and lets the Other-Than-Conscious Mind direct the body, which then hits the ball and achieves the ideal play. The strength, direction, and quality of your outer tennis strokes are determined by this inner relationship. When you pursue and find this ideal mental state, you will be playing in the zone.

Playing Zen-Sational Tennis

An example is to be found if you think about how you drive a car. Your Conscious Mind has a huge purpose as it has to see where you are going so that you don't hit any other cars, people, bicycles, etc. It also has to see where the road goes and needs to read the road signs if you need to find a particular street. However, when you steer the car, hopefully you don't think about how you move the steering wheel and I know you don't think about how your foot presses the gas pedal or the brake pedal. You just do it.

Well, playing tennis is no different. It is just more complicated. Because we have been taught that we must control our bodies so that we can hit the ball correctly, you may not have even thought about just letting your body hit the ball without conscious control.

Your Conscious Mind has a role to play but you need to learn how to get it out of the way when it comes to hitting the ball. Please believe me when I tell you, your body is what hits the ball and it knows far better how to do it than the Conscious Mind telling it how.

As a natural by-product, your enjoyment will be enhanced. This is because you will be calmer and more relaxed, and of course, you will be playing better.

Before we get into the jobs of the Conscious Mind and how we figure out how to really let the body play, I want to talk a little about the ultimate goal and winning.

Why I Don't Want You To Try To Win & The Ultimate Goal

Do you think that winning is the ultimate goal? I hope not and if you do, I will try to change your mind.

In the meantime, would you like to learn how to win every time you play?

If this is your ultimate goal, then I have a deal for you. If I can tell you how you can win every time you play, and I can, will you pay me $10,000? No?

OK, maybe winning is not that important so how about paying me only $1,000?

Well, you can save your money because I will tell you how you can win every time anyway, and for free. In order to win every time, you just need to play a 2-year-old. If you can't beat a 2-year-old every time, then you are in really big trouble.

Maybe now you can begin to see that winning may not be a goal that will bring you the most satisfaction or pleasure even though winning can be a lot of fun and is the icing on the cake, especially when you win a close match.

I have another trick question for you and let's see if you can get the answer. I can tell you who has won every match that has ever been played, and I can tell you who will win every match that will be played in the future.

How can I make this statement?

39

Playing Zen-Sational Tennis

Here is the answer: The player who plays better on that given day will be the winner. So, if you play better than your opponent today, you will win. Did you get the answer right?

The point is that winning will take care of itself, and if you strive and learn to play at the top of your game and that "top" is better than your opponent, guess what – you will automatically win. And if you play twice as well as you ever have but still lose the match, most likely you will still be a happy camper. Oops, I meant to say a happy tennis player.

If you don't like how well you played (even though you played at the top of your game), then you need to figure out how you can play better in the future. This means that you will need to practice more of both the physical and the Mental Game.

So, how do you play at the top of your game? By spending more and more time figuring out how to get your Conscious Mind out of the way so your body can play its very best. You will also find that when you practice these concepts, your body will learn faster and more easily. I can't describe to you what this state of being feels like, but I can guide you so that you can begin to discover for yourself what it feels like and how to get there.

Let's get back to the ultimate goal.

I believe the ultimate goal is for you to find out how to play your very best every time you play. This automatically will help you win more matches. This goal not only helps you accomplish the old goal of winning but it will happen automatically and without you thinking about it.

Playing Zen-Sational Tennis

Thinking about winning when you are playing in a tight game is death and will not lead you very often to playing your best and not playing your best may mean that you will lose.

Trying hard to win will not always lead you to playing your best and may not lead to winning.

Trying to not lose doesn't work that well either.

How many times have you blown it in a tight situation? I don't think you blew it because you weren't trying hard to win. I believe it is because you were focusing on winning instead of focusing on the things that you needed to do to play well enough to win. I see this happen all the time, even with professionals.

Most of you know who John Wooden is. Some people say he is the greatest athletic coach ever and not just the greatest basketball coach. Do you know how often he talked about winning to his players? If you guessed never, then you would be correct. So, there must be a good reason why the greatest coach ever, never ever talked about winning and he didn't want his players thinking about winning either.

Do you know why thinking about winning is not productive? Do you know how it affects your body? Thinking leads to trying which leads to tension which may lead to not playing very well, especially in a tight match. Thinking about and doing what you need to do to play your very best is by far better and will lead to helping you to win more matches.

Now I do see, from time to time, some athletes try really hard and it works for them and they play better. These players are few and far between. If you are one of these players, then you may not get much out of the techniques I will be teaching you.

41

On the other hand, if you are like most of us, the harder you try, the worse it gets and this information I am presenting to you here will be your salvation, because you will learn how to "try" properly.

Lesson No. 2: A Huge Issue That Is Damaging Your Game

If you haven't already, please read or listen to the first part of this book up to this second lesson. There is some foundational stuff there that you need to know. Please do that now as you will be tested on it next week.

The issue presented in this lesson can be very dramatic for you in improving your play. It is not an easy one and needs to be paid attention to at all times, as it is likely to creep into your mind when you are not looking.

Please begin to work on it today.

If you are going to be playing the Mental Game, there is one huge issue that will cause you to often lose or play badly. **"That issue is Judgment."**

If you judge yourself, your shots, how well you are doing, etc, you will need to change your thoughts as they will interfere with you playing your best. Therefore, one of the most important concepts you can learn is to let go of judgment. I am not saying you shouldn't be aware of what is going on and what is working and not working. I mean judgments as to whether you are doing good or bad or whether you hit a good shot or bad shot. There are no bad shots. There are only shots that didn't go where you wanted them to go. Likewise, there are no good shots. There are only shots that went where you wanted them to go.

When you judge your shots, your strokes, how well you are playing, or anything else, it is unproductive and can even cause you to play worse.

The natural response to judgment is to try harder. For example, if you judge your last shot as being a bad one, what is your response? You may say to yourself, "OK, I hit a bad shot last time and from now on I will only hit good shots." This leads to using your Conscious Mind to start controlling your body, thereby becoming more tense.

The same thing happens when you hit good shots. You will try harder the next time to keep hitting good shots and your body will probably more get tense, leading you to miss more balls. This becomes a vicious cycle.

Although trying harder may seem to work in the short run, you will find that when the match gets tight or when it comes time to win, your game may break down.

The letting go of judgments is not easy, but even if you just begin to deal with them even if it is only 5% of the time, you will see things happen to your game and maybe even immediately.

A few years ago and after working on my Mental Game for over 18 years, I thought I had really let go of judging things in my tennis. That was certainly true of winning and losing and in my strokes, but one day while I was playing I realized I was judging every ball. Balls that didn't go deep enough or didn't go to where I wanted it to, or was hit too short. I even judged when other balls were good which is equally as bad.

I was really shocked and amazed that after all those years, I was still judging so much.

As soon as I began to let go of these judgements, I started to hit much better and hit so many more what I call easy shots that without letting go I often missed. I was even hitting winners without trying or even thinking about them.

Though I had difficulty stopping my judgments completely, even letting go a little bit helped my play immensely and immediately. I still struggle with this at times and I have to monitor it, but to the degree I can let go of my judgments, my shots go ever so much better.

Lesson No. 3: The Core Principles Of The Mental Game

These Core Principles are absolutely necessary for you to know. You will need to keep these principles in mind when working with just about every lesson. Please take a lot of time studying and learning these principles. They are that important.

There are four primary parts to the Core Principles of the Mental Game: Consciousness, Focus, Relaxation and Judgment.

The Principle of Consciousness

We all have a Conscious Mind and an "Other-Than-Conscious Mind." Tim Gallwey uses Self One and Self Two to describe the two parts that must work together so that we can perform at our best. I have chosen to use Conscious Mind and Other-Than-Conscious Mind because my friend and Neural Linguistic Programming (NLP) master Dave Dobson coined this phrase and it seems to me to better describe what is going on in the body.

The Mental Game encourages you to keep your Conscious Mind calm and, clear. It will also focus on what it needs to and stay out of the way while letting your Other-Than-Conscious Mind emerge. You can and will learn to program this Other-Than-Conscious Mind with visualization and/or talking to yourself. I will teach you how in later lessons.

The Principle of Focus

Focus lets your Conscious Mind continually notice or pay attention to some aspect of the game. You use focus to put your attention on things like seeing the ball, breathing or some part of your body that you want your Other-Than-Conscious Mind to respond to. For example, when you are seeing the ball really well, this information is just what your body needs to have in order to time the hit perfectly.

The Principle of Relaxation

Although relaxation is the general principle, breathing is the most important and biggest component. Breathing supplies the rhythm of relaxation and proper breathing helps keep your upper body from getting tense, thereby allowing your Other-Than-Conscious Mind to use your body to its greatest potential. It also keeps distracting thoughts from coming into your mind by keeping you in the here and now.

Relaxing other parts of your body, especially your grip and wrist, when you hit makes up the complete principle of relaxation. An example would be when you have hit the ball and it absolutely feels effortless because you have turned over control of the shot to the part of your body that knows how to hit it.

The Principle of Playing Without Judgment

When you judge your shots, your strokes, how well you are playing, or anything else, it is unproductive and can even cause you to play worse. The natural response to your judgments is to try harder. This leads to using your Conscious Mind to start controlling your body, thereby becoming more tense. Although trying harder may seem to work in the short term, you will find that when the match gets tight or when it comes time to win, your game may break down. You can see this judgment in just about every player when they pump their fist, when they make a good shot, or when they get angry with themselves when they miss.

In the following lessons you will find the details of the Core Principles that should be anchored into your Other-Than-Conscious Mind. By activating these principles before you play and as needed during play, your Conscious Mind, your Other-Than-Conscious Mind, and your body will be in the best possible place to work together so that you can play at the top of your game.

The Mental Game Core Principle Statements

Remember that the idea here is to truly get your Conscious Mind out of the way and turn over your play to your Other-Than-Conscious Mind. The Conscious Mind's role is also to help you focus on the ball and your breathing. By programming yourself with these principles, you will be able to quickly and easily get into this state of mind. It just takes practice and discipline.

The following statements make up the Core Principles: Please go to www.maxtennis.com/core_principles.php to print a copy of these Principles. This is absolutely essential.

Here are the Core Principle Statements

The Core Principles

- Soon I will be able to pay attention and follow the ball all the way to my racquet so that I can see the ball spinning. This is Core.

- As I follow the ball to the blur of the racquet, I keep my focus on the contact point for a short period of time. This is Core.

- As I learn to pay this kind of attention, I will soon be able to follow the ball and see it spinning to when it contacts my opponent's racquet. This is Core.

- As I become more competent in paying attention to the ball, my breathing will become more natural, and I will learn to be exhaling with a sigh before making contact with the ball and exhaling through and long after contact with the ball. This is Core.

- I finish my follow-through on every groundstroke **NO MATTER WHAT**. This is Core.

- The fingers on my racquet are always very relaxed on every shot especially when I make contact with the ball. This is Core.

- I move for the ball and hit the ball **"knowing"** where I want it to go without effort and without judgment. Without judgment means truly letting the ball go where it goes, truly accepting how well I am seeing the ball, truly accepting how well I am breathing, and truly accepting anything else that is happening while I am playing. This is Core.

- I observe my breathing and I watch the ball even between points. This is Core.

- After missing a ball, if I feel it's necessary, I immediately visualize or talk to myself about hitting the ball the proper distance over the net and into the court to the spot I would have liked it to go, using a perfect stroke, consciously seeing the ball perfectly, and consciously exhaling before and after contact with the ball. This is Core.

- My Conscious Mind stays calm and clear and I let my Other-Than-Conscious Mind direct my body to move to where I see the ball coming. This is Core.

- Between points, I sometimes inhale deeply and exhale slowly with a sigh to relax myself and clear my mind. This is Core.

- My strokes are smooth and relaxed through the entire stroke and my grip is very relaxed, especially at the point of contact. This is Core.

- My Other-Than-Conscious Mind is hitting the ball to where it **"knows"** to hit it while I am consciously seeing the ball and consciously exhaling before and after my hit. This is Core.

- When changing sides (always in tournaments) I sit down, clear my mind, relax my body and, if necessary, reprogram my Other-Than-Conscious Mind to do any of the above. This is Core.

- My Other-Than-Conscious Mind communicates to me any strategy changes to be made. If I am behind in the score, I will use the "wondering technique." This is Core.

-

- In doing all of the above I am letting my Other-Than-Conscious Mind figure out how to make it happen, rather than trying to force myself to do anything by using my Conscious Mind. This is Core.

You will need to read and re-read these Core Principles before every match and/or until they are truly a part of your very being

Lesson No. 4: You Need To Drill And How To Do It

Since you have chosen to buy this book and are reading it, I am assuming that you really do want to improve your game. Do you want to know the fastest and proven way? In case you haven't guessed, here is the answer. You absolutely need to drill.

In the lessons that follow, I include some drills for you to do. However, all the drills that I believe are essential for improving your tennis are listed at the end of the book.

Please read these next two lessons as they will explain about drilling.

How often should you drill? At least twice a week. If you normally play for 1.5 hours, it is best if you drill for 45 minutes and then play sets for 45 minutes using the things you worked on in your drills. If you spend some serious time drilling, you will see a huge improvement in just 6 months to a year. I know you are saying that is a long time, but it really is a short time in tennis years. It just takes a long time to get really good at this game.

Playing Zen-Sational Tennis

In some of the lessons and in the drills at the end of the book, I am going to give you drills that will improve just about every aspect of your game. There are lots of other drills out there and everyone says their drills are the best and there may be some drills out there as good or better than mine. The difference is that mine are designed around using the Mental Game to speed up learning. Of course, once you get good at playing the Mental Game you can use those principles with any drill.

When you get to the lesson about Ron Waite and his e-book and articles which I recommend for you to read, he liked my drills so much that he had his college team use them. From my way of thinking, that says a lot about these drills I am going to give to you.

Doing drills is the only way to really hone your accuracy, consistency, and strategy. Please take drilling to heart and spend at least half of your time on the tennis court doing them.

Here are some other ideas for you as you drill. I find that if you place a small orange road cone on the court as a target, this will help you be aware of where your ball is actually landing in relation to your ideal.

Any time you practice and do the drills I am going to tell you about, please don't just hit down the middle. I see so many people hitting for an hour and just hitting balls over and over again right down the middle. You don't want to hit down the middle in a match so why would you do it so long in practice? When I drill, I just spend very minimal time hitting down the middle when I am warming up. I go into the drills as soon as possible.

Instead of hitting down the middle you will want to hit forehands cross-court, backhands crosscourt, forehands down the line, and backhands down the line. You can do the same when working with your volley. Always have a specific place that you are aiming for when you drill, no matter what you are working on.

After working on any drill for a while, play a game up to five points and at 4-4 play sudden death. This will simulate playing points in a match. I see a lot of players playing a game up to 21. The reason I don't like this is that it doesn't simulate a match. The games in tennis are short so even playing up to five is on the long side.

When I was in college, my roommate and I played a lot of ping pong. As you know in the game of ping pong you play up to 21. My roommate would sometimes have a "hot streak" and I would not be able to catch up so one day I said, "Let's play to 51." When we played to 51, I never lost to him because I was more consistent. The problem was that this is not how ping pong is played. So, play the shorter game of five because that is closer to the games in tennis.

Another concept to keep in mind while drilling is to always try to simulate a game. That means you don't hit the ball in the air if you are behind the baseline and you get all balls on the first bounce. If you get a short ball that normally you would hit and go to the net, you do that in the drill. If you are doing volley drills, you let out balls go out. If you are hitting backhands crosscourt and your opponent hits it late and the ball goes down the line, you still play it as if you were playing a match. The point here is to play as you would in a match.

After working on a drill and the next time you play a practice match, work on utilizing the same things you worked on in the drill. If you were working on hitting forehands crosscourt, hit more forehands crosscourt when you play. If you were working on serving and volleying, then serve and volley every time when you start playing games. Even if you lose! Remember, you are working on improving, not working on winning. Winning will come automatically.

The final thought on all the drills is, "When you start playing the game, do you still hit as well as you did in the drill?" If you can, you have arrived.

The way I see someone getting the most out of these drills is take this book with you when practicing so that you can refer to the drills and do them correctly.

Lesson No. 5: How To Drill When No One Will Drill With You

Ok, you really want to drill, but no one wants to drill with you. Is this true and you can't find anyone who wants to drill? I hope this is not the case.

It is too bad that more people don't want to do drills. As I said earlier, doing drills is absolutely critical if you really want to take your tennis game to the highest possible level. The good news is that you can "fake" doing them when you play. It can be more difficult but doable.

Here is what you need to do. When you play games, decide that you are going to play a different game. Choose what you want to work on and just focus on it.

For example, you could decide that you will hit all of your balls to the backhand side **NO MATTER WHAT**. Even if you know that it is the wrong strategy. And while you are doing this, make sure that you do this while working on seeing the ball, keeping your focus on the contact point for a short time, breathing properly, or working on relaxing your grip and wrist. After doing this for a while, hit all balls to the forehand side.

Here are some other variations.

- Hit side to side. Again, no matter if it is the wrong strategy.
- Hit two balls in a row to the forehand then two balls in a row to the backhand.
- Hit two to one side then one to the other.
- Hit a dropshot, then lob when he/she comes in.
- Serve and volley on every serve and hit your volley to one side only on every volley.
- When you are serving, wait for the return of serve and hit an approach shot and go to net.

Again, you will do all of these drills even if you miss every ball and lose 6-0, 6-0. You get the idea?

So as you go through the rest of the lessons in the book, please do your tennis game a favor and do a lot of drilling.

Lesson No. 6: See The Ball! Do You Really Know What That Means?

In this lesson you will learn some things about seeing the ball that I will bet you have not heard before. Seeing the ball the way it needs to be seen is not easy and needs to be worked on bigtime.

As you already know, seeing the ball is important. But, do you know how important? Do you know that seeing the ball the way I believe it should be seen just may blow you away? Do it and see if it affects your game dramatically like it has so many others.

This is a long lesson but it is the most important of all the lessons, period! Please read it all the way through.

You know that you are supposed to watch the ball, right? Do you think you see the ball when you play? Of course you say you do. Otherwise you would not be able to hit the ball at all. But, do you really see it the way it needs to be seen?

I will tell you that there is a 98% chance that you don't and that percentage is based on giving "My Test," which absolutely demonstrates how to see the ball. I have given this test to hundreds of people and it is surprising to me how many people just don't see the ball very well or properly.

Here is the good news. When you really see the ball the way I know it should be seen, your tennis game will improve immediately and sometimes dramatically.

Playing Zen-Sational Tennis

In case you haven't guessed, seeing the ball is the single most important thing to do when playing and, unfortunately, most people don't see the ball properly even after being shown how to do it and being told how important it is. I am hoping that you won't fall into that category.

"See the ball." "Watch the ball." "Look at the ball." Yes, I know you have heard this so many times. But do you really **consciously** see the ball all the way to and from your racquet? It is not as easy as it sounds. And as you get into really seeing the ball, it becomes easy to think that you are seeing the ball well when you really aren't.

When I talk about how important it is to really see the ball clearly, some of my students try so hard to focus on the ball that they tense up too much. Remember that you don't need to try hard to read the words when you are reading, and likewise you don't need to try hard to see things if you were to look up and around the room. The same principle applies to seeing the ball on the court. Don't try, just see. What may be hard is to keep your focus on the ball for an entire point, game, or match, and this, like any other skill, will need practice.

How do you know if you are seeing the ball well? This requires awareness. **When you are playing, are you able to answer the following questions with absolute certainty?**

- Am I really **consciously** seeing the ball and the direction all the way from my opponent's racquet?
- Am I really focusing on the ball as my ball crosses the net and bounces up to my opponent's racquet? . As you see the ball hit your opponent's racquet, be sure to look for the direction and the speed of the ball as soon as possible after the ball comes off the racquet.

56

- If someone were to ask, could I tell them whether the ball was spinning fast, slow, or medium as it was coming to me and after I hit?

- Have I ever seen a ball that has no spin? Those balls should stick out like a sore thumb because they are so different from the rest and very rare.

- Am I able to see the ball spinning all the way to the blur of my racquet when it makes contact with the ball?

You need to be able to answer these questions beyond a shadow of a doubt. If you find yourself saying that "I think" the ball was spinning slowly, then you didn't see it. If you really saw it you would say without a doubt, "Yes, I saw that one."

When I am giving a student a lesson for the first time, I usually start out by having them just see the ball. I explain that I don't want them to think about their strokes or to think about hitting the ball into the court or aiming. Instead, I want them to just focus on seeing the ball spinning all the way to their racquet and all the way back over the net to their opponent's racquet. Please do this the next time you play and see what happens.

After rallying with them for a few minutes, I then ask them if they saw the ball very well. Most of them will say that they did, and many times they will say that they saw the ball better than they ever had in the past.

The reason they can say this is because I have taken away most of the things they normally think about and just had them watch the ball. And, many times they are aware that they are hitting the ball more consistently solid and in the court.

Playing Zen-Sational Tennis

It is then that I give them "My Test." This test is the best way for me to tell if they are seeing the ball the way I want them to see it and it demonstrates to them beyond a shadow of a doubt how the ball needs to be seen.

Here is what I say to them before I do the test with them. I say that I am going to give them every hint in the book so that they can get the "correct" answer to this test. I will tell them that I will be hitting four balls to them, two to their forehand and two to their backhand. I will hit the balls as easy as I can and that I will stand at the net so that I can hit the ball really easy. I will tell them that all four balls will have the identical spin, and I want them to explain to me what direction the ball is spinning all the way from the time it hits my racquet to the time it hits their racquet. I tell them the three "key" words that practically give away the answer. Those words are "all the way" from my racquet to their racquet. I also tell them that there are three ways the ball can spin: Sidespin, topspin and underspin.

When I do the test, I always use new balls so it is easier to see the spin of the ball. Would you believe that 98 percent of my students can't correctly tell how the ball is spinning? Sometimes I even give them another chance after explaining to them again the three key words, and they still don't get it right. Once I tell them how the ball is spinning and I hit them more balls, they see it immediately.

I once had a student who got really mad when I told him he didn't get the test correct because he was so sure he saw the ball correctly. The point I am making with this test is that people think they are seeing the ball well when they are really not. Almost 100% of those who got it correct had no idea that the ball did what it did.

A few years ago, I gave this test to a friend of mine named Ken Stuart who came up from California to play doubles with me in the

Playing Zen-Sational Tennis

National Indoor 60s tournament in Seattle. Back in the old days, Ken was a world-class player. He is still a great player today, even though we have both aged a little.

After I told Ken about watching the ball all the way to his racquet and after we hit a few balls so he could get somewhat comfortable with focusing on the ball, I gave him the test. Well, he was one of the 2 percent who got it right the first time.

Because it was so easy for him, I was sure he thought I was lying about how many people got this test wrong just to make him feel good. About three weeks later he called me and said that he gave my test to 10 or so other players and all of them got it wrong.

I told him, see, I wasn't just trying to make you feel good. He now knows how special it was that he was able on the first try to see how the ball was spinning the way it needs to be seen. Did I tell you that when he could see the ball well, he really noticed the difference in how well he played?

Ken also told me another story about seeing the ball this way. He was invited to play doubles with 3 other 6.0 players. Ken told them that he wasn't good enough anymore to play with them. They all said that they didn't care, they needed a fourth and they really wanted him to play with them.

Because Ken felt the pressure of playing well, he really focused on the ball. After the match was over, Ken said that he was the best player on the court. When you see the ball this way, it really can have a dramatic effect on the way you play.

Ken is the owner of the Palisades Tennis Club in Newport Beach, Calif., so if you ever get down there, give him a call and tell him I sent you and that you would like to play at his club. His staff has a terrific way of matching you up with players of your own level. If you get a chance to play there, you will see one of the best-run tennis clubs in America. They also host one of the largest senior tournaments there called the Pacific Southwest Senior Tournament.

Are you wondering by now what the correct answer to my test is? Since I am not there to give you the test in person, I want you to try to give yourself the test. It won't be the same, but I am hoping that you will get the idea, not only about how you may not be seeing the ball as well as you could, but how really, really critical seeing the ball accurately is to your playing.

Here is what I want you to do. The next time you play, really work on seeing the ball as it comes to you, and notice which way it is spinning. After you get home, go to the super secret page on my website and get the answer to the test. Here is the web address: **www.maxtennis.com/secret_answer.htm.**

On this page you will get all the answers to how the ball is really spinning as well as all the answers to the universe. It is absolutely critical that you go to this secret page because you will find information there about seeing the ball that you won't find anywhere else. Including in this book.

If you can't wait until the next time you play, ask a friend or family member to throw a ball to you. Have them throw it so that it bounces so that you can then catch it after it bounces. Don't forget to see the ball spinning from the throw, to the bounce and then all the way to your hands as you catch it.

Have your friend toss it with any spin they want 4 times. If you cheat and just continue to read without doing this exercise, you will miss much of these techniques. After you see the spin, continue reading and I will tell you the secret. Now stop reading and do the little throwing test.

In the scheme of things, it doesn't matter if you cheated and just kept reading to get the answer. What does matter is that you learn the answer to the test and how the balls are spinning. Here is the answer to how the ball was spinning as you were catching it.

The secret is that no matter what the spin is before the ball bounces, the ball will always have topspin on it after the bounce. Did you know this? Did you know that even when your opponent hits an underspin, the ball will still have topspin on it after the bounce?

Whether you played first as I asked or did the little throwing test, you absolutely must go to the secret page on my website as it has more critical information that you must have in order to fully understand about seeing the ball. Again that web address is: **www.maxtennis.com/secret_answer.htm**

Seeing the ball the way I have described on my secret page may be a challenge for you. It took me years to get good at it, but when you really know you are seeing the ball, you will absolutely see a difference in your game.

Some of the benefits of seeing the ball really well will be fewer miss-hits, more consistency, and more relaxed strokes. You will also begin to experience what it means to get your Conscious Mind out of the way and let your Other-Than-Conscious Mind direct your body.

Here are some games you can play that will help you to focus on the ball:

The Bounce-Hit Game

In Tim Gallwey's book, *The Inner Game of Tennis*, he talks about a game called "Bounce-Hit." Every time the ball hits your racquet or your opponent's racquet, say out loud or to yourself "hit." Every time the ball bounces on the ground, say out loud or to yourself "bounce." Check to see if you are saying "hit" with a relaxed voice or a tense one.

And check to make sure that you are saying these words exactly when it is happening and not before or after. You may not be able to do this very well at first, but please challenge yourself until you can do it even in a game situation. The benefits will be worth it.

Another game to play is to say out loud or to yourself what direction the ball is spinning. When you hit the ball, say what direction it is spinning as it is going over the net and again when the ball is coming back toward you. Don't forget to consciously see the spin after the bounce. And we all should know what direction the ball is spinning then, right?

Here is one more game to play. Watch the trajectory of the ball as it comes to you and as it goes back to the other side. Ask yourself whether the ball is still rising, has reached its peak, or is dropping when you hit it. Do the same when your opponent is hitting the ball.

As you learn to let go and just see the ball the way I describe above and on my secret web page, you will see amazing things begin to happen. If nothing much happens, then maybe you are just not seeing the ball properly.

Playing Zen-Sational Tennis

Please contact me so we can figure out what is going on with you. My phone number is 360-305-7084. Call anytime between 9 am and 9 pm. My e-mail address is **david@maxtennis.com**

If you want to get a visual picture of what it looks like when someone sees the ball all the way to contact, watch Roger Federer's head as he makes contact with the ball. He sees the ball better than any professional I know of.

I use this visual picture when I am playing and am having difficulty seeing the ball. I just remember how Roger's head moves when he hits the ball and immediately I begin to see the ball better.

The final thing to understand about seeing the ball is that even though it is your Conscious Mind that is seeing the ball, you want to have your Other-Than-Conscious Mind make it happen. This means that, for example, when you read, you are not trying hard to read, you just do it. Do the same for seeing the ball. Just see it.

One final thing. Anytime you read or hear me say see the ball, I am talking about seeing the ball the way I described it in the answer to the test. **If you have not gone there yet, you must stop reading and do it now.**

If there is one thing in my book and in the lessons that is a must, this is it. If you have read this before, you may want to go over it again. **www.maxtennis.com/secret_answer.htm**

Lesson No. 7: Drills For Seeing The Ball

After learning about seeing the ball, I trust that you worked on it or will work on it bigtime. Because seeing the ball is so important, I am going to have you work on it again but this time you can use the drills that are in this book and on the CDs. I kept the drill numbers the same as in this book and in the CDs to make it easier to find them there if you so desire. If you want to see all the drills in one place, go to the Drills section at the end of this book.

Please go through all the drills below as they are great drills to help you see the ball the way I believe it should be seen.

Drill No. 1: Seeing The Ball

The next time you play spend it just seeing the ball. Seeing the ball means focusing on the ball and being able to tell yourself at all times what direction the ball is spinning, especially after the ball bounces as it comes to you.

Seeing the ball means **consciously** seeing what direction the ball is spinning as the ball comes over the net, after the ball bounces, all the way to the blur of your racquet, keeping your focus on the contact point for a short time and as your ball bounces to your opponent's racquet. It also means **consciously** seeing the ball spinning when you miss the shot long, wide, or into the net. You may want to read again Lesson No. 6 on seeing the ball.

Playing Zen-Sational Tennis

In order to see the ball properly, keep thoughts about your stroke or hitting the ball into the court out of your head. Just focus on seeing the ball spinning. In addition, make seeing the ball easy. Relax your eyes. Just think about when you read. You don't try hard to see the words, you just do. It is also easier to work on seeing the ball when playing the short game. See Lessons No. 11 & 12.

As you do this drill, pay attention to the different balls that you are hitting. Are there any balls that "make" you lose your focus? These will be the balls you really need to work on as you get beyond seeing a normal ball. For example, you might have difficulty seeing a really deep ball to the blur of your racquet, or maybe you have trouble seeing the ball when you hit the ball out.

Anyway, once you get good at seeing the ball, you will constantly need to refine it. If you are anything like me, there will be times when you think you are seeing the ball, but you just really aren't.

Here are some more questions to ask yourself after a point or rally is over so that you can make sure you are seeing the ball correctly:

- Am I **consciously** seeing the ball spinning all the way to my racquet?
- Am I **consciously** seeing the blur of the racquet as the ball hits the strings, in other words, am I seeing the ball to the presence of the racquet?
- Am I **consciously** seeing the ball spinning after the bounce?
- Am I keeping my eyes on the contact point after I see the ball to the blur?
- Am I **consciously** seeing the ball spinning after it crosses the net and to the other side of the court?
-

- Am I **consciously** seeing the ball spinning, even when I hit the ball long, wide, or into the net?

Any "no" answer means that you have some more practicing and letting go to do.

Here are a few more questions.

- Am I worrying about hitting the ball into the court?
- Am I trying to hit the ball into the court?
- Am I worrying about stroking the ball correctly?
- Am I trying to stroke the ball correctly?
- Am I trying to direct the ball to a certain spot on the court?

Any "yes" answer means that you have some more practicing and letting go to do.

Here are two more drills that will help you see the ball well.

By the way, all these drills will help you experience what it means to separate the Conscious Mind from controlling the body.

Drill No. 12: The Spinning Game

Another game to play is to say out loud or to yourself what direction the ball is spinning. When you hit the ball, say what direction it is spinning as it is going over the net and again when the ball is coming back toward you. Don't forget to **consciously** see the spin after the bounce. And you know what direction that is, right? If you don't then you have not done your homework in Lesson No. 6.

Drill No. 11: The Second Generation Bounce-Hit Game

Caution: This Exercise may be hazardous to your Conscious Mind.

This is the most advance of the "letting go" exercises. Use at your own risk. When you do this exercise, your Conscious Mind will not be able to try, think, judge, or do.

At least, not very much.

You should be familiar with the normal Bounce-Hit Exercise, as I talked about it in Lesson No. 6 on Seeing the Ball.

If you are not already familiar with this Bounce-Hit drill, this Second Generation Bounce-Hit drill may not make complete sense to you. If you haven't worked with the Bounce-Hit exercise yet, you may just want to do the original one first in practice until it is familiar before trying to do this advanced one. For more advanced information on doing this Bounce-Hit drill, read ahead to Lesson No. 83.

Many years ago, when I learned from Tim Gallwey about the Bounce-Hit exercise for seeing the ball, I used it when I was rallying or practicing. However, when I used it during a game, I found I couldn't do it. I then proceeded to give up on it and forgot about doing it in a match for many years.

I had been struggling with my Conscious Mind for a while because it kept interfering with my game. It wanted to get involved with hitting the ball in the court. I had visualized letting go many times. I had reprogrammed letting go over and over again and still my Conscious

Playing Zen-Sational Tennis

Mind just kept interfering. When I say interfering, it means that I was choking.

So, over the few months that I was finding myself choking, I was searching for ways to keep my focus on the ball and my breathing for the entire point, especially when the point and the match got tight. I was really good at seeing the ball and breathing during a match, except when it came to the "crunch" time when all I had to do was hit the ball in to win the point. I would then try to hit the ball how and where I wanted to and ended up missing the ball.

As it happens, when I work on a problem, the answer comes. This time it took months. For some reason, I thought about and started to do the Bounce-Hit during my practice. The thought came to me that I should try it when I played a match, as I had not done it for years and years. I wanted to see if I could do it now that I was so good at both seeing the ball and breathing at the same time. I felt that I was now sufficiently "mentally developed," and that I would be able to actually do it right.

It was amazing. Not only was I able to do it (even though it was not perfect at first), I found I did not miss the balls I was missing before. When I played three days later, I did the Bounce-Hit method when I served and volleyed. I found that for the first time in my tennis life, I did not panic on a hard half-volley and my other volleys were so much more relaxed. I still missed some balls, but they were ones that I was still too tight on.

But, here are the "kickers" I discovered while practicing this exercise and why I call it the "second generation."

When you say the word "hit" it is a hard sound. I noticed that when I was saying it, my voice was at a higher octave than normal and it was a tense sound. I began to soften the saying of "hit" and it made a lot of difference. I also noticed that I was doing the same thing when my opponent was hitting the ball, especially when he was serving and when I was serving. I began to soften the word "hit" again when my opponent was hitting the ball as well as on my serve. I saw a big difference in the way I felt and how well I hit. Lo and behold, my Conscious Mind could not get control of my body. At least not very easily.

By the way, I always say the Bounce-Hit out loud, but very softly so only I could hear myself saying it. You would not be able to hear me say it from the other side but you could hear me say it if you were standing close to me. I suggest doing this as it helps you be aware of how you are saying the Bounce-Hit and whether or not you are relaxed when you say it.

Here is the other "kicker." At the same time as I was saying "Bounce-Hit," I started to really see the ball to my racquet like I normally would do when not doing the Bounce-Hit and that added the icing on the cake.

To sum up, make sure that you are saying the word "hit" softly with a very relaxed voice as the ball travels to both sides. This, of course, includes when you serve and when your opponent serves. At the same time you are doing this Bounce-Hit exercise, see the ball all the way until you say "hit." Make sure you are still keeping your focus on the contact point for a short time. And, again, see the ball and say "Bounce-Hit" when the ball is on the other side of the net.

If you can't do this very well at first, all it means is that you have some more "letting go" to do. You may need to work on what I call the "foundational place" of the Mental Game, which is truly letting go of everything. I talk about this in Lesson No. 77.

This means letting go of hitting the ball into the court, letting go of any strategy, letting go of aiming, and letting go of trying to do anything else that you may be thinking of when you are playing. Thinking about these things is your Conscious Mind getting involved. Once you get to this place, you will find doing the Bounce-Hit exercise, seeing the ball and breathing much easier.

And, the dirty little secret is that this is the place you are searching for. This is where you need to be when you play. It is the ultimate place to be so that you play your very best every time you play.

Don't believe me on how amazing this Second Generation Bounce-Hit is. See and do it for yourself.

Drill No. 13: The Trajectory Drill

Here is another game to play. Watch the trajectory of the ball as it comes to you and as it goes back to the other side. Ask yourself whether the ball is still rising, has reached its peak, or is dropping when you hit it. Do the same when your opponent is hitting the ball.

This drill can be an eye opener when you do this when you are volleying. Did you know that probably 99% of balls you hit when you volley are dropping before you hit it. The other 1% is at the peak. If you hit a ball that is rising, then you need to know that the ball would be going long if you didn't hit it. So, let all rising balls go so you will win the point.

Lesson No. 8: An Unknown But Powerful Technique When Hitting: Breathing

Did you read and work with Lesson No. 6 on seeing the ball? If not, please take the time now. Even if you did read it, it may be a good idea to read it again because the concept of seeing the ball is so critically important.

Some of the things you should have noticed is that you were more consistent, you hit the ball more solidly, and your strokes felt better. Did you notice any of these things?

Now that you have mastered the seeing of the ball, in this lesson, I will take you into the world of relaxation starting with your breathing patterns.

After seeing the ball as described in Lesson No. 6, the second most important thing to focus on is your breathing. This is because focusing on your breathing keeps the upper body more relaxed, thereby allowing your body to hit the ball better.

Up until now the breathing part when hitting the ball has been unknown. However, recently you will hear many of the pros exhaling with a grunt or even a loud scream so I have to conclude that these professionals believe that breathing this way is valuable. But – and I have a big important but (no not my behind) – these pros do not breathe the way I know works hugely better. A way I have been teaching for many years now.

Playing Zen-Sational Tennis

If you listen to them breathe, they are starting their exhale as, or after, they hit the ball and this exhale is very tense. This way is not as productive as the way I have been teaching. Please keep reading to learn a much better way to breathe when hitting.

This will be another eye-opener for you as most players don't have a very good idea on how to breathe or even what relaxation really means. Maybe I should have said this will be a mouth-opener as I hope that you will learn to breathe through your mouth and not through your eyes.

In this lesson you will learn something that I know you won't hear anywhere else. Well, you may not hear any information on how to breathe, but you will hear the way most of the pros breathe. However, as I said earlier and from my way of thinking, they do not breathe in a very relaxed manner. I won't mention any names but some of them breathe so tensely and so loudly that you can hear them scream from miles away.

Although this is another long lesson it is a very powerful technique and you absolutely have to work on it.

Just about all my students say it is the most difficult thing to do when they are playing, but it can be the most incredible one you will do. Are you wondering yet what this breathing pattern is?

Have you ever taken a yoga class? What is one of the important things the instructor tells you while you are doing the postures? You quickly learn that breathing is a big part of getting the full benefit from it.

Tennis is no different except that you will be using the breathing to stay in the here and now, as well as using it to help you learn how to keep your Conscious Mind out of the way. And, like yoga, working with your breathing helps you relax properly.

Since breathing is the most important part of the relaxation package, you will need to work on it as much as you do on seeing the ball. I will discuss the full relaxation package in a later lesson. In the Mental Game Core Principles (Lesson No. 3), I talked a little about how to breathe but not about some of the practical ways to work on it.

Here I will go into more detail.

Up until I wrote my first book, *Tennis: Play the Mental Game* in 2006, I have always told my students that the jury was still out as far as the "best" way to breathe because I have always had difficulty allowing my breathing to be the way I felt it should be.

Just before I published my 1st book, the jury arrived at a verdict. For many years I had experimented with just about every possible way to breathe and I believe the way I will describe to you now is the easiest and most beneficial way to do it while hitting.

Do you think you hold your breath when you hit? Have you ever been out of breath and realized that you didn't really run anywhere? If you have, then you are holding your breath.

Early in my days of working on my Mental Game and trying to find out how to play my very best, there was a time when I was playing doubles, and after most points, I found myself out of breath. I thought that this was very strange because, as you know, there is not a lot of running in doubles and I was only a few feet away from where I started. I said to myself, "How can I be out of breath when I didn't run anywhere?"

Playing Zen-Sational Tennis

This was when I realized that I was holding my breath and when I began to discover what the best way to breathe was when hitting the ball. And, as I said earlier, I experimented with many ways of breathing. The thing I found was that no matter how I breathed, I felt so much more relaxed.

The next time you play, begin by just being aware of your inhales and exhales as you are hitting the ball back and forth. Check to see if you are holding your breath when you make contact with the ball. Without this ability to consciously pay attention to yourself breathing, it will be difficult to work on changing your breathing patterns in the way I describe next.

Once you have the ability to pay attention to your breathing, you can start working on the quality and rhythm of it. **Here is what I consider to be the most effective and natural breathing pattern while hitting the ball.**

When you are hitting from the backcourt, start your exhale before, as, or just after the ball bounces on your side as the ball is coming to you. This exhale should be a sigh that is long, slow, and relaxed and should continue well through contact with the ball. In fact, the exhale should last until your ball bounces on the other side.

The exhale is not a blow and if your face or mouth moves when you exhale, you are not exhaling properly.

At the same time, of course, you are consciously seeing the ball all the way to the blur of your racquet. You don't have to concern yourself with your inhales as I guarantee that you will do it.

Exhaling as you hit is a very natural way to breathe, so all you have to do is start your exhale (not a blow) before you hit the ball, make it

74

smooth and relaxed, and make it longer than usual. The ideal length is to keep exhaling until your ball bounces on the other side. It doesn't get any easier than that.

When you watch the pros play, you will hear some of them actually grunt out loud or scream as they hit the ball. Especially Sharapova. Oops, I wasn't going to name names.

If you notice closely you will hear that they start this grunt or forced exhale as or after their racquet makes contact with the ball. I don't think this way of breathing is very helpful since it does little to relax their upper body.

If you listen to Nadal's breathing, it will be closer to what I am describing as the optimum way to breathe. He does sometimes start his breathing before he hits the ball, but he still exhales after hitting the ball. From my way of thinking, he is exhaling too tensely, but I believe it has great value anyway.

When you are at the net, you will notice that your breathing will have to be a little quicker. You will need to start your exhale just before, as, or just after the ball hits your opponent's racquet and allow it to continue well through your hit. Do this, and you may see some amazing things happen with your volleys.

When your opponent is at net, it is also a little trickier because the ball is also coming back sooner than normal, and you will have to start your exhale before you make contact with the ball. You might need to start your exhale just as your opponent hits the ball, or you can still start the exhale when the ball bounces. Again, the important thing is to start the exhale before you make contact with the ball.

Again, while you are working with your breathing, it is ideal to also be focusing on the ball all the way to the blur of the racquet. However, you may want to forget about focusing on the ball for a while and just work on the breathing part.

After you have spent some time with the breathing, you must then see if you can do both at the same time. Achieving both the correct breathing and seeing the ball at the same time, and without judgment, is the ultimate focus and leads to playing in the zone.

One of the ways I help myself pay attention to my breathing is to make a little sound as I exhale. It is not a grunt, and no one else can hear me, but I can hear it inside my head. This way I can stay more aware of what is going on with my breathing.

The breathing will be a little different on your return of serve. I will be discussing the return of serve in more detail later. Until you get to that part, here is what you need to do. You should be starting to exhale just before your opponent hits the ball.

But the exhale is still a long, relaxed sigh (not a blow) and continues well through your hit. This way your upper body has a better chance to stay relaxed even when your body has to move quickly. This is especially important when playing someone with a big serve.

When you are serving, you will also start the long, relaxed exhale before you make contact with the ball. Just start your exhale as you release the ball on the toss. And again, continue to exhale well through contact. You may also find that you will be able to see the ball to the blur of the racquet that much easier.

The important point to remember is that no matter what shot you are hitting, the exhale should always be like a very relaxed

sigh and that you start it before making contact with the ball and continue it long past contact.

This may be a good time to let you know that there will be no shot that you will ever hit where you won't want to see the ball and breathe. This includes drop shots, lobs, overheads, behind the back shot, every shot. Every ball you hit. Again, this is easy to talk about, but may be hard to do. When you can do this, have you seen how much better you play?

Breathing was the last part of the inner game that I worked on. I didn't work on it very much in the early years because I just couldn't let go enough to focus on both breathing and seeing the ball. However, once I did get serious about doing both, my game started to really improve.

Doing both is not easy. It takes a lot of work and a lot of letting go. Please don't let that keep you from working on your breathing.

The obvious way to work on it is to just hit balls and see if you can pay attention to your breathing and for the moment forget about focusing on seeing the ball. If you are just playing a practice match, you can do it then also. However, if you are playing a match that is important to you and can't yet focus on both the ball and your breathing, I would rather have you just focus on the ball.

What I am trying to say is that when playing an important match, it is not the time to practice the way you breathe, but it is the time to have your breathing be as relaxed as possible, even if you can't consciously focus on it.

Another way to work on breathing, and you can even do this in a game, is to play two points or rallies just paying attention to yourself exhaling. This means from the time the first point starts to when the second point ends and includes the time in between points. And, of course, any thought of trying to see the ball, trying to hit the ball into the court, or trying to stroke it a certain way needs to be eliminated. If you happen to see the ball well at the same time, that would be wonderful and an added bonus.

Then play two points just seeing the ball. Again, make sure that you are focusing on the ball from the time the first point starts to the time the second point ends. Likewise, if you happen to feel yourself breathing at the same time, that is better.

Then see if you can pay attention to both your exhaling and seeing the ball at the same time for two points.

The ultimate goal here is to program the Other-Than-Conscious Mind to have the breathing be very relaxed. Just as when you are seeing the ball and the time comes to play the game, you need to get the Conscious Mind out of the way and again let your Other-Than-Conscious Mind keep your breathing relaxed.

Lesson No. 9: Drills For Working On Your Breathing

After learning about how to breathe when you hit, I trust that you have started to work on it. Because breathing is so important, in this lesson I am going to have you work on it again but this time you can use the drills that are in this book and on the CDs. I kept the drill numbers the same as in the book and CDs to make it easier to find them there if you so desire. Go to the Drills section at the end of this book to see all the Drills in one place.

Please do all of them as they are great drills to help you work on your breathing the way I believe it should be done.

Drill No. 2: Paying Attention To Your Breathing

In this drill, you will be working primarily on your breathing. Many of my students tell me that the breathing part is the hardest. Please don't let this keep you from working on it. Even if you are not able to do it very well, it will still have huge benefits and will lead you to the next level. You may want to read again Lesson No. 8 on the breathing.

Here is how you can practice it.

Spend five minutes or any period of time you want just paying attention to your breathing.

The ideal breathing pattern is to allow your breathing to be very relaxed and to use a long exhale with a sigh before you make contact with the ball and to continue exhaling through the hit. Paying attention to your breathing means consciously feeling your breathing, even after the point or rally is over. The idea is to be able to do this over an extended period of time.

To do this exercise properly, you will have to keep thoughts about your stroke or about hitting the ball into the court out of your head. Focus only on your breathing.

You also need to know that you may or may not hit the ball very well. You need to let go of this and not worry about it.

This exercise is not designed to maximize hitting the ball into the court. It is an exercise of relaxing and letting go. However, you may just find yourself hitting better. Again, my point is that you are not to worry or even pay attention to this aspect.

Here are some questions to ask yourself after a point or rally is over:

- Can I **consciously** feeling myself exhaling?
- Is my breathing very relaxed?
- Am I sighing before the hit and continuing it after?
- Am I **consciously** and continuously aware of my breathing even in between points and into the next point or rally? That means both inhales and exhales.
- Am I able to stay focused on my breathing, even when I hit the ball long, wide, or into the net?

Any "no" answer means that you have some more practicing and letting go to do.

Here are some more questions for you to ask yourself.

- Am I worrying about hitting the ball into the court?
- Am I worrying about stroking the ball correctly?
- Am I trying to direct the ball to a certain spot on the court?

A "yes" answer means that you have some more practicing and letting go to do.

Once you have worked with the seeing of the ball and your breathing, you need to work on combining them. This is really the ultimate thing to do when you play if you want to really play well. This next drill is Drill No. 3 which is for learning to combine seeing the ball and breathing.

Drill No. 3: Combining Seeing The Ball And Breathing

After spending some time only watching the ball and then working on only your breathing, now you need to do the ultimate. Here is what you want to do.

Spend five minutes or any period of time you want working on consciously seeing the ball and consciously feeling your breathing at the same time.

Again, you must keep your mind free of thoughts about hitting the ball into the court or about your stroke or you won't be able to do this. Focus only on the ball spinning coming and going and your exhaling before you make contact with the ball and allowing it to continue long after the hit.. Refer to the questions to ask yourself in Drills No. 1 and No. 2.

Lesson No. 10: What Is So Important About Relaxation?

Now that you have the first part of the relaxation package nailed, we need to discuss the rest of the relaxation part. In this lesson I will

81

now get more into what relaxation really means and how you can know if you are relaxed properly in the other areas of your body.

As you know in the last two lessons, I talked about breathing. Breathing is just part of the relaxation package – and please know it is the most important part.

Even though the breathing is extremely important, understanding about the other parts of relaxing when you play can also be very important to your ability to play well.

Again, this is a long lesson so I am hoping that the length of it won't keep you from reading all the way through carefully.

Do you ever hit a shot that feels "wrong" or awkward? How about a shot that felt really hard to do? I believe that the "wrong", hard or awkward shots are the result of being tense somewhere in your body.

On the other hand, have you ever hit a shot that felt absolutely effortless and you wondered how come your ball went so hard and well? If you have, then you know what perfect relaxation means. And, you can learn to hit these kinds of shots more often.

So, what do I mean by relaxation? **When playing tennis, being relaxed properly means using only those muscles that are needed to execute the shot and using the right amount of tension.**

The problem is that there is no person on this earth who knows exactly which muscles those are and how to use the perfect tension every time when hitting.

Playing Zen-Sational Tennis

The good news is that your Other-Than-Conscious Mind does know or it can and will learn. And if you can relax and let it hit the shot, you will be able to produce shots that really are effortless.

One day when talking to one of my students about relaxation, she realized perfect relaxation did not mean being relaxed the way you feel during a massage. You can observe the proper amount of relaxation and tension demonstrated when you watch the professionals in any sport and you say, "They make it look so easy." This is especially true of the way Roger Federer hits.

When we try hard to do something, especially the first time and when learning any new physical skills, we use so many more muscles than we need to and often with much more tension. And we wonder why it takes so long for that new skill to become easy and second nature.

When I teach a student a different way to stroke the ball, they will often have a death grip on the racquet. I tell them this is not a weight-lifting class and the racquet does not weigh 1,000 pounds. The student also often feels that this new way of stroking is not natural or feels funny because they are so used to trying very hard.

I try to help my students discover only the muscles that are needed when hitting a particular stroke. I accomplish this by having them experience relaxation in some part of their body starting with their grip and wrist. By the way, having a relaxed grip when making contact with the ball is the most important part of the body to be relaxed.

Here is one of the little secrets of why relaxation works so well. When you are relaxing and not trying to control your body with your Conscious Mind, your body falls under the supervision of your Other-Than-Conscious Mind and it can then take control of your stroke using only the necessary muscles and tension. Your Other-Than-Conscious Mind will also figure out exactly how to time the ball perfectly and what angle the racquet must be at to hit the ball the way you want. If the body doesn't know, by keeping your Conscious Mind out of the way and keeping it from trying to control your body, your body will learn that much faster.

Let's say for example, that you are hitting the ball too high and it goes long. Do you know what angle of the racquet is needed to make the ball go lower? I don't think so. But some part of your body knows. So, by relaxing your grip and wrist, your Other-Than-Conscious Mind can take over and adjust the angle of the racquet. This principle applies to every part of your game.

So, how do you work on using only the muscles you need, and how do you know if you are doing this? There are some signs that you can watch for.

When you hit a ball and you feel awkward or the stroke feels hard to do, it means you are too tense somewhere in your body. As I told you earlier, if you are hitting a lot of balls long – especially when running for a ball – then your grip and wrist are too tense.

If you have ever paid attention to what your face is doing when you hit the ball, you may notice that it also is not relaxed and you are "making a face." That means you are too tense and maybe even holding your breath from trying too hard.

Speaking of the face, let me tell you about Roger Federer. He does two things better than any other top pro that I am aware of. The first is that he must be seeing the ball all the way to his racquet as I discuss in the watching the ball section. You can see his head follow the ball to his racquet, and his head stays at that point for a period of

84

time longer than any other player I have seen. You will see most other pros move their head to their racquet, but not even close to how well Federer does it.

If you will take a look at when other players miss the ball, and I am talking about the pros also, you will see that often their head and eyes don't follow the ball all the way to their racquet.

The second thing that Roger does that no other top pro even comes close to doing is what he does with his face. Or maybe I should say what he doesn't do with his face.

In every picture I have seen of Roger hitting the ball, his face looks very relaxed, and sometimes it looks like he may be exhaling gently. Even in pictures where he is obviously straining to get to the ball, his face is relaxed.

In every picture I have seen of other pros (male or female), you can see tension in their faces. Please go look in any tennis magazine and look at the faces of the players when they are hitting a ball.

This means that Roger is truly allowing his body to hit the ball and is not using any other muscles or trying to control his body consciously when he hits the ball. This is why Roger will be, and maybe already is, the greatest player the world has ever seen and will be on top for a long time to come.

By the way, do you know what stroke Roger hits without a relaxed face? The next time you watch Roger play, look at his face when he serves. Is it relaxed like the rest of his shots?

Playing Zen-Sational Tennis

OK, back to how to work on the relaxation issue. When you feel you are too tense somewhere, you first have to isolate where the tension is located.

Other than the breathing, the most common place is in the grip and the wrist.

Tim Gallwey says that when you hold the racquet you should hold it like you are holding a bird. You want to hold it tight enough so that the bird can't get away, but not so tight that you squash the poor bird. Do you think you are squashing the poor bird when you hit the ball?

Many of my students think that if they hold the racquet this loose the racquet will turn in their hand. The racquet will only turn in your hand if you hit the ball off center.

Here is the irony of this. If you hold the racquet too tight, you will find yourself hitting more balls off center thereby having the racquet turn in your hand more. By holding your racquet looser (and I mean very loose) and combined with seeing the ball and breathing, your body will be able to find the center of your racquet easier and more often.

In addition, you just might amaze yourself on how well you are hitting.

Here is a pretty complete list of the areas of tension, in order of importance, that seem to be common to most players:

1. Your breathing — holding the breath as you hit the ball or a tense exhalation
2. Your grip and/or your wrist (may be the most important)

3. Your face
4. Your arm at the shoulder
5. Your elbow when you are serving
6. Your elbow as you are hitting your forehand
7. Your elbow as you finish your one-handed backhand
8. Your legs
9. Your left hand if you hit right-handed
10. Your left ear. OK, maybe I am getting a carried away and being a little ridiculous but you get the idea
11. And lastly, any other place in your body that feels tight

Once you have determined what area you think may be tense, all you need to do is **consciously** pay attention to that area when you are hitting the ball.

For example, if you think that your grip or your wrist is too tight, **consciously** pay attention to your five fingers as you hit the ball. If you use a two-handed backhand, **consciously** pay attention to and feel to all 10 fingers as you hit. With this awareness you will discover how not to squash the poor bird.

At the same time you are working on relaxing by paying attention to some part of your body, it is critical that you refrain from trying hard to do anything about the tension. The trying leads to more tension. Let your Other-Than-Conscious Mind figure out how to hit the ball into the court using only the muscles that are truly needed, and get your Conscious Mind out of the way.

As you begin to let go of all the other muscles you don't need when you are hitting the ball, your strokes will become natural and so much easier. Your game will improve, and you will find that you have more endurance because you are using so much less physical effort.

When I was a junior and I played the No. 1 ranked player in S. Calif. Jerry Cromwell, I always felt that I was in terrible condition. This was because after the match, I was absolutely exhausted. Only after my lesson with Tim Gallwey did I realize what was going on so many years ago. I was tensing up every muscle in my body for the entire time I was hitting the ball. No wonder I was so tired afterwards and no wonder I never ever beat Jerry.

As you work on relaxing the different parts of your body, you will experience more shots that feel absolutely effortless. When this happens, you will know that you are in the state of perfect relaxation.

You need to remember those times so that you can begin to duplicate them on every shot. This is what you are striving for. And, all this "letting go" leads to "playing in the zone."

Lesson No. 11: You Must Play The Short Game

Nowadays you see just about everyone standing at the serviceline hitting when they begin to warm up. As an old timer, we never did that ever when we were young or even later on in our tennis lives.

For years I would ask any teaching pro that I was talking with what the value was in warming up this way and I never got a satisfactory answer. As you may have guessed, that has now changed or I wouldn't be writing about it.

Playing Zen-Sational Tennis

It started to change when I read *The Talent Code* by Daniel Coyle. I won't go into detail about what I learned from this book, but suffice it to say that this book is an absolutely fascinating book on how talent is developed.

OK, back to the short game. You will have to trust me when I say that by playing the short game "correctly" it just may be extremely valuable. Be sure to read the Second Generation short game in the next lesson.

To play the short game "properly" here is what you must do. Stand about 3 to 6 feet behind the serviceline. Then you must take a complete swing which means a full back swing and a full follow-through. In order to do this, you must swing very slowly and be very relaxed and your opponent must also swing very slowly or the ball will be hit too fast.

You must make every stroke absolutely correct every time, NO MATTER WHAT. This is a terrific way to work on your strokes.

After working on your strokes (and/or at the same time) you can add the other factors like seeing the ball, exhaling before and after you make contact with the ball, and feeling and allowing your grip and wrist to be very relaxed.

After doing all this for a period of time, begin hitting from behind the base line and see if your stroke, seeing the ball, breathing and relaxation of your swing is the same.

The whole point of hitting the ball in slow motion is to make it easier to groove your stroke and to feel what it is like to swing properly while seeing the ball, breathing properly, and being very relaxed.

89

When you can take the same stroke over and over again the same way every time when doing the short game, your "real" tennis game will have to improve. After all, the sign of a good player is one who can stroke the ball the same every time.

So, the next time you warm up using the short game, make sure you do it correctly in order to get the most from warming up. And, if you are so inclined, pick up a copy of *The Talent Code* and read about how talent is developed. It is not hereditary or just in the DNA.

Lesson No. 12: The Second Generation Short Game

Practicing Ground Strokes

This is just a small variation of the normal short game. Instead of standing on the service line and hitting, you stand back about 6-8 feet and instead of just hitting down the middle, you hit cross-court forehands, cross-court backhands, down the line forehands and backhands aiming for the corners of the service box. You can spend as much time on each direction as you like.

However, when you do this, and because the ball is going so slowly, you can do all of the following. Maybe not at the same time but certainly you can be aware of them to make sure that you are able to do all of them.

Playing Zen-Sational Tennis

Once you have gone through the things on this checklist, you may want to isolate just one of the things on the checklist and work on it for your entire practice session.

For example, one day I was having difficulty consistently seeing the ball spinning from the bounce to the blur my racquet. So I decided to just work on that, and to use my famous words, I would do it **NO MATTER WHAT.**

This means that I would warm up this way, I would give up on any strategy when the game started, and the only thing I would do is consciously see the ball spinning to the blur of my racquet **NO MATTER WHAT.** And you can choose to do this days at a time or even weeks at a time.

There was a time when my breathing was not satisfactory to me and I worked for two months only with my breathing.

Here are the main things to work on when doing the short game:

- Seeing the ball perfectly. That means seeing it to the blur of your racquet to it making contact with your opponent's racquet. And, of course, seeing it means **consciously** seeing the ball spinning.
- Make sure you are **consciously** seeing the ball hit your opponent's racquet.
- Breathing properly. This means starting the exhale when the ball bounces and having the exhale continue until the ball bounces on the other side.
- Being very aware of the grip and wrist to make sure it is very relaxed – especially at impact.
-

- You can even be aware of your stroke to make sure you are doing it correctly. This means, for example, that if you are doing a topspin stroke that your ball actually has topspin on it. And, of course, you know this because you can consciously see the ball spinning after you hit it.
- When doing the stroke make sure that you are taking a full finish. My new word for the short game is that the finish should **"float"** up to the very end. Because your stroke is so slow and relaxed the momentum won't carry the racquet all the way to the end like it would if you were hitting a normal ball from the backcourt. So you have to **"make"** the racquet finish all the way with as little effort as possible. **It is also very important that you "have" your shoulders rotate as you finish.** It is very easy to just use your arm when you are doing this short game. When rotating your shoulders, it should be as slow and easy as you let your arm **"float"** up to the finish.
- When hitting crosscourt, aim for the corner of the service box. When hitting down the line, also aim for the corner next to the singles line. If your aim is off, reprogram it.
- Work on your footwork also. You should not be moving back to hit a ball but should be stepping in properly and moving your feet properly on every ball.

Practicing Volleys And Half Volleys

There are two volley drills that you can do to enhance your volleys when doing the short game. One is just to develop some control and consistency. The other is for developing your half volleys.

The Consistency Volley Drill

For this drill you will stand on the service line and again you will hit the forehand volleys cross-court, backhand volleys crosscourt, down the line forehand and backhand volleys. Again, you can spend as much time on each direction as you like.

You will work on hitting the ball between the head and the waist of the other person being as consistent as possible. This drill is for developing control and consistency and you won't be hitting the balls hard.

And, while doing this you should do the following things:

- Seeing the ball perfectly. That means seeing it to the blur of your racquet to it making contact with your opponent's racquet. And, of course, seeing it means **consciously** seeing the ball spinning coming and going.

- Make sure you are **consciously** seeing the ball hit your opponent's racquet.

- Breathing properly. This means starting the exhale when the ball hits your opponent's racquet and having the exhale continue until the ball crosses the net after your hit. The exhale will be a lot shorter due to the short distance the ball is going.

- Being very aware of the grip and wrist to make sure it is very relaxed. Especially at impact.

- You can even be aware of your stroke to make sure you are doing it correctly.

- As a variation, you can begin to move in until you both are practically touching the net.

Playing Zen-Sational Tennis

The Half Volley Drill

The person practicing the half volley will stand about half way between the base line and the serviceline. The other person will be standing just inside the serviceline and again you will hit the volleys cross-court and down the line. Again, you can spend as much time on each direction as you like.

The person that is standing just inside the service line will start the rally and attempt to hit the ball at the opponent's feet so that they will hit as many half volleys as possible. And then, of course, change places and let the other person hit half volleys while you practice hitting at their feet.

And, while doing this you should do the following things:

- Seeing the ball perfectly. That means seeing it to the blur of your racquet as well as seeing it making contact with your opponent's racquet. And, of course, seeing it means consciously seeing the ball spinning.
- Make sure you are **consciously** seeing the ball hit your opponent's racquet.
- Breathing properly. This means starting the exhale when the ball hits your opponent's racquet and having the exhale continue until the ball crosses the net. The exhale will be a lot shorter due to the short distance the ball is going.
- Being very aware of the grip and wrist to make sure it is very relaxed. Especially at impact.
- You can even be aware of your stroke to make sure you are doing it correctly. However, you need to know that, even on a half volley, it is ideal for you to take a much longer follow-

94

through than you normally would. And, it is not a forced finish but a very relaxed finished.

Lesson No. 13: A Missing Piece Of The Puzzle

As a student of the Mental Game, you know that seeing the ball properly and breathing properly when you play is a huge part of getting to that place called playing in the zone.

You also know that relaxation is also a key factor. Yes, exhaling very relaxed is part of the relaxation package, and in fact is a huge part of it. Another big factor, which I have not really specifically talked about and is part of the relaxation package, is allowing your ground strokes to finish completely on every shot. And, of course, in order to have this happen you must keep the muscles in your arm relaxed so that you don't stop your arm prematurely.

Then you also know that the part of the body I talk about next that needs to be relaxed is the grip and the wrist. However, up to now I have not made it very important to work on it other than to pay attention to it for short periods of time.

I have also recently told you about how important the short game is when you drill. Hopefully you have read the lesson which I call The Second Generation Short Game (Lesson No. 12). It is drilling using this short game that will make it very easy to work on everything and it also makes it easy to become aware of the things that need work.

Playing Zen-Sational Tennis

I have been doing this short game for some time now. I keep thinking that I am not going to be learning anything new or different especially after doing this for so long. So let me tell you what I have discovered in my own game so that you can also benefit.

When doing the short game, I became aware that on my backhand I had a tendency to squeeze my grip as I hit the ball. This was also the case when I did the volley drills. Yes, I worked on relaxing my grip from time to time but I never really spent any serious time working on it.

So one day I thought that I would spend the entire practice session focusing on keeping my grip and wrist extremely relaxed on every hit. During the short game I was still able to see the ball and breathe fairly well, but my main focus was on keeping my grip and wrist very relaxed not only as I hit the ball but during the entire stroke.

After doing the short game and I went on to hitting regular ground strokes from the backcourt and during the volley drills I was able to still allow my grip and wrist to be very relaxed. The result was amazing. I found myself missing very few balls and it seemed that over and over again I was aware of my wrist changing the angle of my racquet in order to keep the ball in the court.

At the end of my practice session where we do serves and return of serves, I was still able to allow my grip to be very relaxed and again the results were amazing.

Yes, you still have to see the ball and exhale relaxed as you hit but I now feel that having a relaxed grip and wrist is a huge part of the things we need to do in order to play our very best.

Playing Zen-Sational Tennis

So working on keeping the grip and the wrist relaxed during the entire practice session was something that I had never done before. I had not really worked on this relaxation aspect of my game for any period of time so that it would happen automatically. And this brings up another idea that I have talked about before but I have not really emphasized it much.

When you practice it may be a good idea to spend the entire practice session on just one aspect of the game. I have spent a great deal of time over the years working on seeing the ball and on my breathing. There was a two-month period of time where I pretty much just worked on my breathing. And I remember a time when I started to play sets I would work on just seeing the ball spinning after the bounce to my racquet.

But what is different about this idea is that I spent the entire session on just the one thing. In the past you may have heard me talk about practicing things in segments. That idea, I believe, is still a very good one. But now I have extended it to working on just one thing the whole time you are playing rather than just spending two or three minutes at a time on multiple issues.

So there you have it. The next time you practice or play, pick just one thing to work on. Let me suggest that you start with the grip and wrist being relaxed to the extreme as I am willing to bet that this part of your game has not been worked on very much.

Don't forget that you want your grip and wrist to be very relaxed when serving, returning serve, volleys, and lunging balls. And also don't forget that you still must see the ball and breathe relaxed to really maximize your play.

97

Lesson No 14: Work On Seeing The Ball In A New Way

If you have worked on seeing the ball the way I believe it should be seen and as I have described in the lesson in my book on seeing the ball, you should know by now what I mean when I say you need to see the ball to the blur of the racket. And hopefully you have experienced this when you play.

As I have said over and over again, playing using the concepts in my book is an ongoing process, one that will continue until you hang up your racket. Let me tell you about my new experiences with this aspect of seeing the ball.

As a new general rule, I have discovered that when I become aware of some aspect of my focus I am not doing very well, I will spend the entire practice session focusing only on that aspect. For example, I realized one day that my grip was tightening up on my backhand. Up to that time, I had only given a little effort to keeping my grip relaxed. This time I got the idea that I would consciously pay attention to my fingers on the racket and allow them to be as relaxed as possible during the entire practice session. Yes, I still saw the ball properly and still allowed my breathing to be there, but my main and primary focus was on my grip and making it as relaxed as possible.

The results absolutely blew me away. My game took a huge jump up. As I was able to relax my grip more, it seemed like I just couldn't miss the ball. Now when I play and I find myself missing too many balls, I check in with my grip to make sure that it is very relaxed. And guess what? The tightness has crept in.

Playing Zen-Sational Tennis

So, onto the subject of this lesson. Again, as I was drilling, I noticed that my ability to see the ball all the way to the blur of my racket was sporadic. I always work on consciously seeing the ball spinning to the blur of my racket every time I play any way, but this time I decided that I would focus only on the blur part. So, as I did with working on my relaxed grip, I spent the entire practice session only seeing the blur part. I did not really concern myself with consciously seeing the ball spinning to the blur. I just followed the ball to the hitting point.

I still did my breathing properly, still kept my grip relaxed, and still saw the ball pretty well. But again, my main focus was to just see the blur of the racket 100% of the time as my racket went through the hitting point. And again, the results blew me away. Again, I just couldn't seem to miss the ball when I did this properly. Lot's of "agains" don't you think? ☺

Since this was the first time that I ever really focused specifically on that one aspect, I thought that maybe the results wouldn't last, because I wasn't really consciously seeing the ball from the bounce to the blur of my racket as I have said you must do in my lessons on seeing the ball. So, I thought I would do this the next time I practiced.

And again, the results were amazing. However, I noticed that I had a tendency to miss hit more balls off center. My balls still went into the court but they just weren't hit as solid. To remedy this, I just allowed myself to more consciously see the ball spinning from the bounce to my racket. What was very interesting was that after spending the entire previous practice session on seeing the blur, I could now consciously see the ball spinning to the blur much easier and still about 100% of the time. This pretty much fixed my miss-hits.

Playing Zen-Sational Tennis

The next time I played, I still made sure that I saw the ball to the blur but now I found myself missing balls that I was making before and I was wondering why this was happening. What I discovered is what I think is the last piece of this concept. I realized that I wasn't keeping my eyes and focus at the contact point for just a moment. Yes, I was seeing the blur of the racket but I was pulling my head up to see where my ball is going. So after spending so much time working on just seeing the ball to the blur, to add this last concept was easy and made all the difference in the world. And guess who always keeps his head at the contact point for a moment when he plays? Yeah, you guessed it; the best player the world has ever seen, Roger Federer.

So please give this way of focusing on only one specific aspect for an entire practice session, or for as long as you like, a chance. In this lesson, I have talked about having a relaxed grip and about the blur of the racket. These are two of the five major components of my Core Principles. If you are having difficulties with any other aspect of my Core Principles or any other part of your game, use this way of practicing with them also.

If you get any spectacular results using this way of practicing as I did, I would love to hear from you about it. Even if you just get some obviously noticeable improvement and if you have a moment, please shoot me an email. I would love to hear from you.

Lesson No. 15: The Process For Learning Anything And/Or Fixing Your Errors

This process, developed by Tim Gallwey, is one of the most impressive ones I have ever seen for learning, changing or fixing just about anything. I have made some changes to the original Tim Gallwey technique but I have found it is still, if not more so, as powerful as the original.

For some reason, most of my students have a hard time remembering the steps to take, so I thought I would write it out and hopefully, they are simple and easy enough for all of you to do. Please print them out, study them and more importantly, use them.

Step 1: Really Know What You Want to Do

You need to know very precisely what it is you are trying to accomplish. Another way to think about it is – this is your goal. For example, if you are working on your backhand, you need to be very clear how you want to hit it.

You must have the image in your mind, you must be able to swing your racquet perfectly without the ball, and you must be able to feel it and get it perfect even with your eyes closed. If you miss a forehand cross-court, you must know exactly how you would have liked your ball to go. That means the speed, direction, how high over the net, where it should bounce, and what kind of spin. If you are working on fixing a mental error you must know exactly what mental pattern you wanted – not just that you did something wrong.

Step 2: Visualize, Re-Program, and do a Shadow Stroke

The Shadow Stroke

Before I get into step two, let me talk about how to take a proper shadow stroke. When you do a shadow stroke, it is critical that you do it perfectly. Just don't go through the motions.

When you do your shadow stroke, not only must the stroke be perfect, but you must do the stroke with perfect breathing, perfect seeing the blur of the racket as it passes through your imaginary hitting point, having a very relaxed grip, taking a full and perfect finish, and visualizing the imaginary ball going into the court the way you would like it. If you don't do all of these things every time you take your shadow stroke, you will be losing a terrific opportunity to speed up the changes and the learning you want to happen.

In addition to the above, you need to take a number of your shadow strokes pretending that you are hitting a high ball, a waist high ball, and a low ball. You will also want to take some very slow and relaxed swings, some medium but relaxed swings, and some very fast but relaxed swings. When you take the fast swings, please guard against tensing up your breathing and having a tight grip. Your breathing and your grip should be relaxed during the entire swing regardless of how fast or slow you swing.

Playing Zen-Sational Tennis

As an aside, if you will spend a minimum of five minutes per day going through all of your strokes (fore hands, backhands, serves, forehand volleys, backhand volleys, overheads) you will see a huge difference in the consistency of your strokes in a very short time.

The key to maximizing the benefit of these shadow strokes is to make sure that you are taking a perfect stroke. If you are not 100% clear on how to take the perfect stroke without the ball, you need to find a good teaching pro that specializes in stroke production. Obviously, if you take incorrect strokes when doing your shadow stroke, this incorrect stroke will be what you will be doing when you hit a ball.

So do your tennis game a huge favor and religiously spend some time doing these shadow strokes. You won't regret it.

Now back to Step 2.

You need to actually fix what it is that you are working on and I don't mean when you are hitting a ball. If your stroke was different from your ideal (in other words "wrong") then you need to stop and visualize a perfect stroke. Even take a few practice swings without the ball. Take as many as you need to really get it right. Feel what it feels like to stroke it perfectly without the ball. If you used the wrong strategy, visualize or imagine yourself in the same situation hitting your shot the way you wanted to. If you had a thought that was not productive or "wrong," make sure that you cancel out the old thought and replace it with a more productive one.

Step 3: Just Let It Happen Without Trying

Once you have done Step 2, you need to forget about trying to make it happen. This is where I believe most people go wrong. Just be aware and feel what is going on.

If you are working on a stroke, just be aware of it by truly feeling it and compare it with your perfect stroke. You can break it down into parts. Be aware or feel your backswing, your follow-through, your footwork, or anything else you feel needs attention. Be aware if you make the same strategy error as before, or if you still have those pesky negative or "wrong" thoughts.

Step 4: Visualize Again, Re-Program Again, and do a Shadow Stroke Again

After you spend time being aware of and feeling whatever you are working on, if you notice that the situation is not getting any better, you need to go back to Step 2. However, this time, you will need to let go more (this means relax more). The reason things are not changing is that you are not allowing your Other-Than-Conscious Mind and/or your body to learn to make the needed changes.

This is a very powerful process. If you can't make it work, then something is not right. You are missing some ingredient of the process. After you have worked very seriously on this process and are still having difficulties or can't make it work for you, then you need to contact me.

Lesson No. 16: Classic Tim Gallwey: Body Awareness Is Very Important

Drill No. 4: Feeling And Relaxing Your Strokes

This drill helps you develop the proper amount of relaxation when you hit the ball and works on really grooving your strokes. Actually, this is a bunch of small drills because you will be doing this drill with every stroke and paying attention to different parts of your stroke.

If you feel like your strokes are not consistent, then you will want to spend more time with this drill.

While you are doing all of these exercises, you need to make the movements as relaxed as possible. Remember that when you relax your body, you are turning control over to your Other-Than-Conscious Mind. This leads to much faster learning.

The other reason to make each stroke as relaxed as possible and with as little conscious control as possible is so that when you actually play in your matches your body will still be stroking the ball the same way even though you are not thinking about it.

Have you heard me say that the follow-through is the most important part of the stroke? When you work on the follow-through, sometimes good things happen in other areas of your stroke and you probably won't even know about it.

Here is what you are to do.

You will want to spend five minutes holding the follow-through until it comes to a complete stop. This means stopping and holding the footwork also. (See Lessons No. 19 & 20) Spend some time combining holding the follow-through with consciously seeing the ball spinning or consciously feeling your breathing. When you do this, it becomes an extremely powerful exercise.

Spend five minutes on each of the following strokes doing the following without controlling or judging:

- **Consciously** feel your complete **forehand stroke** from the time you are in the ready position to the time you recover back to the ready position.
- **Consciously** feel your complete **backhand stroke** from the time you are in the ready position to the time you recover back to the ready position.

- **Consciously** feel your complete **forehand volley** from the time you are in the ready position to the time you recover back to the ready position.
- **Consciously** feel your complete **backhand volley** from the time you are in the ready position to the time you recover back to the ready position.
- **Consciously** feel any other stroke

While you are consciously feeling the stroke, keep thoughts about hitting the ball in the court out of your head. In case you were wondering, feeling the stroke means that you are able to absolutely describe the exact movement of your arm, wrist and the racquet as you are moving it through the stroke.

For example, do you know if your racquet is going up, down or straight back when you are taking the racquet back on your forehand? Since so many of my students have difficulty with being accurately aware of their swings, you may want to take some videos of your swing so that you can be really sure you are swinging the way you think you are. When you get comfortable with feeling your stroke, add seeing the ball spinning or add your breathing, but not both at the same time.

Here are some specific mini drills that you may want to work on. If you know that you are having difficulty with a stroke, paying attention to it and feeling the different parts of the stroke will help a lot.

If you have not done these awareness exercises, then it will be very helpful in improving your strokes. Even if you don't know how to fix a particular stroke, it won't matter. By paying attention and feeling

your strokes, changes happen for the better even if you are not aware of any changes.

Please remember to let your body be as relaxed as possible while doing these drills.

Mini Drill No. 1: Spend some time **consciously** feeling the direction the arm and racquet travels on the back swing from the ready position.

Mini Drill No. 2: Spend some time **consciously** feeling the direction the arm and racquet travels as the racquet starts forward.

Mini Drill No. 3: Spend some time **consciously** feeling the direction the arm and racquet travels as the racquet goes forward and makes contact with the ball.

Mini Drill No. 4: Spend some time **consciously** feeling the path of the arm and racquet after the racquet makes contact with the ball and continues to the finish.

Mini Drill No. 5: Spend some time **consciously** feeling and knowing exactly where your follow-through ends. Remember that the follow-through is the most important part of the swing.

The key to doing these drills is to absolutely know what is going on with your stroke during these specific parts of the stroke. In order to do this, you must be letting go of where your ball goes and even trying to make your stroke "right." Your only job is to just feel what the arm and racquet are doing and relaxing as much as possible.

When you get really good at this drill, you can begin to feel the entire stroke all at once.

These drills are really designed to help you with your strokes. If you spend just a little quality time relaxing and feeling your hand, wrist, fingers, and any other parts of your body, you will see significant changes in how well you stroke the ball and as a result of your strokes being better and more consistent, you will play better. What a concept!

Lesson No. 17: A Short Review Of What To Do When You Play Games Or A Match

When I was in Mexico City working with six tournament players, I wasn't sure if they were really understanding what they were supposed to do when they played their matches so I wrote this summary for them.

It would be a good idea for you to print this out and keep it in your tennis bag to read along with reading the Core Principles before you play your matches.

When you play matches (or points for that matter) here is a summary of what needs to be done to fully play the Mental Game.

- Make the "Core Principles" the most important thing that you do.
- Make sure you don't think about your strokes. However, if you feel your stroke is "off" it would be good to visualize and re-program your stroke mentally, as well as take a practice swing, and then forget about it and go back to doing the "Core Principles." This you would do in between points.
- Every time you miss the ball, **consciously** see where and how high over the net you would have liked your ball to go, re-program it, and visualize the ball going into the court the way you would have liked it to, then forget about it and go back to doing the "Core Principles."

- Remove all judgments (or at least keep them to a minimum). When you judge, it leads to trying which leads to tension, which leads to missing shots. If you miss a ball, let it go and encourage your body to learn to hit it in the court through visualizing and re-programming. If you hit a good shot, give your body credit. Don't try to do it again but tell your body to keep those good shots coming.

- If you think about winning at any time but especially at the end of a game, set or match, take a deep breath, sigh your exhale and say "cancel cancel" letting those thoughts go. Or you can yell as loud as you can to yourself silently "Stop!" Then go back to doing the "Core Principles."

You may want to re-read the following Lessons for the complete explanations: Core Principles (Lesson No. 3), Lesson No. 32, Lesson No. 45, Lesson No. 51, Lesson No. 52, Lesson No. 54. There are many other lessons that you should re-read, but these are some of the more important ones.

I am here to help you. Please feel free to call me or e-mail me anytime with any questions. My phone number is 360 305-7084. Call anytime between 9 am to 9 pm. My e-mail address is **david@maxtennis.com.**

Lesson No. 18: Playing By Instinct

Though the full title of my first book is *Tennis: Play the Mental Game, And Be In The Zone Every Time You Play*, I must confess that most of that book is centered around playing the Mental Game. Yes, when you do it right it leads to playing in the zone and I believe my tools, concepts, and exercises help you get there, but I have not really talked about how to actually get to the state that we call playing in the zone. In this book I have given you many more ideas, concepts, and techniques for getting to the zone state.

I started to think about this a lot more after reading Dr Robert Soloway's book *Tennis in the New Age*. Now, I must say that I have different ideas on how to achieve actually getting to a zone state, but he certainly got me thinking a lot more about how to get in the zone. However, you may think differently and may want to get his book and see for yourself. Dr Soloway does have some really great ideas on how to get into the zone and believes that getting into the zone can be worked on and is not something that just happens. And I certainly agree with that.

He also talks about playing by instinct and he says the most important thing a player needs to be able to do (other than getting in the zone) is to figure out how to hit the ball to the "right" spot at the "right" time. The ideal way to do this is by instinct and not by thinking hard about the shot.

Let me give you some of my ideas on the way to train your mind to hit the ball where you want it to go using your instincts.

Playing Zen-Sational Tennis

So, how do we learn to play completely by instinct? First of all, it is important to have a good understanding of the game. This means that we know good strategy, have a good variety of shots, (offensive shots, defensive shots, topspin and slice, drop shots and lobs, overheads, etc).

An example of doing something by instinct is when you see a cat stalk its prey. It already knows how to crouch, creep up closer before it pounces, and how to focus one pointedly on its prey, and then attack. No one has trained the cat to do these things. It just knows what to do by instinct, or possibly by watching its mom, but certainly not from any formal training.

Now a player could learn to excel by just playing a lot of tennis, or by watching better players, but it would take a long time and a lot of trial and error. So, we help things along by taking lots of lessons, reading books and articles and watching the pros, etc. However, we don't very often make the transition to letting all this go and just play by instinct.

So, again, how do we play by instinct? We get there by quieting the Conscious Mind and staying in the here and now. Remember seeing the ball and breathing? Then we just let our bodies play. Sounds easy, doesn't it? Well, it is pretty easy to talk about.

If you have read this entire book, I talk a lot about "fixing" the shot by reprogramming, by visualizing, by relaxing, by changing the thought processes, etc.

Like I said earlier, you have to have some training in these things (maybe a lot of training), as they will lead you into playing in the zone. However, at some point you have to let go of these things also.

Playing Zen-Sational Tennis

You will do this by focusing on the ball and by focusing on your breathing, even in between points. And I mean every second. Like a cat focusing on its prey. It doesn't let its focus wander to thinking about how good the mouse is going to taste or what is going to happen if the mouse gets away, or what its mate is going to think if it misses or if it succeeds in killing the mouse. All it does is focus on the mouse. Then, I don't think it thinks about how it is going to kill the poor little mouse. Are you feeling sorry for the mouse yet? ☺

When you focus on the ball (or even a ball in the next court) and your breathing every moment, at some point you will put yourself into a trance-like state where you are just playing by instinct. It may take a few minutes or a lot of minutes to get there but as you practice this, it will get easier to attain a zone state.

Let me spell it out again very clearly. **You focus on a ball every second, even in between points.** It can be any ball, even a ball on the next court or a ball that is in your hand. It doesn't matter. During the point, you will also be focusing on your exhaling at the proper time, but as soon as the point is over you will begin to focus on both your exhales and your inhales. Both focusing on the ball and on your breathing keeps you in the here and now, which in turn helps keeps destructive thoughts away, which then helps lead you to being in the zone.

In addition, when the point is over and you are focusing on your inhales and exhales, you will find yourself relaxing more and more not only between points but during the points.

Now that we know how to get into the zone, there is another aspect of playing by instinct that needs to be understood.

Playing Zen-Sational Tennis

I talk about this again in Lesson No. 57, but I want to talk about it here first.

Think about when you are warming up. You just **know** that you want to hit the ball down the middle, and without thinking very hard, if at all, you just do it. You **know** this before you even get on the court.

The same applies when you are hitting your balls crosscourt, down the line, or anywhere else. It is simply a **"knowing"** of where you want the ball to go and then just doing it. Trying hard, thinking hard, making it important, or trying to consciously direct the ball won't work in the long run or when you are under pressure.

Like when you warm up and you are doing drills, you already know in advance where you want the ball to go. However, when it comes time to choose where to hit it, the process is a little different.

The analogy I like to use is this: you need to get to an important appointment and you were a little late getting out of the house and when you went to get the keys to your car, you couldn't find them. So, you panic a little and try as you might, you can't think of where your keys are. But, instead of finding them, you go get your spare set of keys, get into your car and drive away. As you are driving and now knowing that you will be able to get to your appointment in plenty of time, you relax.

Then out of nowhere, you remember that your keys to your car were in the top drawer of your desk. You were not trying to remember and the thought just came to you.

Well, the same approach needs to be used when hitting a tennis ball to where you want it to go. **You let the thought come to you and** then you just see the ball and exhale properly as you let your body hit it to where you now know it should be hit.

Thinking hard about where you want to hit it is death and may cause you to miss even easy balls, as it tenses up your body and tends to keep your focus away from the ball and your breathing. When you are thinking too much, missing shots may happen bigtime if you are playing an important point or if the match is close or if you are playing a tiebreaker.

Still, it does take practice figuring out what I mean by **knowing** and how to let this knowing come to you. Unfortunately, I can't really tell you how to do this except to tell you to keep your mind calm and clear so that these thoughts can, in fact, get through.

I can tell you that when you do learn to do it, you will be able to hit the ball anywhere you want effortlessly and without thinking, which is to say by instinct. And, the more you work with all of these concepts I have in this book and on my CDs, the more it will become easier for you to understand what **knowing** means.

Lesson No. 19: How To Know If You Are Playing The Mental Game Properly

Do you think you are playing the Mental Game properly? How do you know?

Playing Zen-Sational Tennis

I have heard from players who have said that they have read *The Inner Game of Tennis* and are playing the inner game. However, if you watch them play, they really aren't playing the inner game at all. There must be some way to know if you are on the right track.

I assume that by now you have read most or maybe all of the lessons up to this point and hopefully you have begun to put these lessons into practice. You may also be "sick to death" of hearing about seeing the ball, breathing, letting go, relaxing your grip, and the Core Principles. I hope not because you will be reading about it a lot more.

I go over and over these so many times because we have learned all of our lives to try hard, make it happen, beat your opponent, etc and it will take some serious effort to "correct" these thought patterns. With repetition, I am reinforcing these new patterns of thought.

You can see that there are not that many things you need to do to play the Mental Game. Using the Core Principles when you play is really all there is to it. You just need to strip away all the unproductive thoughts that get in your way but it is always nice to know if you are playing the Mental Game properly, or at least making progress.

Here are some questions you can ask yourself which will give you the knowledge that you are on the right track. Please read and use Lesson No. 89 also for a more complete analysis.

- Does your play improve during a match?
- Have you seen at least one ball to the blur of your racquet when you are playing sets or matches?
- Has your focus stayed on the contact point for at least one ball?

Playing Zen-Sational Tennis

- Have you felt yourself exhaling properly for at least one ball during a match?

- Have you re-programmed any of your misses either in practice or in a match? This means that you have remembered to take practice swings when you miss.

- Have you been aware of any unproductive thoughts and had the presence of mind to stop, say Cancel, Cancel, or you have yelled as loud as you can to yourself silently "Stop!"and re-programmed?

- Even if you are not able to focus very well, are you constantly re-programming yourself to see the ball better on every point and working with letting go more and more?

- Are you making the Mental Game the most important thing to work on when you play? I am talking about using the Core Principles.

Any 'yes' answer to the above questions should tell you that you are on the path of playing the Mental Game.

As I have said before, this is a lifelong process. Assuming that you are continuously working on it and are making it important, the improvement in focusing and letting go will continue until you retire from the game.

When you work with this aspect of tennis, you will also find that your enjoyment of the game will be greatly enhanced.

So, after you play a match, go over these questions and/or use the Match Analysis Sheet (Lesson No. 89) to determine where you may need some work.

Playing the Mental Game also means that you constantly are aware of not only your play but of also what is going on in your mind on and off the court.

Lesson No. 20: The Mother Of All Tips

Have you ever wanted a technique that pretty much did it all when it comes to practicing your strokes, consistency, focus, and your relaxation? The mother of all tips comes pretty close to doing it all. Wow! How good is that?

I do believe that this is one of the "miracle" tips, but it will take some focus and concentration so you can do it correctly.

Here is what you are to do.

Start by holding your follow-through until you see your ball bounce on the other side of the net. This means that your arm and racquet will come to an absolute stop. You must do this even if you miss the ball. In fact, it is even more valuable to hold it longer when you miss.

When you are holding, pay attention to the location of your follow-through and how relaxed you are. This is the time you will relax your grip and arm, maybe to the extreme.

Ask yourself, if someone was standing next to you, could they take the racquet out of your hand without much effort? That is how relaxed you must work toward.

I also did not say to try to follow-through correctly or to make anything happen. You are just letting your arm and racquet go wherever it wants to end up naturally. You will also hold and relax your footwork.

Here are some things to watch out for when doing this exercise.

- You will have a tendency to not hold the stroke when you miss and not even know it, so you must be very aware and allow yourself to hold even longer at these times.
- In addition, you will have a tendency to not allow the stroke to come to an absolute stop every time, even on a regular stroke, so you need to be especially aware of this.
- Remember that this is not the time to worry about hitting the ball into the court. It is much more important to hold your follow-through, even if it means that you miss the next ball because you are not ready for it.
- You will also need to be aware of whether you fall off balance when you are holding your footwork. If you find that you are off balance, it means that your legs are too tense, so you will have to relax them until your body can figure out how to keep your balance.

After you get comfortable with the holding and relaxing, work on seeing the ball to your racquet some of the time, and some of the time work on your breathing. If you can do all three in the same period of time, that would be ideal.

This exercise has a lot of benefits, some of which you may not even know about. The foremost is that it will absolutely groove your strokes. It will make you more consistent in hitting the balls in the court. It will force you to learn how to be balanced with your footwork. And best of all, it will help you break the pattern of reacting physically and judging your shot.

Speaking of reacting physically to your shots, do you know when you do react and/or judge your shots and what it looks like? Here are some questions to ask yourself to see if you ever react to or judge a shot:

- Do you ever make a verbal sound when you miss? Some of my students make a sound but are not even aware of it until I point it out to them.
- Do you look away immediately when you miss or look away even if you hit a great shot?
- Do you look down at the ground or hang your head after a shot is missed?
- Do you pump your arm when you hit a winner?
- Are you aware of any other physical patterns that you do when you either miss a shot or hit a winner?

If you answered yes to any of these questions, use it as a wakeup call to remind yourself that you need to let go more, let go of any judgments, and stop trying so hard.

The short version of this Mother of All Tips exercise is to just allow your arm and your footwork to come to a complete stop before you recover to the ready position. However, if you have difficulty with this, then you will need to go back to holding your follow-through until your ball bounces on the other side.

When you use the Mother of all Tips, it will help you, bigtime, on the problem of letting go of your physical reactions. Please spend some quality time with it.

Playing Zen-Sational Tennis

Let me tell you a story about how well this tip can work.

When I was at a tournament where my book was being sold, one of the players who bought my book asked me if I would give him "the test" in person. Since I love giving the test, I said sure. Well, he was one of the 2% who got the test correct, but his strokes were not very grooved. I told him that I wanted to show him the Mother of all Tips, which I did. It took me about 10 minutes to get him to do this technique to my satisfaction.

He was still in the consolation mixed doubles with a partner who he had not met previously as the tournament had fixed him up with this partner. After his match, his partner said to him, "What happened to your game? You improved 1,000%!" Now, I think she must have exaggerated a little, but it gives you an idea as to how powerful this technique can be. And in only 10 minutes.

This technique is not to be used in match play. It is to be used when you warm up and practice. However, if you want to use it in a game situation, then you can do it but only if you truly make it okay to miss more balls and you make it okay to sometimes not be ready for the return ball. Remember, this is to help you groove your strokes and not to maximize your play. However, you just might find yourself playing hugely better like the man in the story above.

I would like to think that my strokes are pretty solid after playing for over 50 years, but I still use this exercise. It is one of the most all-around incredible exercises that I have ever developed.

You can do it while practicing seeing the ball. You can do it while working on your breathing, and even better, you can do this while combining seeing the ball and breathing.

Please don't underestimate the value of this lesson. I have never seen this exercise fail. Not only to make the stroke consistent but also to hit more balls in the court. This is not a bad thing. Notice that I didn't say "more consistent." I said "consistent" period.

It absolutely makes your strokes consistent when you do this properly. **If you want a visual picture of this exercise, search for "mother of all tennis tips" on Google to watch the video on YouTube that I made.**

Lesson No. 21: Finish The Follow-through, No Matter What

I'm assuming that you have been using the Mother of all Tips (Lesson No. 20) exercise from time to time. Here is a variation of it that I'm finding absolutely critical to my play. It will be critical to your play as well when you do it.

In fact, I have found this concept so critical to playing well that I have added it to the Core Principles.

Here is how I discovered it.

I tape all matches when the big tournaments are on TV so that I can then go back and watch Roger Federer play. He is the only player I really watch because of the way he plays. I find it inspiring.

Playing Zen-Sational Tennis

During the U.S. Open one year I was fast-forwarding through the matches looking for a Federer match and sometimes I would stop and take a look at the other matches.

Well, I ran across the quarter final woman's match where Elena Dementieva was playing. When I watch matches, I look for different things than the average spectator.

As I was watching, I saw the way she worked the point. Her strategy was as perfect as I have ever seen. Most players don't seem to have any strategy to their play, so when I see a player who does, I am amazed.

Anyway, as I was watching I noticed something about her backhand. On every backhand stroke and literally every time, Elena took a perfect and complete finish.

Her finish was perfect even when she had to lunge for a ball and even when she had to hit a hard and/or reaching return of serve. I was fascinated by this as I always teach that the follow-through is the most important part of the stroke.

The next time I played I began to take a look at my own follow-through. I noticed that there were a whole bunch of times that I tensed up and did not do a full finish. So I began to "let" my arm finish completely on every hit. I even did this in a match. I always tell my students that they need to let go of any stroke thoughts when they play but I did it anyway in a match, mainly so that I could practice finishing my follow-through.

An amazing thing happened. I began to hit the ball with more power, more consistency and more accuracy. Even on the return of serve. How good is that? Of course, I still saw the ball properly and either exhaled properly or did the Bounce-Hit method, as well as kept a relaxed grip.

Shortly after working with finishing my follow-through completely, I was driving home from California. I usually stop in Ashland, Ore. to visit a good friend and play tennis with one of my students at the local club there. Up to then, I had never beaten him. However, this time I beat him pretty easily just because I allowed myself to finish every stroke completely. That was the only difference.

Do you know why doing this works so well? The reasons I talk about in why you should do the Mother of All Tips are the same. However, being very aware of your follow-through and letting it go more is a huge refinement of that exercise.

If you have spent any time doing the Mother of All Tips you should have noticed how well it works. Once I was aware that I was not doing the full finish every time, and especially on certain shots like wide running balls, approach shots, return of serves, and easy balls, I was then able to let my follow-through finish completely. And the results spoke for themselves.

Let me remind you that you still must do the other parts of focusing. Finishing the follow-through works best with proper seeing the ball and exhaling properly, or doing the Bounce-Hit and with a very relaxed grip. I have also found that I am able to finish properly now without a lot of attention to it, but I still find that many times when I miss a ball, I can trace it back to being too tense on my finish.

I have been having all my students work on being aware of their finish. Again, just about every time one of my students misses a shot, I can see that the tenseness of the follow-through plays a part. Yes, you can miss a shot even though you take a fully relaxed finish, but

124

there is a much better chance you will hit the ball in if you finish each stroke completely.

If you talk to my students, they'll tell you that I have 3 new words that I use a lot. I tell them that they are to finish their stroke, **"NO MATTER WHAT."**

The next time you play, try paying attention to your follow-through and just let it finish completely, **NO MATTER WHAT**, and see what happens. It may just surprise you.

Lesson No. 22: Focus Your Awareness In Segments

When you play, you know what to focus on, right? However, you may think that you are focusing properly, but when you start to miss balls you may want to take another look at how you are focusing and what you may be missing. Sometimes the Conscious Mind tries to hide from you what you need to do to play really well so you may want to go through these check points to make sure you are not missing some focus points.

When I play and I start missing, most of the times it is one little area in my focus that is "off", so I have compiled a list of focus areas for you to look at and to practice to make sure you are focusing properly.

To make sure you are focusing properly and also to help you strengthen your focus in areas that you are weak in or are not doing at all, is to focus your awareness in segments. So spend some period of time being aware of all of the following. Do them one at a time or two at the most to make sure that you are not missing any of these areas of focus.

In case you haven't figured it out, I have bolded certain words to emphasize their importance. **Consciously** is one of the very important words so please make sure you are being very aware when I use this word.

On Normal Ground Strokes

1. **Consciously** see the ball spinning after the bounce.
2. **Consciously** see the ball to the blur of the racquet.
3. **Consciously** see the ball spinning before the ball bounces.
4. **Consciously** keep your focus at your contact point for a second.
5. **Consciously** see the ball spinning after you hit it as it goes over the net.
6. **Consciously** see the ball bounce on other side.
7. **Consciously** see the ball and the direction as it comes off your opponent's racquet.

8. **Consciously** feel the grip and the wrist to make sure your grip and wrist is very relaxed at impact as well as during the rest of the stroke.
9. **Consciously** feel and allow a complete finish. Sometimes the momentum will allow you to make a complete finish or on an easy ball the follow-through will feel as if it floats up to a complete finish.

When Breathing

1. **Consciously** start your exhale when the ball bounces as it comes to you.
2. **Consciously** focus on continuing your exhale until the ball bounces on the other side.
3. **Consciously** focus on making your exhale more relaxed.

When Serving

1. Focus on starting your exhale as you release the toss.
2. Focus on keeping your exhale until your ball bounces on the other side.
3. **Consciously** see the ball hit your opponent's racquet.
4. Focus on making your exhale as relaxed as possible even though you are serving hard.

When Volleying

1. **Consciously** start your exhale when your opponent hits the ball.
2. **Consciously** focus on keeping your exhale through your hit.
3. **Consciously** focus on keeping your exhale until your ball bounces.
4. **Consciously** see the ball and the direction as it comes off your opponent's racquet .
5. **Consciously** see the ball spinning at it comes to your racquet.
6. **Consciously** see the ball to the blur of your racquet.

7. **Consciously** feel your grip and wrist at impact to make sure it is as relaxed as possible.

When You Return Serve

1. **Consciously** start your exhale before your opponent hits the ball.
2. **Consciously** focus on keeping your exhale throughout your hit.
3. **Consciously** focus on keeping your exhale until your ball bounces on the other side.
4. **Consciously** see the ball after the bounce as it comes to you.
5. **Consciously** see the ball to the blur of your racquet.
6. **Consciously** feel and allow a complete finish.
7. **Consciously** feel your grip and wrist at impact to make sure it is as relaxed as possible.

Lesson No. 23: Do You Ever Listen To The Ball?

I must confess, I have not been very good about spending any time listening. That does not mean, however, that listening to the ball hit your racquet, your opponent's racquet and the ground is not valuable and important to do. It all helps letting the mind learn to release control and having you experience what letting the body do the work feels like.

Playing Zen-Sational Tennis

Let me tell you a story. I have a friend who is a Buddhist and one day we were talking and I asked him how he practiced being one. He said

that there were a lot of meditations that he did and I asked him to give me an example. He said that he would just meditate and listen to all the sounds around him with no thoughts or judgments, but just being aware of them.

I thought that would be an interesting idea for when I am playing tennis as it would keep me in the here and now and keep my mind calm and clear. I had not done any listening on the court before. I had not been able to play for about 4 months because of an elbow injury, but I thought that I would just listen for the ball hitting the ground and hitting my racquet when I got back into playing.

Before I was able to play again, I read Ron Waite's latest article on the Tennis Server website (see Lesson No. 88) and lo and behold he talks about listening on the court. Go to this link: **www.maxtennis.com/articles.php** on my website and scroll down to read his article called "Listen to Your Game."

I would strongly suggest that you read it. He has already had a lot of experience in listening. It is all about letting go and having a calm mind when you play, and I really believe listening when you play will help.

After I started playing again, I began to listen to the sound of the ball hitting the ground and the ball hitting the racquet on both sides of the court. If you have done the Bounce-Hit exercise that I explained in Lesson No. 7, then this concept of listening is very similar except that you are hearing the ball instead of saying "bounce" or "hit."

Of course, you will want to see the ball at the same time. Anyway, I have found it a very calming way to stay in the here and now as well as a technique to learn how to further let go of consciously trying to control your play.

As with some of the other drills and ideas that work on letting go, I don't believe that you will want to do this in a match that is important. You may use it when you are playing practice matches as it will be a good test for you to see if you can let go of your strokes and everything else enough to still hear the ball and see the ball at the same time. As always, the ultimate way to play the Mental Game is to use the "Core Principles."

Lesson No. 24: Important Things To Do When Practicing

Here are some very important things you need to work on. Remember to work on these in segments either when you warm up, drill or even in practice matches. Then work on combining.

Even though I have given you much of the same things to work on in Lesson No. 22, it never hurts to be reminded as these things are so important to do.

Here they are again in a little different format:

- **Consciously** see the ball all the way to your racquet. Don't forget to see it go over the net as it comes to you. On the

130

Playing Zen-Sational Tennis

return of serve, it is especially important to **consciously** see the ball spinning after the bounce as it comes to you.

- On groundstrokes, start the exhale when the ball bounces as it comes to you keeping the exhale going until your ball bounces on the other side.

- On return of serve, start the exhale before your opponent hits the serve and keep the exhale going until your ball hits the ground on the other side.

- When you are at net, start the exhale when your opponent hits the ball and keep the exhale going until your ball hits the ground on the other side.

- When serving, start the exhale as you release the ball on the toss and keep the exhale going until your ball hits the ground on the other side.

- In all cases the exhale is a relaxing sigh and you keep the exhales going until your ball hits the ground on the other side.

- Relaxing the grip and the wrist all the way to the end of the stroke.

- Letting the follow-through finish completely **NO MATTER WHAT**.

- Releasing the elbow on the forehand.

- When serving, speed up the swing as your arm starts to go into the bend behind your back.

- Alternate breathing and the Bounce-Hit when you play games or points. You get to decide how long you do each but make sure that you spend time with both. Remember, doing the Bounce-Hit takes the place of the exhale but you still see the ball properly when doing both.

- Release the grip at the end of the stroke to the point of almost dropping the racquet.
- If your ball goes long, reprogram it the way I talk about doing it in Lesson No. 51. The same for when the ball goes into the net or wide.

Lesson No. 25: Give Yourself A Lesson Every Time You Play

Do you ever wish that you didn't have to pay for a million lessons every time you want to improve or learn a new stroke?

Once you really learn this technique, you can give yourself a lesson on any stroke or any part of tennis that you may ever want to learn. If you remember, I gave you a summary of "The Process" in Lesson No. 15. Here I will address using it to learn tennis strokes.

You probably think that I am repeating myself again and you would be right. This process is so important for you to learn that I wanted you to read it again. In this lesson the process is more specific to learning tennis things. So please don't skip over this lesson unless you have it completely memorized. It is an extremely powerful process.

Step 1: You first must know exactly how to hit the stroke you want to practice. This is your goal or ideal stroke. You must know it so

well that you can teach it to a beginner. If you don't know exactly how you want to hit your stroke, you can still use this technique, but
132

you will bypass step 2 and start with step 3. Or you will need to actually take a lesson from a teaching pro or watch a video of a pro hitting the stroke so that you are very clear on how to hit it.

Step 2: Take some practice swings without the ball, starting from the ready position and making certain you are able to do these practice swings absolutely perfect every time. Take as many of these swings as needed until you can stroke it relaxed and without thinking too hard about how to do it. **Please review The Shadow Stroke found in Lesson No. 15.**

In order to make sure that you are taking the practice stroke correctly, you may need to follow your stroke with your eyes as the racquet goes through your entire swing and especially into the backswing. Remember, the follow-through is the most important part of the stroke so make sure that you pay extra attention to it.

Before you start hitting the ball, decide what part of the stroke you want to work on. Choose only one part at a time, and plan on spending a few minutes on each part.

I would start with the follow-through because, as I said earlier, I believe this is the most important part of the stroke. Then I would spend a few minutes on the grip and the wrist to make sure that they are very relaxed. Next I would go to the backswing, followed by the path of the racquet as it goes forward to the contact with the ball, and then the footwork.

Step 3: When you start hitting the ball you will want to compare your actual stroke with your ideal stroke. A good place to start this

133

comparison is with the follow-through. As you swing, just be relaxed, feel and be aware of the arm and the racquet as it moves to wherever they both finish up. This needs to be done with as little conscious effort as possible.

When you make your stroke as relaxed as you can, your body will learn very quickly how to follow-through correctly, and later on when you are not thinking about the stroke, your body will still stroke it the way you were practicing it. This is what you are aiming for.

As you compare your stroke when you are hitting with "your ideal stroke" and you are aware that your stroke is not doing what you want it to, then stop hitting the ball and take a number of practice swings again without the ball using an absolutely perfect swing. It would also be helpful to visualize this perfect swing and/or talk to yourself about the swing. Then go back to Step 2 and just be relaxed and feel your stroke again.

If your stroke is not getting close to your practice swing or is not improving, it means you are trying too hard to control your stroke, and you will need to relax some part of your body more. Another issue you may have is that you may be trying so hard to just hit the ball that you didn't do a very good job of feeling the stroke.

While you are following the instructions listed above, do not be concerned about where your ball is going or try to hit the ball into the court. You are playing a different game. Your awareness is to be on your stroke or what I call body awareness and not on the ball.

As you get better at feeling your stroke, it would be helpful to add seeing the ball or being aware of your breathing. Do not try to do both at the same time. If you find yourself missing too many shots, you could fix this by visualizing your ball going into the court and then letting go of any thoughts about this and just getting back to being relaxed and feeling your stroke again.

Remember, you are working on your stroke and not working on hitting the ball into the court.

Lastly, you are not to use this technique in a match. This is only for practice and/or warm-up.

Lesson No. 26: Secrets Of Winning The Mental Game And The Steps You Need To Take

Here in this lesson, I will review the long-held secrets of the steps you need to take to win the Mental Game.

Are you doing everything you can to learn all there is to know about playing the Mental Game?

Being the compulsive tennis instructor that I am, I feel an obligation to you that just reading this book, listening to my CDs or taking a few lessons is not enough. Until you actually understand and are able to incorporate these ideas and concepts into your game, I feel that my job is not done.

You will still need to implement this Action Plan, which is designed to give you a complete road map on all the steps you can take so that you can continue practicing the Mental Game.

Here are my ideas on the most efficient way. These ideas will also speed up your learning and the mastering of the Mental Game.

The Action Plan

- Go to **www.maxtennis.com/download.php** to get Dick Leach's doubles booklet if you haven't already. Dick Leach was the coach at U.S.C. for a number of years. He is retired now, but he was and is a master of doubles strategy. He has given me permission to give out his booklet and you get it free with my book and my CD's.

- Listen to the entire CD series or read my book over and over. You will be re-enforcing what playing the Mental Game all is about and what you have already learned.

- Re-read or read for the first time, Tim Gallwey's book, *The Inner game of Tennis*. If you haven't read this book, it is required reading in order to get the most out of the Mental Game.

- Read Ron Waite's e-book *Perfect Tennis, 10 Steps to a Much Better Game*. This e-book compliments the information I give you in this book and on my CDs and gives you easy and necessary steps for you to take to facilitate improving your game. It is only $10 and it is absolutely a must if you are really serious about improving. Go here to order. **www.tennisserver.com/turbo/perfect-tennis.html**

- Know that your ultimate goal is to find out what state your mind and body needs to be in to play your very best every time you play. This book and my CDs will guide you to this place as you work through the Lessons.

- Re-read and review the "Core Principles" before you play your matches and especially tournament matches. These principles will be the foundation to everything you do when playing the Mental Game. Print them out if you have not already done so. The web address for printing them is **www.maxtennis.com/core_principles.php**

- Letting go of winning is a huge key to playing the Mental Game. Just knowing that winning takes care of itself and letting go of judgments on how you play are huge steps into discovering how to play your very best every time.

- Listen to or read the lessons on Seeing the Ball and Breathing all the way through again. I have given you "the test" talked about in the seeing of the ball lesson. If you haven't gone to the web page and gotten the answer to how the ball must be seen, then you must do it now. Here is the web page again. Please stop now and go here. **www.maxtennis.com/secret_answer.htm.** This is an absolutely critical part of seeing the ball. Spend more concentrated time where the only thing you are doing is seeing the ball as described in the seeing of the ball lesson. Read or listen to this lesson at least three times during this next week so that you don't miss something important when you are working on seeing the ball. Also, make sure that you "play" the other little seeing the ball games as described in this lesson.

- Spend a week (or a lifetime), working only on your breathing. Again, listen to or read this lesson three times during this week. Just because you find the breathing difficult to do, please do not ignore working with it as it is a critical part of playing the Mental Game.

- Spend a week, working only on the relaxing of your body. Really work on relaxing your grip, your wrist, your arm at the shoulder, and any other part of your body that seem to be too tight. You do this by feeling or what I call "body awareness".

- If you haven't already, start doing the drills that are found on the Drills CD or in the back of this book. Once you have worked on the seeing the ball, breathing, and relaxing, now is the time to work on combining seeing the ball and breathing if you haven't already. While you are doing this, pay attention to what is going on. Your mind will guide you to what you need to pay attention to. For example, if you are hitting a lot of balls long, you will need to focus on the corrections which are all found in Lesson No. 51. This is why I want you to listen to my CDs or read my book over and over so when these issues come up you have all these "corrections" memorized and you can fix them immediately.

- Spend a week doing The Mother of All Tips (Lesson No. 20) at least 10 or 15 minutes each time you drill or warm up. Remember this is not to be done in a match or game and only when you are warming up or drilling. Really work on doing exactly what it says. Holding the follow-through means having your whole body and racquet come to an absolute and complete stop. While you are holding, check to see if the various parts of your body are relaxed being especially aware of your arm, wrist and fingers. Remember, you can watch this technique on YouTube by searching for "mother of all tips."

-

- Go through the rest of the Lessons one at a time and spend as much time working on them as you feel you need to.
- I have a personal checklist that I use when practicing. You can use them and customize the checklist for your own needs. To print these checklists, go to **www.maxtennis.com/my_check_list.php**.
- Every 3 months listen to the complete CD series or read my book all the way through for the first year.
- Realize that playing the Mental Game is a process and a lifelong endeavor. Give it a chance by making it the most important thing to do when you play.

Contact me if you have any questions, I am here to help you. Please feel free to call me or e-mail me anytime with any questions. My phone number is 360 305-7084. Call anytime between 9:00am to 9:00pm. My e-mail address is **david@maxtennis.com**.

So, there you have it. The ball is in your court. I hope you are going for it, as this way of playing truly is a better way to play this wonderful game of tennis.

Lesson No. 27: Stop Getting Nervous Before A Tournament Or Important Match

Have you ever tried really hard to stop being nervous before a tournament or before playing an important match and just couldn't relax and calm yourself?

Playing Zen-Sational Tennis

Well, you just can't stop being nervous until you deal with the cause. People get nervous for a reason.

See if any of these possible reasons apply to you:

- Are you worried about losing?
- Are you making the match too important?
- Are you worried about playing badly?
- Are you worried about letting someone else down like a parent, husband, wife, girl or boy friend, or maybe letting your school team down if you don't win?
- Are you worried about any other issue?

All of these possible reasons boil down to wanting to win. Remember winning will take care of itself. You don't have to worry about winning or losing, because if you play better than your opponent, you will win. Just focus on the Core Principles and you will be playing as well as you are capable.

You also have to let go of making the match important. When you make the match important, you will tense up, probably try too hard and therefore not play as well as you could. Remember, this is not life or death. Even if you are playing for a million dollars, making it important will not help you play better and most likely will hurt your play.

When you use the Mental Game Core Principles it will be impossible for you to be nervous when you are on the court because you will be playing a different game. You will be playing an inner game, which will help you play your best, and if that best is better than your opponent, then you will win.

If you don't win, you will need to practice more on your weaknesses and maybe even on letting go. But being nervous because you are worrying about winning, won't lead you to playing your best. You may still win, but you probably won't feel so good about it.

On the other hand, if you go out and have some fun, play the Mental Game, and let winning take care of itself, you just may find yourself playing very well. If you didn't win, most likely you will still feel pretty good about your game.

Lesson No. 28: Ground Stokes: A Check List Of Things To Practice

You have most likely taken some lessons on your ground strokes. Some of you have taken lots of lessons, but, do you know what to practice? You now know how to practice because I have given you the process for giving yourself a lesson every time you play (Lesson No. 25) but have you ever kept a check list of things to practice? I will bet that you haven't and here is your chance to be awesome.

This checklist is just a guideline for you. It includes some issues that I feel are important to take a look at from time to time. As you practice, you should be adding your own personal stroke issues to this list and it is important that you keep a personal check list on your computer so that you can easily add to it and print it out so you can take it to the court with you.

When you practice, you should use the process that I discussed in Lesson No. 25 to work on any of these issues.

Here is the checklist.

- Hit all balls harder that are above the net and not too deep.
- Hit more top spin on low balls, short balls, and down-the-line balls.
- Make sure you do a complete follow-through **NO MATTER WHAT,** especially on reaching balls, return of serves and when your opponent is at net.
- Exhale through the mouth in a relaxed way, with a sigh just before and through hitting the ball and allow the exhale to continue until your ball bounces.
- When returning serve, gently exhale with a sigh just as your opponent hits the ball and continue exhaling through your hit and until your ball bounces on the other side.
- Take a split step just as your opponent hits the ball.
- If you are missing the return of serve, hit the ball a little easier, using a more relaxed stroke.
- If you are having trouble returning serve, hold your follow-through until it comes to a complete stop. Of course, make sure you are seeing the ball and breathing properly.
- If the stroke is not feeling proper and if you feel the need, take a practice swing without the ball. This is a good idea to do after every miss.
- Allow the racquet to rotate over the ball gently as contact with the ball is made when you are hitting topspin.

Please add some of your own issues and then spend some time working on them. By having a check list, you won't forget the areas that you need to work on and you will get the most from any lesson you take on your strokes.

Lesson No. 29: How To Stop Getting Angry With Yourself

Do you think that getting angry helps you play better? Do you think that getting angry is a good thing? Does getting angry ever make you feel good?

I am assuming that your answer to these questions is no and that you understand that getting angry with yourself is usually unproductive.

Why you get angry with yourself is pretty easy to understand. You get angry because you have tried to do something over and over again and you still are making the same mistakes or you are expecting a different outcome.

When you miss an easy shot, for example, you tell yourself that you should have been able to hit that ball into the court, especially because it was so easy. So the next time you get an easy ball, you try even harder, using your Conscious Mind to get it in, and because you have tensed up more by trying harder, you miss it again and get even more upset with yourself.

However, the really big question is "How do you stop getting angry?"

The obvious answer to this is for you to let go of trying to hit the ball into the court and let go of judging yourself or caring if you miss. I know this may be a little difficult to accept and even counterproductive, but letting go of judgments will help you hit more balls into the court. It really does work, and it is a really important part of the Mental Game. And, guess what? By letting go of these things, you will not get angry.

143

Playing Zen-Sational Tennis

Do you know who is hitting the ball when you play? You probably answered, "I do." Trust me, it is not you. It is your body that is being directed by your "Other-Than-Conscious Mind." If you think about it, if I cut off one of your arms, you are still completely there. It is just part of your body that isn't there.

When you allow your Conscious Mind to control your body, your body most likely won't function properly all the time, especially when the match gets tight. This is because your Conscious Mind does not know exactly what muscles to use, what the angle of the racquet must be, what the perfect timing of the shot is, etc.

Your body, however, knows far more than your Conscious Mind about how the ball needs to be hit. And if it doesn't, it will learn better and faster without you or your Conscious Mind trying to control it. You must work on getting your Conscious Mind out of the way.

The job of your Conscious Mind is to set the goals for your body and then step aside. We accomplish this by relaxing the grip, seeing the ball, breathing properly, and letting go of everything else. In other words you will use the Mental Game Core Principles.

There are many ways to quickly release your anger and here are a couple of them. However, the main goal is to not get angry in the first place.

- Just remember to lighten up and have fun. Remember that tennis is supposed to be a fun game, and even if you become the greatest player who ever lived, you will still miss some balls. Even easy ones. I often wonder why players think they should never miss a ball. It's just part of the game. Accept it.

- Put your game in perspective and don't make it so important. Because, guess what? It really isn't that important, is it? Even if you are playing at a professional level, making it important when you are on the court will not help you play better.

Now that you know how to stop getting angry, go play the Mental Game and you will miss fewer balls, which should make it easier for you win more matches and will enhance your enjoyment of the game.

Lesson No. 30: Why "Slow" Or "Easy" Balls Are Not Easy

I will bet you never miss easy balls, do you? Oh, you do? Why is that? If they are so easy, then how can you possibly miss them?

People always think that a ball that is coming slow and is a "set up" is easy to hit and when they miss this set up they get mad. Let's take a look at these easy balls and see why they really are not that easy and how to make them easy once you understand "the animal."

Let me put my physics professor hat on for a minute. What do you know about an easy ball? Well, first of all, it is traveling slowly. Duh! Ok, but what is really different about them? If you see the trajectory of a slow ball, you will notice that it is more up and down. On a fast ball, this trajectory is pretty much parallel to the ground when you are hitting it.

Playing Zen-Sational Tennis

The analogy I like to use is two cars at an intersection. If the two cars are coming at right angles, the speed of the two cars and the timing has to be perfect for them to have a crash. But, if they are coming from opposite directions, the speed can be anything and you will hit the other car. You can even close your eyes and the cars will still crash.

When you are going to hit a slow easy ball, the ball is traveling more up and down and you are going to swing at it more parallel to the ground. You will also want to swing with more speed because you have to generate your own power since you won't be getting much power off the speed of the ball. These factors make the timing of hitting an "easy" ball more difficult.

So, what do you need to do on these slow balls in order to get the "right timing?" Do you know yet what I am going to say?

In order to get the timing perfect, you really need to see the ball to the blur of the racquet so that your body can learn to time it correctly. And how about exhaling very relaxed and having a very relaxed grip?

Hitting these kinds of balls should be easier to do since the ball is coming slowly, but let's look at what the mind is saying. It is saying, "Ok, this is a really easy ball and I am going to hit it hard for a winner and win the point." When you think this, your focus is no longer on the ball, you probably will tense up your stroke, your grip and your breathing, and therefore you have a good chance of missing. Then you get mad, and on the next one you try harder and the pattern continues or gets worse. Or, maybe, you hit the last easy

ball really well so you try to do it again which may lead to tension which in turn causes you to miss the next time you get an easy ball.

146

The next time you play and you get these easy balls and you start missing, really see the ball to the blur of the racquet, keeping your focus on the contact point for a short time, keep a relaxed grip, don't try hard to hit a winner and see what happens. Don't forget that your breathing needs to also be relaxed and you should be exhaling as you hit the ball. As you know, this breathing helps keep your upper body relaxed.

Now you know the secret to making a "slow" and "easy" ball truly easy. Pretty easy, eh?

Lesson No. 31: Volleys: A Checklist Of Things To Practice

Just like the ground strokes I have talked in lesson No. 28, you have most likely taken some lessons on your volley. And again, you now know how to practice but have you ever kept a check list of things to practice on your volley? Again, I will bet that you haven't.

This checklist is just a guideline for you. It includes some issues that I feel are important to take a look at from time to time. As you practice, you should be adding your own personal volley issues to this list and it is important that you keep a personal check list on your computer so that you can easily add to it and print it out so you can take it to the court with you.

When you practice, you should use the process that I discussed in Lesson No. 25 to work on any of these issues.

This checklist is for when you practice your volley. Hopefully, you are adding some of your own personal issues to this list.

Here is the check list for the volley.

- Keep the head of the racquet higher than the handle at all times. If there is one thing you should do when working on the physical stroke, this is it.
- See the trajectory as the ball comes to your racquet.
- Hit any volley that is above the net hard.
- Take a split step at the moment your opponent hits the ball.
- Show the emblem on the backswing.
- Exhale through the mouth in a relaxed way, using a sigh just before and long after hitting the ball.
- Have your racquet continue 12 to 18 inches after hitting the ball. This means that you want to hit through the ball as if it isn't there.
- Keep the face of your racquet facing in the direction of where you want the ball to go as best you can.
- Keep your grip very relaxed.

Lesson No. 32: What To Do To Prevent Choking

Any time you are in a close match or set and then you lose, you need to take a look at what happened as the end of the match approached. You need to ask yourself, "Did I lose the match or set because I missed easy balls, or did my opponent win by hitting winners or forcing me into errors?"

If you lost because your opponent played better than you at the end and you didn't miss balls that you were hitting earlier, then the only conclusion as to why you lost is that he or she played better than you did on that day. You may want to figure out how your opponent played better, where he or she was hurting you, and where your weaknesses were, and then work on them.

On the other hand, if you missed easy shots or played worse than you did earlier, then you "choked.

The good news is that you can learn to not choke.

Here are some questions you need to ask yourself so you can begin to learn about why you choked:

- As the match got closer, did I think about winning?
- Did I have any thoughts about losing?
- Did I have thoughts that said, "All I have to do is hold serve" or "If I win this next game I will win the set or match"?
- Did I have thoughts that said, "I better not lose my serve" or "If I lose this next game I will lose the set or match"?
- Did I try hard to win or to hit the ball in the court?
- Did I try hard to "not lose"?

Did I hear any "yes" answers? Did you answer yes to all of them? If you answered yes to all of them, you are in serious trouble and we will need to do a frontal lobotomy. Please make an appointment.

Playing Zen-Sational Tennis

Here is the ultimate answer to choking. It is one that must be taken very seriously if you want to control your choking or eliminate it all together. So, here it is.

Any thought of winning or losing when the match or set is close is Death. Trying hard to do anything, especially at this time of the match, is Death. Any thought of winning or losing at any time of the match is Death.

Again, what happens at this time is that you start to try harder, and therefore you start tensing up. As you miss more, you try even harder, you get more tense, and the cycle continues.

So, what do you do? You do the opposite.

First of all, as soon as you are aware of any of the unproductive thoughts I just talked about, you must stop these thoughts in their tracks. One good technique is to say "Cancel, Cancel" or you can yell as loud as you can to yourself silently "Stop!" and then reprogram as follows.

You relax more. This means that you will take a deep breath and do a complete relaxing sigh. Then trust your body to hit the shots, focus on the ball better, without trying hard, of course, while you exhale properly, keep a relaxed grip and let your body play.

You will also want to use these kinds of productive statements.

"OK, body, I can't win this. You will have to do it. I will stay out of your way and I will just see the ball, breathe, and keep a relaxed grip." Or, "I am going to just let my body play and let the outcome be what it will be." In other words, you will get back to doing just the Core Principles.

150

Playing Zen-Sational Tennis

The closer the match, the more you want to trust your Other-Than-Conscious Mind to make your shots. This means that you focus well, keep your Conscious Mind out of the way and keep it from controlling your shots. And, of course, this happens when your body is relaxed.

At the same time, your opponent is doing what you used to do. He or she is trying harder because at this time of the match he or she is thinking that winning every point is very important and therefore will most likely be the one tensing up and choking. I can't tell you how many times I have seen this happen when I get into a close match, and especially in a tiebreaker situation.

I was playing in a league match a few years ago. It was a pretty close match and I had won the first set. I am not exaggerating when I say that when I went to the net and my opponent lobed, he hit the lob within a foot of the baseline every time.

Likewise, when he went to the net, and I lobbed, he didn't miss one overhead and hit winners every time. Ok, here we are in the tiebreaker in the second set. The score was 5–5. I get a short ball so I hit my approach shot well enough so that I force my opponent to hit a lob. Guess what. His lob was a setup for me and I won the point.

Now it is match point for me. He is serving and he comes to the net and forces me to hit a lob and I hit a short one. I say to myself that the point is over and I start walking to receive the next serve. Well, to my surprise, he actually shanked the overhead and missed it. I couldn't believe it. Here he had hit winners all day long but on match point for me he missed it.

I see this kind of play all day long in players of all levels, including the professionals. The man I played in the league match was trying so

151

hard not to lose or thinking some other unproductive thought and because this was a tiebreaker where in his mind he made every point so important, that he just couldn't play like he did the rest of the match.

I know that not trying to win goes against a lot of the way we were taught, but changing your thinking to what I have described above and in other lessons in this book does work. Please try it.

Lesson No. 33: The Power Of Active Visualization

How many of you are using visualization when you play? If you are not or if you are doing so only sporadically, I would like you to consider getting into the habit.

Visualization is a very powerful way to improve your game. It can be used to "fix" any and all issues you may have when you play.

Here are some of the situations where you may not have thought about using visualization along with the obvious ones.

- When you miss a shot over and over
- When you miss a shot that you may only get once in a while like a running short ball that you tried a drop shot on but held your breath
- When you use an inappropriate strategy in a given situation and then ask yourself "Why did I do that?"

- When you have lapses in your focus under a specific situation (for example, when I get into a long rally, I find my focus leaving and I start trying harder to end the point)
- When you notice that your stroke is not working the way you want it to
- When you are aware of any mental lapses at certain times of the match like thinking about winning at 5-4 when all you have to do is hold serve
- Before the match even starts you can visualize your strategy, your strokes, your focus or anything else you feel needs attention
- When you are missing easy balls
- When you are missing balls you wanted to hit hard

I am sure that you get the idea. The sky is the limit on how or what you visualize. Of course, you need to know that, from my way of thinking, all these situations are mental issues and you must treat them as such. In addition, you must include the Core Principles in all your visualizations. All errors stem from some part of these principles not being done properly.

When I work with new students, I ask them to analyze every ball they miss and then visualize the correction. I have them do this until they remember to visualize when it is really important in their matches. **Caution! Make sure that you let go of trying to make things happen once the match continues. Just let go of whatever it is that you visualized and get back into doing the Core Principles.**

You can do a very thorough job of visualization when you change sides but you can also spend a few seconds on it in between points. The more you practice visualizing the more effective and easy it becomes.

153

If you are not in the habit of using this powerful tool, please start now.

Lesson No. 34: Consistency: The First And Last Resort

If your life depended on you hitting the ball in the court, would you know a way to do it so that you would survive? It is surprising how many players don't have a good idea how to hit the ball consistently.

The whole idea of playing the game of tennis is to hit the ball into the court more times than your opponent. Depending on your level of play, using just the strategy of consistency may be what gives you the win.

Here I am going to tell you how you want the ball to travel in the air so that you can hit every ball in the court. We have already talked about how to make it happen. Do you remember? I hope so. If you answered, see the ball, keep your focus on the contact point for a short time, breathe and relax your grip, then you get another gold star.

There are three obstacles to hitting the ball into the court that must be overcome.

The first is that you must hit the ball over the net. OK, so how high do you think you should hit it? How about six to ten feet over the net. Maybe you would want to aim your ball closer to the ten feet or more distance so that you will have a pretty good margin of error.

The next obstacle is the baseline. When you hit the ball ten feet over the net, you cannot hit the ball too hard; otherwise it will go long. So you must hit the ball fairly easy.

The third obstacle is the sidelines. The obvious way to overcome this is to hit the ball right down the middle.

So, by hitting the ball high over the net, fairly easy, and right down the middle, you will cut down drastically on missing the ball. Use this strategy if and when you start missing your regular shots. Then, when you get your groove back and regain your focus, you can start to hit the ball harder and with more placements closer to the lines and lower over the net.

Drill No. 5: A Consistency Drill

After you are comfortable focusing on the ball and feeling your breathing, you are ready to work on maximizing the number of balls going into the court. So, how do you make the ball go into the court over and over again? You should know the answer to this by now. Did you say just focus on the ball, focus on your breathing, and keeping your body relaxed? Very good. You get an A.

Every time you miss the ball, **consciously** look at where you wanted the ball to go, **consciously** see the spot over the net that the ball must go, and **consciously** look at how high over the net you wanted the ball to go. Then take the time to visualize or talk to yourself about exactly where you wanted the ball to go and take a practice swing as you visualize. If your stroke doesn't feel right, relax it more the next time. If after re-visualizing and/or talking to yourself, your

155

balls don't get more consistent, then you are too tight somewhere in your body and you must relax more. Start with relaxing your grip and/or your wrist.

See if you can hit 10 balls in a row. Then see if you can hit 15, then 20 in a row. Doing this will help you discover what state of mind you need to be in to hit consistently. It will also help you learn to stay focused for longer and longer periods of time.

After working on hitting 10 or more in a row, play a game of up to five points as I explained in Lesson No. 4. Look to see how, if at all, your focus and concentration are affected.

If your shots change once you start the game of five, then you know that you have some more letting go to do. Also pay attention to the way you hit the ball. Did it change? Do you all of a sudden hit the ball easier so that you don't miss it? Ideally, you should be hitting the ball the same as you did before the game of five starts. So, if you aren't hitting the same, you need to "just do it" to use a popular saying.

This game of five that you do when hitting forehands crosscourt, backhands crosscourt and down the line shots are really consistency drills. When you hit to only one place, you will not be able to really hurt your drill partner as you can't make them run and likewise, they can't make you run, so it is the person who can hit the most number of balls in the court that is going to win.

If you have trouble focusing or you find that you are missing shots you were making before playing the points, ask yourself these questions:

- Am I trying to win? If yes, you must know by now that trying doesn't work. Only seeing the ball, keeping your focus on the contact point for a short time, breathing, and relaxing properly does. Remember: if you play better than your opponent, winning will take care of itself. Your job is to find what state of mind you need to be in to maximize the consistency of your play.

- Am I trying to stroke the ball correctly? Am I thinking about my stroke? If you answer yes, you will need to let go and trust that your body will do this for you.

- Am I making **consciously** seeing the ball spinning, keeping my focus on the contact point for a short time, and **consciously** feeling my breathing the most important thing in my life when I am playing? Here is one of the little tricks that might help you stay focused. If I told you that every time you see the ball correctly and breathe correctly when you hit the ball I would pay you $1,000,000, do you think you would make doing these things more important? Most people would say yes. I think the only person who would maybe say no would be Bill Gates. Even if you make it important, you don't need to try hard to do it. You just need to do it.

Working on consistency is another way to work on your ability to focus for a longer time. As you do this, you will find your ability to stay focused in a match easier.

Lesson No. 35: What To Do When You Are Ahead In A Game Or Set

Have you ever been ahead in a match, and started thinking about how close you are to winning the set or match? Join the club. I think all of us have done that. The next question is, "Did you end up actually winning the set or match easily or did your opponent close the gap and you either squeaked the win out or you ended up losing?"

When you find yourself losing or playing badly after you have been ahead, you will need to ask yourself this question: "Is my opponent winning the points by hitting winners or forcing me into errors, or am I just missing shots?" If your opponent is winning the points, there is little you can do except to hit better balls so that he or she can't hit those winning shots. You may need to also change your strategy.

However, if you are just missing shots, then there is something you can do. Here are some questions you need to ask yourself:

- Did I think about "winning"?
- Did I think about "losing"?
- Did I have thoughts that said, "All I have to do is win this next point" and/or "If I win this next point I will win the game, set, or match"?
- Did I have thoughts that said, "I better not lose my serve" or "If I lose this next game I will lose the set or match"?
- Did I try hard to win or to hit the ball in the court?

Playing Zen-Sational Tennis

Any thought of winning or losing at this time of the match is Death. Any thought of winning or losing at any time of the match is Death. Trying hard to do anything, especially at these times of the match, is Death.

Again, what happens when these thoughts occur is that you start to try harder, and therefore you start tensing up, and as you miss more, you try even harder and get more tense, and the cycle continues.

So, what do you do? You do the opposite.

First of all, as soon as you are aware of any of the unproductive thoughts I just talked about, you must stop these thoughts in their tracks. One good technique is to say "Cancel, Cancel" or you can yell as loud as you can to yourself silently "Stop!"and then reprogram as follows.

You relax more. This means that you will take a deep breath and do a complete relaxing sigh. Then trust your body to hit the shots, focus on the ball better, without trying hard, of course, while you exhale properly and let your body play.

You will also want to use these kinds of productive statements.

"OK, body, I can't win this. You will have to do it. I will stay out of your way and I will just see the ball, breathe, and keep a relaxed grip." Or, "I am going to just let my body play and let the outcome be what it will be." In other words, you will get back to doing just the Core Principles.

The closer you are to winning the match, the more you want to trust your Other-Than-Conscious Mind to make your shots. This means that you will focus well yet keep your Conscious Mind out of the way so that it does not control your shots. And, of course, this happens when you keep your body relaxed.

When you read Lesson No. 32 on choking, you may have noticed that the solutions to both of these problems are the same. In fact, you may have noticed that I keep repeating the same things over and over.

I am hoping that by my emphasizing these points, you can see how to overcome the unproductive patterns you have developed over the years. You would not be needing these ideas had your solution, if any, worked. You need to reprogram your mind and adopt a different approach when you are in these situations. When you are able to incorporate these ideas into your play, you will see that they really work.

A future lesson will deal with tiebreakers and how you need to deal with them. As you will see, the solution will be almost identical to the last two dealing with choking and when you are ahead in the score. Please don't skip this one and say to yourself, "I know this already." Your Conscious Mind just may not be telling you the truth. And, even if you know this already, the really big question is, "Are you able to use this information when you are on the court and in these situations.

Lesson No. 36: Why Pumping Your Fist May Not Work

Trying to pump yourself up during a match seems like a good idea, doesn't it? After all, you have to do something to get yourself to pick up the pace and play better, don't you? This is especially true in a tiebreaker or at 5-4 in the third set and all you have to do is to hold serve. And, so many of the top players do it, don't they? All except Federer, even though he seems to be doing it more and more.

I am here to tell you why this may not work. And, if all this pumping and yelling worked, you would see the person who yelled and pumped the best would be the No. 1 player in the world.

Three good examples can be found in the finals of Wimbledon between Nadal and Federer a few years ago. I hope you saw the match as it was very interesting if you look at it from a mental perspective.

Here is what I saw.

In the third set where Nadal won the set in a tiebreaker, what did you see? You saw Nadal pumping and yelling every time he won a point. Yes, he hit some great shots, and he went crazy after he won the set. But look what happened in the fourth set. Did all this pumping up stuff work? Obviously not. He lost the fourth set and the match.

Now let's look at Federer. In the tiebreaker in the third set at 2-1, he hit a great shot to make it 2-2 and he caught the pumping bug from Nadal, or from all the other players who pump, and yelled and pumped his arm. I am telling you that I called the next shot. I told

161

Playing Zen-Sational Tennis

myself that I will bet that he will lose the next point and sure enough he missed a nothing shot. He then went on to lose the tiebreaker. Then in the fourth set at 4-1 when Federer broke Nadal's serve and went up 5-1, Federer again yelled out "come on" and pumped his fist. All Federer had to do then was to hold serve to win the match, but he lost his serve easily. Fortunately, he had another serve to win the match.

So, what happens when this yelling and pumping occurs. You are saying to your body, "Body, you can't play this game. You need me to yell at you. You need me to tell you how to play. You can't move your feet unless I tell you how," etc, etc, etc." If someone you cared about yelled at you this way, would you like it? Would you then feel like going out and playing your best?

When you yell and pump, your Conscious Mind has taken back control of your play. It wants to take credit for making the great play. It then tries to hit the ball as well or better again the next time and as in the above three examples you can see what can happen. The body tenses up and misses balls for no apparent reason because the Conscious Mind does not know how to make the body play well. It just thinks it does, but really only the Other-Than-Conscious Mind does.

Here is the sad part. Sometimes pumping and yelling "come on!" works. Sometimes all this trying works at the beginning of the match or at other times when winning or losing the point isn't so important. However, when the match gets tight, if you really analyze it, you just may see that at those times it just doesn't work very well and, in fact, you may play worse.

And what is even sadder, is that sometimes pumping even works when the match is close and the Conscious Mind then tells you, "See,
162

you need to yell at your body to make it work" and you believe your mind and pump even more.

You will need a third party to observe this when you play, because your ego mind (Conscious Mind) will not always tell you the truth. You may think all this pumping works and you need to do it in order to play well when the reality of it you do not play as well.

Here is another sad part. (There are lots of sad parts here, aren't there? Are you crying yet?) There are some players that when they do all this pumping and yelling they really do play better. I believe Jimmy Connors was one of these players. And because we see one great player who is able to pick up their game this way, we think that this is the way to get ourselves to play better.

Please, don't believe me in this. Check it out yourself. When you are watching matches whether at the pro level or not, take a look at what happens over and over when the points and games get close. You will see a lot of missing nothing balls being missed for no reason.

So many times you will see the person try so much harder and therefore react more and more intensely. Then take a look at Roger Federer when the match gets close. Yeah, he is human and sometimes tries too hard but for the most part he is playing at the top of his game and sometimes spectacularly and he does it looking very calm and without yelling at himself.

The main point I am trying to make is that it is ever so subtle. The Conscious Mind just creeps back in and tries to take control again and again when you aren't looking or paying attention. Check out Lesson No. 87 for another perspective on the ego mind.

Have you ever really experienced this difference between trying and letting the Other-Than-Conscious Mind and body play? Trust me, if you haven't, try it, it works far better. Maybe not every time, but it feels so good when it does. And sometimes it may even work spectacularly.

So, all of this mental stuff that I am trying to drill (I mean have you put) into your head is to let go of having your Conscious Mind control your play. Then I want you to let go more of having your Conscious Mind control your play. And finally, I want you to let go even more of having your Conscious Mind control your play. Have I mentioned letting go yet?

Every concept in these lessons tries to lead you in that direction. That is the purpose of the "Core Principles."

Now that you know this, you just have to keep on practicing letting go. This will be a lifelong process but the results can be remarkable.

Lesson No. 37: More On Fist Pumping

More and more I see the professionals and other players do a lot of this fist pumping and yelling at themselves to "come on" or whatever else they say when they hit a good shot. I think it is a contagious habit and that when players see other players do it they think it's cool or whatever and so they start incorporating it thinking that it helps them play better. Even the media thinks it is cool as you see a lot of pictures of players pumping their fist.

Playing Zen-Sational Tennis

Not only do I not think that it is beneficial, but I believe that it is actually destructive. Why would you want to tense up your whole body and pump your fist and scream out something when you could and should be conserving energy? And why would you want to promote trying?

I believe that fist pumping and yelling actually leads to having your Conscious Mind or ego mind start to control your play and lead you in the opposite direction of playing in the zone. Playing in the zone is accomplished by mindless play, relaxed play, flow or letting go and not by trying harder.

So my idea is that if you want to pump your fist, do it in a very relaxed way, without yelling out, and use it to congratulate your body for hitting a good shot and encouraging it to hit more. When you do it in a calm and relaxed manner you have a better chance of communicating to your body and to your other than conscious part to actually hit better shots.

Just as a reminder, here is the script that you could use when talking to yourself about hitting a great shot. "Body, that was a great shot. Thank you and keep them coming." Or you can make up your own self-talk but you get the idea.

So I'm hoping that you have not caught the fist pumping and yelling disease and, if you are, you are using it or something similar to congratulate your body for hitting a great shot and encouraging it to hit more.

Lesson No. 38: You Must Change Your Unproductive Thoughts

When unproductive thoughts come into your mind, do you know what to do to recover from them?

Maybe the first question should be, "Are you even aware of your unproductive thoughts?" Because, only when you are aware of them can you begin to deal with them.

Here are examples of unproductive thoughts.

- I just need to hold serve in order to win this set.
- I am playing terrible.
- I am ahead and I will just play safe so that I will win.

The "official" definition of an unproductive thought is any thought that not only doesn't help you play better but also thoughts that are destructive and will sabotage your play.

Here is how you can deal with these thoughts and you must deal with them immediately. Please don't wait until the match is over.

The moment you are aware that you had an unproductive thought you say to yourself "Cancel Cancel", and take a sighing exhale or you can yell "Stop" as loud as you can to yourself silently. Then make a statement that is productive.

The kinds of productive statements that I am talking about are as follows: "OK, body, I can't win this. You will have to do it. I will stay out of your way and I will just see the ball, breathe, and keep a very

166

relaxed grip." Or, "I am going to just let my body play and let the outcome be what it will be." In other words, you will get back to doing just the Core Principles.

By the way, you don't need to wait until you have an unproductive thought to use these statements. They are powerful just by themselves and can be used anytime. Especially if you are in a tiebreaker or the score is close at the end of the set or match.

Please don't use a negative like "I am not going to try to hit the ball into the court" because as they say in NLP circles your sub-Conscious Mind does not hear the "not." It just hears "I am going to try …" and hopefully you know trying doesn't work very well.

The other thing you can do if you find yourself "thinking too much" is to occupy your mind by watching a ball and listen to your breathing in between points. You should be doing this anyway and this should sound familiar as it is one of the Core Principles. When you do this it will keep you in the "here and now" and it will be harder for "other thoughts" to intrude.

Here is your assignment should you choose to accept it. For the next week, pay attention to your thoughts when you play your matches, especially as the match gets close to the end and change any unproductive thoughts you might have. Your goal is to have enough awareness to change at least one. Once you do that, it will be easier to do it anytime one of these pesky thoughts intrude.

You may also want to re-read Lesson No. 32 on Choking. There you will find some other unproductive thoughts that need to be addressed should they come up.

Lesson No. 39: Cause And Results: What Is This All About?

So many times when I am teaching, I will ask my students what happened when they missed a particular shot. And, many times they will say, they didn't move to the ball, or they were too tense, or they didn't follow-through properly, or they didn't move their feet, or any other of the many things that can go wrong when you miss a shot.

Do you know how I answer them? I tell them that these are all things that, in fact, happened, but that they are the result and not the cause. Yes, maybe they were too tense, and yes the tension made you miss the shot, but there is something that caused the tension in the first place. Let's take a look at how this all works.

It is really important that you find what is really causing you to miss because if you don't, how are you going to change or fix it. Fixing the result won't work for very long.

The analogy I like to use is this. If you are walking down a dark alley late at night in a bad section of town, you would, most likely, get pretty tense and start really looking around or calling 911 if you thought someone was following you. And, no matter what you did, you would have a really hard time relaxing until you were safe at home. So, yes, you were tense, but it was the result of something, not the cause. The cause was the fact that you were in a dangerous place and someone was following you.

Well, unless you find out what is causing you to be tense when you miss a shot, re-programming yourself to relax or telling yourself to move your feet, etc, won't work until the cause is eliminated. Yes, re-

168

programming yourself to relax may work in the short run, but the tension will come back over and over again until you deal with the real cause.

Do you know what some of the obvious causes are that will result in just about every kind of error?

- How about "trying" to hit the ball into the court?
- How about "trying" to win or to not lose?
- How about "trying" to hit a winner or just "trying" to hit a ball to a particular place? Maybe even "trying" to stroke it correctly.

Are you nodding your head as you read these causes? I think you get the idea here.

Now that you know the cause (or as you become aware of them), you just re-program or visualize, or talk to yourself about releasing these unproductive ideas or thoughts and get back into focusing and executing the Core Principles. Maybe even getting to your "foundational place." See Lesson No. 77.

When you fix your missed shots by really dealing with the root cause, you will find that you will not be making these same errors over and over again. You will then have a huge advantage over the other players out there because you will now know how to really "fix" what you did wrong.

Lesson No. 40: When You Don't Play Well

What do you do when you don't play well? The mind play is very interesting when you begin to pay attention to it as you are doing now that you are playing the Mental Game.

I have been playing the Mental Game for over 25 years and still my mind tries to take control and won't let my body play without it interfering. I still have to struggle to let go. Sometimes even my body rebels and doesn't function very well. However, there are two important differences from those who do not play the Mental Game from those of us who do play it.

The first difference is that we now know why we miss the ball. Most other players do not have clue as to why they missed the ball and the only way they know to do better is to try harder, yell at their body to hit the ball into the court or to blame something like the wind, or the other player etc.

The second difference is that even though we know why we miss, we can begin to make the changes in our mind which in turn helps our body play better. We don't need to go home and practice hours and hours before we can improve like the non-Mental Game players. Practicing hours and hours is a good thing, but in the middle of a match it is not possible. The only place you can practice during a match is in your mind.

But what happens if you know what to do, you "try" to do them and either your mind or your body just won't cooperate? This happens to me a lot if I haven't been playing much. Here is the answer. You just
170

keep relaxing and letting go of that part that you think is interfering. You keep making your play less and less important and just staying with the Core Principles. At some point, the mind will give up and let your body play. And nobody knows how long this will take so just keep doing it.

I know what some of you are going to say. That this way of thinking doesn't make sense. If I make it less important, I won't run for the ball, move my feet, or hit the ball hard or I will only hit the ball down the middle. All I can say is that if you do it properly, it works and here is how you can tell.

No matter how well you play when you start the match and if your play doesn't get better as the match progresses, then you need to change something. That doesn't mean that you will always win, but you should be improving during the match. When this does happen, no matter how slight, you can be sure you are playing and winning the Mental Game. See, I do want you to win.

Lesson No. 41: The Three Major Weaknesses And How You Can Exploit Them

I am going to switch gears in this lesson and talk a little about strategy and how to win. Even though you should not be thinking about winning (remember, winning takes care of itself if you play better than your opponent), that doesn't mean you don't use the best strategy and hit your balls to make it difficult for your opponent. And

Playing Zen-Sational Tennis

in some of the lessons to come, I will be talking about more strategies, most of which I will bet you have not read about before.

In addition to using these strategies, you still need to play the Mental Game so that you can execute your strategy. This means that you need to do the "Core Principles" (see Lesson No. 3). As I have said, these Core Principles are the absolute foundation to every tip, idea and instruction that I have for you.

I would like to suggest that you keep my book with you and read these Core Principles before every match or every time you play sets and games. You can also print them out and/or put this book on your e-reader (Kindle, Nook, or iPad) so you can read any of these lessons no matter where you are.

Although exploiting these weaknesses apply mostly to singles, if you play mostly doubles, you still must know what these weaknesses are.

There are three (3) major weaknesses that most players have. However, these weaknesses tend to disappear as the player advances in skill.

Here they are:

1. **Backhands -** Again the exception may be if the player hits a two-handed backhand. Then you need to pay closer attention to see if this is indeed weaker. And if their forehand and backhands are both good, you can make your determination on which side they hit harder and/or more accurately and therefore force you into an error more often.

2. **Running and hitting** is also a weakness. It is easier for you to hit the ball when it comes to you than when you have to run for it. The same is true for your opponent.

3. **Hitting the ball deep** is also harder for your opponent to hit. Many times a deep ball will come back short or they will miss it.

How To Exploit These Weakness When You Play

Of these three weaknesses, which one do you think is the easiest one to exploit? If you said, "Hit to the backhand" you would be correct. It is easier to hit to one side of the court than it is to make someone run or hit deep.

So, pound (this means hit a lot of balls) the backhand side and wait for a relatively easy ball that you can hit to the forehand to make them run. And, of course, unless you are going for a short angle or drop shot, work on hitting all of your balls deep.

After you have hit to the forehand side to make them run, hit the next ball to the backhand side again to make them hit a running backhand. This way you can do two weaknesses at the same time.

You should be hitting anywhere from 3 to 10 balls in a row to the backhand before you make the shot to make them run (Especially if they have a really good forehand). This way when you do give them a forehand, not only will you be making them run, but they may just miss it because they have lost their groove and/or rhythm.

When I tell my students to hit to the backhand, I usually have to remind them again and again so I am going to spell it out for you here. **After you serve or after you hit your return of serve, hit a minimum of three balls in a row to the backhand side. Then you can keep hitting there until you get an easy ball which you can then hit to the other side.**

If you do this, you will be amazed at how many points you will win on the first three hits to the backhand side. Don't believe me. Try it and see for yourself.

Lesson No. 42: A Basic Singles Strategy

Are you clear with yourself on what your strategy will be when you are playing singles? When I am working with first-time students and I ask this question, I rarely get a clear answer. Let me help you with some clear ideas that are pretty easy to think about as well as execute.

I have talked about consistency being the first and last resort for strategy. This is still the No. 1 basic strategy.

I have also talked about hitting to the backhand. Many times I have my students only hit to the backhand until they can do it very well. Doing this most of the time is absolutely the next best strategy.

Using this strategy of hitting to the backhand with some variations would be the third basic strategy and it is what I will talk about now in more detail. Even though I call this a basic strategy, it is very powerful and I use it bigtime myself. Maybe I shouldn't call it basic.

For the explanation of this strategy, I am going to assume that the backhand is the weaker side and that the player is right-handed. There are many variations to this that you can use depending on the patterns of how your opponent returns the ball and how he or she moves, but this is meant to be just the beginning step in the area of singles strategy.

I will use the term "appropriate ball" throughout this lesson. Here is what I mean by this. When you have hit a ball so well that you have forced your opponent wide to the backhand and you get an easy ball in return, I would say that this is an appropriate ball. It is appropriate because you can now hit this ball to the forehand side to make your opponent run for a forehand and if you hit it good enough, it just may be a winner.

Another appropriate ball would be any easy ball that your opponent hits to your forehand, allowing you to then hit the ball to their forehand side, generating a good angle cross-court. This will work especially well if you have hit four or five balls to the backhand side. Your opponent will still be thinking the ball will be coming to his or her backhand and/or will be standing over on the backhand side because that is where you have hit the previous balls.

Let's get back to the strategy.

Here Is What You Do When Serving In The Deuce Court

1. Serve to the backhand side 85 percent of the time. Serve to the forehand side 15 percent of the time, keeping them mixed up. Serving sometimes right at the person can also be a good idea.
2. Hit the next ball and keep hitting the balls to the backhand side until you get the appropriate ball (which I defined above), then hit the ball to the forehand side.

3. Then go back to the Step 2 which is to hit the next ball and keep hitting the balls to the backhand side again until you get another appropriate ball. Hit this appropriate ball to the forehand side again.
4. As a variation, hit two in a row to the forehand side.

Here Is What You Will Do When Serving In The Ad Court

1. Again serve to the backhand side 85 percent of the time. Serve to the forehand side 15 percent of the time still mixing them up. Serving sometimes right at the person can also be a good idea.
2. Hit the next ball to your opponent's forehand side.
3. Hit the next ball and keep hitting the balls thereafter to the backhand side until you get the appropriate ball, then hit the ball to the forehand side.
4. Then repeat hitting to the backhand side until you get another appropriate ball, then hit the ball to the forehand side again.
5. As a variation, hit two balls in a row to the forehand side or hit the first ball to the backhand side.

As you may have gathered, the idea of this strategy is to maximize hitting to your opponent's weaknesses. You have hit the ball to your opponent's weaker side and made your opponent hit running forehands and running backhands. And if you hit any of your balls deep, you have made your opponent hit balls that are that much more difficult for them. By hitting two balls in a row to your opponent's forehand as a variation, you may be able to "wrong foot" them, therefore keeping them off balance.

Here Is What You Do When Returning Serve And The Ball Is Served To Your Forehand

1. Hit all forehand return of serves to the forehand or left side as I talked about in Lesson No. 58.
2. Hit the next ball and keep hitting the balls to the backhand side until you get the appropriate ball, then hit the ball to the forehand side.
3. Then go back to the previous step which is to hit the next ball and keep hitting the balls to the backhand side until you get another appropriate ball. Hit this ball to the forehand side again.
4. As a variation, hit two balls in a row to the forehand side.

Here Is What You Do When Returning Serve And The Ball Is Served To Your Backhand

1. Hit all backhand return of serves to the backhand or right side as I talked about in Lesson No. 58 on return of serve.
2. Hit the next ball to the forehand side. As a variation, hit this next ball to the backhand side.
3. Hit the next ball and keep hitting the balls to the backhand side until you get the appropriate ball, then hit the ball to the forehand side again.
4. Then repeat hitting to the backhand side until you get another appropriate ball, then hit the ball to the forehand side again.
5. As a variation, hit two balls in a row to the forehand side.

Notice that when a ball is served to your forehand, the strategies are the same in both the deuce and ad court.

Notice that when a ball is served to your backhand, the strategies are also the same in both the deuce and ad court.

One last thought about this strategy. You still must be able to execute it. If you are having difficulty, start with just hitting all of your balls to your opponent's weak side and work on being consistent. Remember, consistency is the first and last strategy to use against your opponent.

And, of course, you still must use the Core Principles to make this work.

Lesson No. 43: Singles Strategy For Everyone, Including Younger Players

In the last lesson, I gave my thoughts on singles strategy. In this lesson, I will go over some thoughts on singles strategies for younger players. However, this lesson can apply to just about all of us to some degree.

Anyway, I have received many great questions from my book owners. Here is the one that was about strategy for young kids.

"Do you by any chance have any suggestion to good strategy books or software that is really good for younger players? (teen and younger)"

178

Playing Zen-Sational Tennis

My answer:

I do not know of any books on good strategy for younger kids. However, from my way of thinking good basic strategy for kids (or anyone) is not difficult. I think that too many people try to make strategy too complex and therefore difficult. Here is what I know works and what I tell my all my students. Even the very advanced ones.

When serving, hit all balls to the backhand. First serves and second serves. Once you are able to do that, start mixing up the first serve and hit 85% of serves to the backhand and 15% to the forehand. If you have a fast serve you can try hitting right at the person. Hit 98% of second serves to backhand. Have you noticed where Roger Federer serves his second serves almost 100% of the time?

When returning serves, hit the returns like I talk about in Lesson No. 58. If you haven't read that far along in my book yet, I suggest hitting all forehand return of serves to the left side of the court and all backhand return of serves to the right side.

After the serve and return of serve, hit all the balls to the backhand. I do mean all.

Once the student can do this, I have them hit at least the first 3 or 4 balls to the backhand, then keep hitting to the backhand until they get an easy forehand then hit that forehand cross-court to make them run. If the opponent returns it, go back to hitting to the backhand.

Again the basic singles strategy I talked about in the previous lesson (Lesson No. 42) describes this strategy more formally.

The important thing that I don't see very many players doing is hitting the first ball (after the serve and return of serve) to the backhand. And this applies to advance players.

Here is an example as to how well this can work. A few years ago, I was coaching a young 15 year old who pretty much was winning all the tournaments here in Seattle area. After telling him to hit most balls to the backhand, he still didn't do it. In his next match, I told him I wanted him to always hit the first 3 balls to the backhand even if it wasn't the best strategy. It was amazing (even for me to see) how many times he won the point on the first 2 or three hits just by going to the backhand side.

There are many variations to this, of course, but this basic strategy works bigtime at all levels. I use it when I play unless I discover that my opponent's forehand is truly weaker.

Lesson No. 44: The Value Of Playing Tournaments

Do you play tournaments? If you don't, you may want to re-think this. Tournaments will help you immensely with learning and improving your Mental Game. It is like taking on-going "final exams" and by looking at the results of these tests, you will learn so much about how your mind and body work together.

Playing Zen-Sational Tennis

Tournaments bring out how powerful your Conscious Mind is and how much it wants to control your play. Only through tournaments will you have the opportunity to put your Conscious Mind in its right place.

Notice I haven't said anything about winning. Tournaments bring to the table the thought that all of a sudden winning is important. Of course, by now we know that this is **"Death"** to playing well and tournaments are the best environment in which to work on letting go of winning.

Tournaments are also important because for some unknown factor, you will improve your game just by osmosis. How this happens I don't know but just being around so much tennis and watching the other players somehow improves your own game. Be sure that you guard against unproductive habits like pumping and yelling "come on" etc. that you may see other players engage in.

In tournaments (unless you win the finals), you get to play someone better than you as well as a wide range of players. When you lose (and sometimes even when you win) you can look at it as a terrific learning opportunity. You will discover where your weaknesses are so you can work on them.

In tournaments, you get to see how you stack up against other players your own age. This can be important as you get older because you can see where you stand among your peers, even if you can't run as well or can't hit the ball as hard as you used to.

To sum up, tournaments are a must for those of you looking to really improve not only your Mental Game, but your physical game as well.

Lesson No. 45: What To Do When You Play A Tiebreaker

Tiebreakers are fun, aren't they? What is interesting about a tiebreaker is that you and your opponent have played very evenly up to that point. Now the winner will depend on who can play better for a very short period of time and this is where being mentally tough pays off.

Since you have been on the Mental Game journey for a while now, here are some questions you need to ask yourself.

- Are you seeing any changes in how you play in a tiebreaker?
- When you lose a tiebreaker, are you aware of where your focus or your mental thoughts may have broken down?
- How about when you won a tiebreaker? Were you aware of anything that helped you win, or did your opponent just blow it?

Again, all these questions are important to ask because awareness of what is happening during these different situations is very helpful to learning to play better.

Here are some more questions that need answering as well as more thoughts on playing tiebreakers.

- Do you change the way you play when you are in a tiebreaker? If so, what direction do you go?
- Do you go in the direction of thinking that because every point is so important now that you try harder?

- Or do you go in the direction of relaxing more so that your body can play maybe even better than you were playing earlier in the set?

In a tiebreaker, all of a sudden each point becomes very important. So, what do we normally do? We try harder. When you start to try harder, you start tensing up, and as you miss more, you try even harder and get more and more tense, and the cycle continues.

So, what do you do? You do the opposite.

You need to let go of the notion that each point is important. You do this by relaxing more. This means that you will take a deep breath and do a complete relaxing sigh. Then trust your body to hit the shots, focus on the ball better, without trying hard, of course, while you exhale properly, keep a relaxed grip, and let your body play.

The closer the match, the more you want to trust "your Other-Than-Conscious Mind" to make your shots. This means that you focus well yet keep your Conscious Mind out of the way so that it does not control your shots. And, of course, this happens when your body is relaxed. Your opponent will still be doing what you used to do. He or she will be trying harder because winning every point is now very important and will most likely be the one tensing up and choking.

Here is what I actually say to myself when I start a tiebreaker. Because I have a strong auditory sense, I talk to myself but if you are the visual type, you can translate this into a picture in your mind.

I say to myself, "Body, I can't win this so you will have to do it and hit the shots. I will get out of your way and just focus on the ball for you, breathe very relaxed for you, keep a relaxed grip for you, and just let you play."

Sometimes, I hit some no-brainer winners or I will hit some shots that I had not been able to hit earlier.

I remember one time, I was playing this guy who had a really big serve and I was struggling to just get it back. In the tiebreaker in the third set after I gave my body the idea that it would have to win for me, I hit an unbelievable return of serve for a winner on one of his big first serves. I had not come anywhere close to hitting a return like that up until that tiebreaker. Unfortunately, it doesn't happen in every tiebreaker and believe it or not, even I choke and lose some tiebreakers, but if I can get my Conscious Mind to cooperate, playing better in a tiebreaker happens way too many times for me to believe that it is just a fluke.

I find that I will win most of the tiebreakers I play when I can really relax and let go more at this time. When I lose a tiebreaker, my opponent wins it. I don't lose it very often by missing "nothing" balls. And it is amazing how many times my opponent loses points that by all rights should be theirs.

If you have to lose a tiebreaker, you want your opponent to win it. You don't want to lose it by missing "nothing" balls.

As you work with letting go in these situations it may amaze you how many times your opponent loses points that by all rights should be his and how many times you actually may play better.

Lesson No. 46: How Well Are You Doing The Core Principles?

When was the last time you read the Core Principles? If it has been a while, please read them again right now. You will find them in Lesson No. 3.

Are you reading them before every match?

Reading them often and before every match is an absolute must as in just this one section you will find all you need to do to play out of your mind. Everything else I talk about (except for my lessons on non- mental stuff) is centered around these Core Principles.

So, please read these Core Principles often and really begin to use them. They are very powerful.

If you can do these principles completely, you will have no need to read my book any more. However, if you have been working with these principles for any period of time, you will see that like any worthwhile skill, it takes practice and letting go.

Please use this lesson as a reminder for you to spend more time studying and really working on using them. At the very least read them before every important match, and continue to make them the "only" things you do when you play matches.

If you are not making these principles the most important thing you do when you play, you are missing "the key" to playing the Mental Game.

185

It also may be a good time to review Lesson No. 17 on the summary of what to do when you play a match.

Lesson No. 47: What You Might Be Missing When You "See The Ball"

Since it may have been a while since you have read Lesson No. 6, you may want to read it again and re-read Lesson No. 22 and practice Drill No. 1: Seeing the Ball again.

It is always a good idea to review these concepts because many times when I am working with my students, they think they are seeing the ball well, but I find out that they are missing some part of it.

One part of seeing the ball that you may be missing is the part when the ball is passing over the net and bouncing up to and off your opponent's racquet. As you see the ball hit your opponent's racquet, be sure to look for the direction and the speed of the ball as soon as possible after the ball comes off the racquet. The next time you play, be especially aware of this.

One of the "signs from above" that you may not be seeing this is if you don't even begin to move for a ball when it is hit back to your side of the net.

If they had hit a winner you may not have been able to reach it, but if you don't even begin to move in that direction it means that you did not see the ball to and from your opponent's racquet properly. In
186

addition, if you were aware of what you were thinking, you may be aware that you were thinking about where the ball was going to be hit rather than seeing where it was hit.

Another time to pay more attention to how you are seeing the ball is when you miss the return of serve. Make sure you see the ball from the bounce to your racquet, with proper breathing and a relaxed grip, of course.

When I am serving, the thing I personally have to do is to make sure I am seeing the ball all the way to my opponent's racquet. I tend to look at the spot where my serve landed and by the time I focus on the ball again, it has come back and I end up missing it. Once I focus on the ball bouncing up to my opponent's racquet, I do not miss this return of the return very often.

So, re-read Lesson No. 6, and Lesson No. 22 on seeing the ball and then check to see if you are truly focusing on the ball the entire way both to and from.

As I have said before, seeing the ball is the most critical of things to do and will, in turn, lead to you playing your very best.

Lesson No. 48: Are You Still Working On Your Breathing?

The breathing part of hitting a ball is the second most important thing for you to do. It is part of the relaxation package and can really help you get to the next level of play.

Playing Zen-Sational Tennis

Please read again Lesson No. 8 about breathing and then spend some time doing the exercises (Lesson No. 9) again even if you have done them already.

All of my students say that the breathing is the most difficult thing to do. Please don't let that keep you from working on it.

Be determined to play another game for a while. Say to yourself that all you are going to do is to pay attention to your breathing when you hit the ball.

If you're having difficulties with your breathing, spend some serious time (maybe for a week or 2) working on only your breathing.

Here are the things you need to be aware of to help you work on the rhythm of your breathing.

- When you are hitting ground strokes, start your exhale when the ball bounces as it comes to you and let the exhale continue until your ball bounces on the other side.
- If you are serving, start your exhale just after you toss the ball into the air and continue exhaling through your hit and until your ball bounces.
- If you are returning serves, start your exhale just before your opponent hits the serve and let the exhale continue through your hit and until your ball bounces on the other side.
- If you are hitting volleys and your opponent is hitting from the backcourt, start your exhale when your opponent hits the ball and continue your exhale through your hit and until your ball bounces.

Using these absolute times to start and finish your exhale will make sure that you are starting the exhale before you make contact with the ball and continuing it long enough after you hit. After working on these times, you will find that starting your exhale will become more automatic.

Now that you are starting your exhale before you make contact with the ball, move to the next step and make sure you are exhaling long after you hit the ball. You should still be exhaling until your ball bounces on the other side.

And always remember that the exhale is a very relaxed sigh.

So, work on your breathing when you warm up, when you do drills, and even in practice matches (not in tournaments).

Work on it in segments. Start with paying attention to when you are starting your breathing in relation to making contact with the ball. After doing that for a while, pay attention to how relaxed it is. Then, pay attention to the length of your exhale. And, finally, see if you can allow the entire exhale to be absolute complete.

You may also want to pay attention to what your face is doing as you exhale. If you are "moving your lips" or "making a face," you are not exhaling properly

Once you have worked on just the breathing, see if you can combine seeing the ball and breathing at the same time.

If you are playing points, spend two points (or rallies) seeing the ball. Spend the next two points breathing properly. Then spend the next two points combining both.

I guarantee that when you can do this, your game will be at a much higher level.

189

Lesson No. 49: What To Do When There Are Visual And/Or Noise Distractions

Have you ever let the noise of an airplane distract you? How about a car horn honking or someone yelling about a missed ball on the next court? What about seeing a ball rolling in the back of the court and because you didn't see it in time to call a let, you lost the point because you let it distract you? All of these and any other distractions can really play havoc with your tennis if you let it.

Again, as in many of my lessons, the concept to help you deal with these distraction is pretty simple but it may take some time and practice. Here is what you need to do.

Just acknowledge the distraction.

Know that it is part of life and no one is out to get you, and without judgment just let it go and go back to seeing the ball and feeling your breathing. Remember also, these distractions happen to both you and your opponent, but now you know how to deal with them. You can only hope that your opponent will still be bothered by them.

I can't tell you how many times in the past I have lost the point because I was distracted by a ball that rolled onto the back of either my side or my opponent's side.

One day I thought enough is enough so when I played practice matches, I would never call a let if a ball came into the court. The only exception was if the ball actually rolled in front of us or if there was a danger of either of us stepping on it.

With a little practice of letting it be OK for the ball to be there, staying with my breathing and seeing the ball, I found that I wasn't losing those points anymore.

Do the same for any distraction that comes up. Remember, these distractions are also a part of the game and if you are letting these distractions bother you, you need to know that you are not focusing properly.

Lesson No. 50: What To Do When You Play Better In Your Warm-Up Than You Do When The Game Starts

Have you ever played better than you did when you warmed up? I think most of us have experienced playing worse. Do you know what the real differences are between the warm-up and the game? Once you know these differences you can begin to deal with them and you can learn how to play as well or better once the game starts.

First of all, you must understand what is so different. There are three differences when the game starts.

1. One difference is that you will now want to do something with the ball other than hit it down the middle.

2. The second is that your opponent will not be hitting the ball down the middle any more either, and what he or she does with the ball affects your shots.

3. And the third is that all of a sudden everything is more important. When you were just warming up, it didn't matter if you missed the ball. You were not trying to aim your shots or even trying to hit the balls into the court (I hope). You were just hitting the ball down the middle.

If you really think about it, making the game important all of a sudden just because the game has started is the main cause of playing differently and usually worse. Once the game starts, if you can "trick" yourself into thinking that the game is not any more important than the warm-up, then you will have a better chance to play the same or better.

Here are some things that will help you play better once the game starts.

- Stop trying to aim or hit the ball into the court. Your body already knows how to do this. You did it in the warm-up.
- Stop trying to hit a perfect stroke. This is not the time for working on your strokes.
- Stop trying to win. Reprogram any thoughts you may have about losing. Remember, if you play better than your opponent, winning will take care of itself.
- And, most importantly, use the Mental Game Core Principles. They work.

If you can do these things, the only difference between the warm-up and when you start the game will be what your opponent does with the ball and the effect that has on your ability to play well.

Playing Zen-Sational Tennis

Now that you have been reading these lessons for a while, you should know by now that letting go is always the direction you want to go when you find yourself not playing well or, in this case, not playing as well as you did in the warm up.

As I have said before , if all you did was the "Core Principles" you would be in the zone.

So, the next time you are not playing as well as you would like, do the opposite. Start letting go of the different things you would usually do. Like trying harder, thinking about or trying to fix your stroke or telling yourself to move your feet, etc.

Resist the idea that you (your Conscious Mind) can fix things. The temptation is to believe that you can fix things because sometimes it works, but it will not work very well when the match gets close.

Please jump ahead to Lesson No. 77 on the foundational place. This is a must read for you.

This is one of the best ways that you can get to the place in your mind where you are actually doing the "Core Principles."

Lesson No. 51: What To Do When You Miss Shots And How To Fix Them

Are you like most players who don't have a clue as to why you miss a particular shot? If you do know why you missed the shot, do you know how to fix it on the spot?

If you don't know why you missed a shot or if you don't know how to fix it, I am going to tell you how in this lesson. And, I am talking about a technique that really works and not one where you just try harder to hit the ball in. This is a very powerful technique, but it is a little involved and it will take a little time to learn.

When you miss a shot, you usually miss it in one of three ways: long, wide, or into the net. All three of these can and should be addressed as a non-stroke issue. If you miss when you are practicing your strokes, there may be a stroke component in why you miss, but if you miss when you are playing points which means you are in a match, the following concepts should be applied.

These corrections may be done when you miss the first time and you may want to make these corrections on every miss at the beginning so that you can get into the habit of doing it. However, if there is a pattern as to where you are missing the ball and two times missing the ball in the same place is a pattern, then you must address the issue immediately.

If you miss a ball in the same place three times, then you have to go into overkill and absolutely make these corrections. Don't wait until

194

the match is over and then say, "Boy, I sure missed a lot of shots long." Or "My backhand down the line wasn't working today." These need to be addressed on the spot.

What To Do When The Shot Goes Long

Before you can really do justice to correcting a ball that goes long you must first ask yourself this question. Did my ball go long because I hit it too hard or did it go long because it went too high over the net?

There are times when you hit the ball and no matter how low over the net you have hit it, the ball will go out because it was simply hit too hard. These are usually low, short balls and because the distance is shorter to the base line, the ball needs to be hit easy enough for it to travel up over the net and then down again into the court. Yes, a ball can go long because it is not only hit too high but also hit too hard and there can be a fine line as to which is which, but you should be able to determine the overriding reason as to why your ball went long.

If you determine that your ball went long because you hit it too hard, you will need to re-program by visualizing or talking to yourself so that the next time you get that particular shot, you will hit it easier. Hitting a ball easier is a code word for being more relaxed. In this case, you will need to relax the muscles that you use to swing your arm at the shoulder so that it moves slower the next time.

While you are reprogramming your ball to go slower, you will also reprogram yourself to hit the ball over the net at the proper distance. By the way, do you know how high over the net your ball needs to go, on average, in order to go into the court and bounce where you want it to? Depending on how hard you hit the ball this will be about 1 to 4 feet over the net and sometimes up to 6 feet. The way I hit the ball, I program it to go 1 to 2 feet over the net and I would say it will be 3 to 4 feet over the net for most players.

No matter where you miss the ball (long, in the net, or wide) you will always do the following part of reprogramming first. You will consciously with your eyes look at the spot you would have liked the ball to go and consciously with your eyes look at the height over the net you wanted to ball to go.

This part of the reprogramming is extremely important so don't skip this part. In fact, if this is all you do, it may be enough for most of the balls you miss, but to really make this concept of reprogramming to work, you must do it all.

And, the last part of the reprogramming technique is that you will visualize or talk to yourself about seeing the ball perfectly to the blur of your racquet, keeping your focus on the contact point for a short time, having perfect breathing, keeping a relaxed grip, seeing where you would have liked the ball to bounce, and visualize where you want the ball to cross the net and how high. You might even want to take a practice swing without the ball as you visualize.

If you determine that your ball went long because it went too high over the net, the first and easiest thing to do is imagine or visualize that from now on you will relax your grip and your wrist a little bit more when you make contact with the ball. Because you don't know what the "correct " angle your racket needs to be in order to hit the ball the proper distance over the net, by relaxing your grip and wrist, your body will make the change for you or it will learn how to do it.

196

Secondly, because your ball cleared the net too high, then along with the first correction, take the time to consciously see and imagine that from now on your ball will clear the net by 2 to 6 feet.

And thirdly, since it is a relaxation issue, you may want to check your breathing to make sure you are not holding your breath at contact with the ball and that your exhalation is very relaxed.

And again, the last part of the reprogramming technique is that you will visualize or talk to yourself seeing the ball perfectly to the blur of your racquet, keeping your focus on the contact point for a short time, having perfect breathing, keeping a relaxed grip, seeing where you would have liked the ball to bounce, and visualize where you want the ball to cross the net and how high. And again, you might want to take a practice swing without the ball as you visualize. Please read about taking The Shadow Stroke in Lesson No 15.

In both of the processes I have just described and after you have "reprogrammed" yourself, you must let it go and get back to seeing the ball, relaxing your grip, and exhaling before and after you hit the ball. This forgetting about and letting it go is a huge part of the process of reprogramming. So many times when reprogramming doesn't work it is because after you visualize, you then try hard to make it happen. Please don't let this happen to you.

What To Do When The Shot Goes Into The Net

Missing the ball in the net is also a relaxation issue and not a stroke issue.

No matter where you miss the ball (long, in the net, or wide) you will always do the following part of reprogramming first. You will consciously with your eyes look at the spot you would have liked the ball to go and consciously with your eyes look at the height over the net you wanted to ball to go.

This part of the reprogramming is extremely important so don't skip this part. In fact, if this is all you do, it may be enough for most of the balls you miss, but to really make this concept of reprogramming to work, you must do it all.

The way to fix this issue of the ball going into the net is to relax your arm and wrist so that your backswing and racquet head can get lower automatically and without effort. This will allow your arm and racquet head to swing up to the ball so that the ball goes over the net. In addition, imagine or visualize your ball going 2 to 6 feet over the net.

After you have reprogrammed yourself, let it go and get back to seeing the ball, exhaling before and after you hit the ball, and using a very relaxed grip, of course. And again, you might want to take a practice swing without the ball as you visualize. Please read about taking The Shadow Stroke in Lesson No 15.

What To Do When The Shot Goes Wide

I have found that when I hit the ball wide, it is because I have tried too hard to hit the ball down the line or cross-court, and as a result, I was unable to see the ball to the blur of my racquet and keep my focus on the contact point for a short time. So, in this case, you may need to let go of your effort to direct the ball and make seeing the ball, keeping your focus on the contact point for a short time, your breathing, and keeping a relaxed grip more important.

The way you stop directing the ball is by relaxing your arm, letting the stroke go its natural way so that you take a full follow-through and keeping a relaxed grip.

In any case, no matter where you miss the ball (long, in the net, or wide) you will always do the following part of reprogramming first. You will consciously with your eyes look at the spot you would have liked the ball to go and consciously with your eyes look at the height over the net you wanted to ball to go.

This part of the reprogramming is extremely important so don't skip this part. In fact, if this is all you do, it may be enough for most of the balls you miss, but to really make this concept of reprogramming to work, you must do it all.

As in the previous situations, imagine or visualize your ball landing on the spot you want it to. After you have reprogrammed yourself, let it go and get back to seeing the ball, keeping your focus on the contact point for a short time, exhaling before, as, and after you hit the ball, keeping a relaxed grip, and visualizing where you want the ball to cross the net and how high. In other words, do the Core

199

Principles. And again, you might want to take a practice swing without the ball as you visualize. Please read about taking The Shadow Stroke in Lesson No 15.

Now that you have learned how to fix the various errors, the big thing now will be for you to remember to use these techniques. You will need to develop a strategy so that you can remember to do these things on the spot. It is too late to do them after the match is over.

So, please print this lesson out and refer to it often. Reprogramming this way will give you a huge advantage over your opponents because they will not know how to fix their misses and may get frustrated or angry while you are busy fixing your misses so that you can be more consistent.

Lesson No. 52: What To Do When Your Whole Game Starts To Go Badly: The One Minute Method

Have you ever found yourself playing good one minute and then all of a sudden your game fell apart? Do you know how to get it back on track, and in one minute?

Why do you think so many of the players out there get angry with their shots? It is because they just don't have a clue as to how to fix their game much less how to make the ball go into the court. This one technique, (as well as the technique learned in Lesson No. 51) when you learn it, will set you apart from all the other players out there.

Here is what you are to do. When you change sides, sit down, take a deep breath, do a relaxing exhale, clear your mind, and reprogram what you want to do.

Pretty easy, eh? This, of course, means letting go of all other thoughts like trying to hit the ball into the court, your strategy, thinking about winning or losing etc. Then start refocusing on using and only using

the Mental Game Core Principles. This technique actually takes less than a minute but then again, you have to remember to use it.

When I was in Victoria, B.C. working with one of the top players there, I saw over and over this technique work with him. He was far better than I was, but there were times he would begin to miss balls he should have been making.

One day, when we were playing and he started to miss again, I would talk to him about seeing the ball, breathing etc, but nothing really seemed to get him out of this metal lapse. So, I had him sit down on the bench and take a deep relaxing breath, calm his mind and re-program his whole approach to playing.

This, of course, was what I was telling him before but now it was much more formal. This took about 30 seconds. When he got up to play, again, he hit four winners in a row and completely turned his game around and I was lucky to get a point thereafter. You can do this also, but you must remember and take the time to do it.

This technique can be very powerful, so will you ever use it?

One of the biggest problems with doing anything, is that for some reason, we just don't remember to actually do it at the time. When the match is over it is too late.

Do you have in place a strategy so that you will remember to actually do some of these reprogramming techniques? If not, you need to figure out a way to remember.

Here are some ideas to help you remember.

- How about writing a note on your hand?

- How about putting my book by your water bottle so when you change sides and take a drink your memory will be jogged?

- How about taping a note on your racquet?

I am sure that there are many more ways for you to remember. Will you now take the time to figure out one that will work for you? I hope so.

Lesson No 53: Why Preprogramming Is As Important As Reprogramming

What is the difference between pre-programming and re-programming? Maybe the first question should be, "Do you ever re-program when you miss a ball?" Re-programming is extremely important because it is the only way you can "fix a shot," immediately, while you are playing.

The difference between pre-programming and re-programming is that when you pre-program, you plan what you want to do in advance. For example, if you are returning serve in doubles you may want to pre-program your return of serve to go cross court or down the line. Or maybe you are having difficulty focusing on your breathing and you will pre-program your breathing to help you to exhale during the next point. Re-programming is what you do immediately after you miss a ball.

So you will re-program your shot after you miss and pre-program before the point has started. Pre-programming is usually something that you want to do, rather than "fixing" an error. Using this combination of techniques will help you immensely.

Let's go over again on how to re-program and then I will talk to you about how to pre-program.

At this time, I am going to only talk about how to generally re-program no matter if you miss the ball long, wide, or into the net. In my book, I have some additional and specific ways to re-program based on where it is that you missed your shot and you can and should read it at your leisure. However, if all you did is re-program in this general way, it will be hugely helpful for you.

The first thing you want do immediately after you miss a shot is to **consciously** see where you wanted the ball to bounce, where you wanted the ball to cross the net, and how high over the net you wanted the ball to go. Once you have done this, and it will only take you a second to do it, you will then want to take a perfect practice swing using a very relaxed grip, using a relaxed exhale that starts

203

before you hit the imaginary ball, and consciously see the blur of the racket at the point where you would like to make contact with the ball. If, during your practice swing, you can mentally visualize your ball going over the net where you **consciously** looked at previously, that would be good.

All of this will take less than 5 seconds and you will want to do this every time after you miss a ball until you are in the habit of doing it. Then you will want to re-program as needed. Re-programming as needed means that there is a pattern as to where you are missing, and two misses in the same place in a very short period of time may be considered a pattern. Please don't wait for the game, set, or match to be over before you use this re-programming tool.

After you have re-programmed, the way you execute this "correction" is to let it go from your mind and go back to doing the Core Principles. Hopefully, by now you know the four main Core Principles, which are seeing the ball the way I believe it should be seen, exhaling properly, hitting the ball with a relaxed grip, and with a full and relaxed finish. To get the most out of your re-programming please go back and read all of the core principles.

Obviously, you can use your pre-programming for any number of things that are going on with you when you are playing. If you are having difficulty finishing the stroke you can pre-program that so that every stroke will finish properly. If you're having problems with seeing the ball to the blur of the racket, you can pre-program this before the point has started. You should, by now, be pre-programming before each serve and be pre-programming where you want your return of serve to go. You may want to re-read the lesson on where I think your return of serve should be hit. I sometimes even pre-program my strategy for the first two or three hits. The sky is the limit on how you can and will use this pre-programming.

Again, you can pre-program using a perfect stroke without the ball and/or by visualizing how you would like the ball to go as described above, when I talked about how to re-program. Or, you can have a little talk with yourself about what you want to happen when you are playing the next point.

And again, the way you will execute this pre-programming is doing the Core Principles.

Now that you know how and when to pre-program and re-program, the big issue will be is, "will you remember to do it or will a big eraser come across your mind as you play?" If you suffer from this "Big Eraser Syndrome" on a regular basis, then you will have to figure out a way to cure yourself and remind yourself to use these tools. These tools can be very powerful, but you need to know that they will not work every time. That being said, what other tools do you have that will enable you to improve your game immediately as you are playing? I don't think there are any or at least I have not ever heard of any.

The ball is now in your court to see if you can remember to use these tools and to see how you can make them work for you.

Lesson No. 54: What Do You Do And/Or Think About In Between Points?

Do you know what you think about once a point is over and you are getting ready for the next point to start? Are you thinking about something that is really going to help you play better? If you are, is it working?

Do you know what the pros do in between points? Have you ever observed the body language of players as soon as the point is over?

What you do in between points can really make a difference in how you play.

Maybe you are just thinking too much and need to stop. Do you think that is the case for you?

The time in between points can be a very productive time if you use it correctly. This lesson will give you some insights into what may help you during this time so you can encourage your body to play better.

If you have already read this lesson, it would be good to review and ask yourself if you are really doing this productively. You can always improve and refine your thoughts.

If you did not miss the shot or you have won the point and are doing what I suggest in the Mental Game Core Principles, ideally you would continue seeing the ball and being aware of your breathing when the point is over and until the next point starts. This will keep you focused and in the here and now.

Some instructors say to focus on something neutral like the strings on your racquet. I say why waste time focusing on something that is not going to help you play better? Instead, by keeping your focus on the ball and your breathing between points, you will be ready to see the ball, and your body will have a chance to be relaxed and ready for the next point.

If you become aware of negative or unproductive thoughts, just say, "Cancel, Cancel," or you can yell as loud as you can to yourself silently "Stop!" and then change the thought into something more productive, and focus again on the ball and your breathing.

If you have hit a good shot, it is OK to thank your body (after all, it is your body who hit it) and ask your Other-Than-Conscious Mind to keep those shots coming. However, if you have missed the shot, then you may want to do the following.

If a thought comes to you about your stroke, then you can mentally reprogram the stroke by visualizing how you want to hit it. This does not mean that you think about what you are doing is wrong. **Always think about what you want and not about what you don't want.**

You can even take a practice swing doing the stroke correctly. This practice swing must be absolutely perfect and must be a complete swing. This practice swing must include not only the perfect swing but also seeing the imaginary ball, breathing properly, keeping a relaxed grip, and hitting the ball into the court.

Please don't do what I see some people do. They actually take a practice swing using the incorrect stroke they just used when they missed the shot.

After you have done this reprogramming, let go of and forget about your stroke. Go back to seeing the ball, keeping a relaxed grip, breathing properly, and let your Other-Than-Conscious Mind figure out how to make the stroke change.

If you are aware of missing a certain shot more than once, immediately visualize hitting the ball into the court to the spot you would have liked the ball to go using a perfectly relaxed stroke, consciously seeing the ball perfectly, and having your body breathe properly. After you have done this, go back to seeing the ball and breathing as the next point begins.

If you are aware of missing the shot because of an error in seeing the ball or in breathing, again imagine or visualize yourself seeing the ball perfectly all the way to your racquet and all the way to your opponent's racquet with perfect breathing.

If you find that you are having difficulty with your focus, then you must begin to address the causes.

Ask yourself the following questions:

- Was I trying to hit the ball into the court?
- Was I thinking about hitting the ball to a particular place on the court?
- Was I trying to hit a winner?
- Was there anything else going on that would have kept me from seeing the ball all the way to my racquet?

If your answer was "yes" to any of the above questions, just be aware that this way of thinking is going to interfere with you playing your best. So make your mental correction, let it go, and get back to focusing on the ball, breathing, keeping a relaxed grip, and letting your Other-Than-Conscious Mind direct your body on how to hit your shots.

Now you know what I believe is the most effective way to deal with this time between points. All you have to do now is be aware of your thoughts and be proactive in changing these thoughts, which will of course, help you play your very best.

Lesson No. 55: What To Do When You Hit The Ball Off Center

Do you think that you hit more of your share of mis-hits?

Maybe I should ask first, "Are you even aware of when you mis-hit a ball?"

Do you think you know how to hit the ball on the center of your racquet? If you answered yes, then you are the only person on this earth who does. So, if you don't know who does know?

Remember when I asked earlier about who hits the ball and I told you it was not you but your body? Well, it is your body that knows how to hit the ball in the center of the racquet and if it is having trouble learning, the good news is that there are some things you can do to help it.

Playing Zen-Sational Tennis

One or all of the following can cause you to hit the ball off-center:

- Your grip and your wrist are too tight, usually at impact.
- You are not **consciously** seeing the ball all the way to the blur of your racquet.
- Maybe your breathing is too tense or you are holding it.

If you think that you are mis-hitting often, you will need to spend some time paying attention to your grip and your wrist at impact and know that you want them to be more relaxed.

Do you know what Tim Gallwey said about how you should hold your racquet? Hold it like you would hold a bird – tight enough that the bird can't get away, but not so tight that you would squash it. Do you think you are squashing the poor bird?

Check your grip out and see what happens when you relax it even more. If I was standing next to you, I should be able to take the racquet out of your hand with no effort as you hit and finish the stroke. Could I?

Seeing the ball and breathing relaxed is critical, but if you still try hard to hit the ball in the center of the racquet, you may still be hitting it off-center. Trust that your body knows how to hit the center of your racquet. Or, it will learn how to do so if given the chance. That is why the grip and the wrist must be relaxed at the same time as you see the ball and as you are breathing properly so that you are not consciously controlling your body.

The more you relax, the more you are giving your body the chance to learn where the center of your racquet is.

Lesson No. 56: How To Help Your Body Learn To Hit Accurately

Don't you think it is amazing how talented the body is when it can learn how to do something without you even knowing how?

Do you know that your body can actually learn to hit the ball with extreme accuracy?

Here is how you can help it to do just that.

This is the same process that I have developed for learning to do anything physical which I talked about in Lesson No. 15.

In this lesson, I will use this process to show you how to hit your shots very accurately when you play tennis. Hopefully, you realize that this ability to hit accurately will take time as it is a learned skill, but it will take a lot less time than if you were to keep doing it the traditional way. Don't believe me? Do it and see for yourself.

I am going to use hitting forehands crosscourt for the purpose of this discussion. You can, of course, substitute any place on the court or any stroke that you want.

The first step in the process is to know where you want to hit the ball. I am not just talking about saying to yourself that you want the ball to go crosscourt or over there. I am talking about a very specific place.

Playing Zen-Sational Tennis

The example I like to use to demonstrate this concept is this. If you asked me to come over to your house today and I had not been to your house before, I would ask you where you lived. If you said, "I just live over there," it would take me a long time for me to find your house.

Because I am a smart guy, I bet you I could eventually find your house, but I would really have to work at it and it would take me much longer to get there. Give me your address and I will go to MapQuest on the Internet and I will get very specific directions.

It is the same with hitting the ball crosscourt. You must have very specific directions. So, the first thing you need to do is to **consciously** see the spot on the court where you want your ball to bounce. I like to place a small bright orange road cone on the court so that the spot really stands out.

Then you need to see and know where the ball will pass over the net. On a stroke other than the serve, the spot over the net will be a whole range of places because it will depend on where you are on the court when you hit the ball.

Then you will need to know how high over the net your ball must go in order to hit your spot. Have you ever thought about that? Maybe you have now because I talked about it in an earlier lesson. But, most likely you haven't thought about it until now. You will want your ball to travel about 2 to 6 feet over the net for your average ball. These distances may change depending on the particular shot and how hard you hit.

Now that you have the goal down, you will just visualize your ball going over the net 2 to 6 feet and landing on the spot you picked out.

Playing Zen-Sational Tennis

This is step No. 2 in the process. The first step was determining your goal.

Step No. 3 is when you actually hit the ball. You want to turn over control to your Other-Than-Conscious Mind so that it will direct your body to learn how to hit your target. You do this, of course, by seeing the ball, keeping your focus on the contact point for a short time, breathing properly, and proper relaxation which is to say you need to keep your grip very relaxed. Please don't try to hit the target. Let your Other-Than-Conscious Mind direct your body so that it can do it. Your job is to just observe.

If you see that the patterns of your balls are not very close to your target or that your body is not learning very well, then you need to go back to step No. 2 and reprogram how and where you want your body to hit the ball.

This is all there is to it. By just working over and over with this process, you will see your body becoming so much more accurate.

I can't tell you how many times when I am working with a new student on developing their accuracy that it amazes me how accurate the body can be when hitting a tennis ball. Here is a short scenario that I see over and over. I start by explaining to my student how to make the ball go the direction they want and to hit the target.

When they start hitting balls, I usually begin to see more of a pattern of the balls going closer to the target but very seldom do any balls actually hit the road cone. They come close but always miss. I then stop them from hitting and I ask my student if they see that their patterns are better and they usually say yes.

Then I ask them if they are trying to hit the target. Because this is so normal for the Conscious Mind to get involved and because my student has not yet assimilated what letting go really means, my student usually tells me that, yes, they are trying hard to hit the target.

However, even in spite of this trying, their balls begin to go better.

As soon as I remind my student to let go of trying to hit the target, it is amazing how many times within the next 10 hits that the target is actually hit. Sometimes it happens on the very next hit.

Lesson No. 57: How To Decide And Then Hit The Ball Where You Want It To Go

When you are playing, how do you make the decision to hit the ball where you want it to go? Do you really know how, or is your idea just some vague process? Do you think that you do it by directing your racquet in that direction or maybe it has something to do with your feet or how you turn your body? These things obviously have something to do with it but the big question is how do you "make" your body do it.

When it comes to how you decide where you would like to hit your ball, it is actually pretty simple. And, like most things I talk about here, it will take some time and practice to do it well.

Think about when you are warming up. You just **"know"** that you want to hit the ball down the middle, and without thinking very hard, 214 if at all, you just do it. You even **"know"** this before you even get on the court.

The same knowing applies when you are hitting your balls crosscourt, down the line, or anywhere else. It is simply a **"knowing"** of where you want the ball to go and then just doing it. Trying hard, thinking hard, making it important, or trying to consciously direct the ball won't work in the long run or when you are under pressure.

The best way to achieve this **knowing** and therefore hit the ball where you want it to go is to see the ball all the way to the blur of your racquet, keeping your focus on the contact point for a short time, keeping a relaxed grip, and trust that your Other-Than-Conscious Mind will direct your body.

Still, it does take practice figuring out what I mean by **"knowing."** Unfortunately, I can't tell you what this **"knowing"** feels like. I can tell you that when you do learn to do it, you will be able to decide to hit the ball anywhere you want effortlessly. The more you work with all of these concepts I have been telling you about, the more it will become easier for you to understand what **"knowing"** means.

Obviously, if you have not developed the skill of accurately hitting the ball to the corners (or anywhere else) to your satisfaction, then you must spend more time practicing using the drills found in the Drill Section. And, of course, you will be using the concepts I talked about in the previous lesson. (Lesson No. 56)

Please keep in mind this concept of **"knowing"** when you are practicing.

Lesson No. 58: Why You Should Hit All Serve Returns Cross-court

The return of serve is one of the most important shots in tennis, yet I don't see much said about it nor do I see it being practiced very much. Are you aware of how important it is? If you are aware how important it is, then why don't you practice it more? If you do practice it, how often? Do you know how the return is different from other shots?

I admit that I have not done any actual studies of the return in doubles, but it is my contention that the team that gets the most return of serves back in doubles is the team that wins. Notice I said that just getting the returns back. I didn't say anything about hitting great returns. I will talk more about doubles a little later, but first I want to address the return of serve for singles.

The Return Of Serve When Playing Singles

When playing singles, I believe that you should hit all returns cross-court. Assuming you are a right-hander this means that all forehands are to be hit to the left side and all backhands should be hit to the right side, regardless of which side of the court you are returning from. Just saying hit cross-court may be confused with hitting an inside out forehand from the ad court. Technically, that would be cross-court, but that is not the cross-court I am referring to here in the singles part.

Here is my reasoning. See if you agree.

It is an easier and more natural stroke to hit the ball cross-court and a key element of breaking your opponent's serve is just to get the return back in play, hopefully well enough that you don't give him or her a setup. By hitting the easiest and most natural shot, you will be able to hit that many more returns back into the court.

In addition, it is harder to hit a return down the line because when the ball is coming fast, you have less time to turn your body enough to make it an easy shot. The only exception may be if the return is very wide and your body is already turned sideways.

If you are returning from the deuce court and hitting a cross-court forehand, not only is the distance to the baseline longer, but you will also be hitting the ball over the low part of the net. The only disadvantage is that you are returning to your opponent's forehand.

In the ad court and if you are hitting a backhand return, you also will be hitting over the low part of the net as well as having a longer distance to hit to. In addition, your ball will be going to your opponent's backhand which is a good thing.

Here is another reason for hitting the return cross-court. If you think about it, breaking serve is rare. So by hitting the ball cross-court, you want to accomplish three things other than just getting it back.

1. First, you want to make your opponent hit a running ball which if you remember is a weakness for most players or at least more difficult.

2. Second, you are pulling your opponent wide and off the court.
3. And third, you want to get control of the point on the first hit.

The nature of the serve gives the server an advantage because, assuming you or your opponent has a good serve, most of the time the server is in control of the point from the beginning. So, when your opponent is serving, all you need to do is to string together a couple of good returns so you can take control and win the point. This will put that much more pressure on your opponent, and with some of his or her errors, you will have broken the serve.

Another terrific benefit is that you won't have to think about where you are going to hit your return, as you have already planned it. This in itself is important because it will allow you stay that much more relaxed, and you will be able to concentrate on seeing the ball, keeping a relaxed grip, and on your breathing.

Do you think your opponent will know in advance where you are going to hit your return if you have this pattern of hitting cross-court? Don't worry. Believe me when I tell you most players will not have a clue. I have played many good players and asked them afterward if they saw a pattern on my serve return, and about 95 percent of them said no, they didn't know where I was hitting it.

However, here may be a concern. If your opponent knows that you have read this lesson, they just might know where you hit your returns. And, if you ever play against me, you will absolutely know where I hit it, but, you know what? I don't care if you do know and here is why.

Playing Zen-Sational Tennis

If I hit a good return, I will be making you run wide and I will be taking control of the point. The issue here is that you are to play your game and that game is that you want to hit as many returns back as you can and you will do this by preprogramming where you are going to hit it and that place is going to be the easiest and most natural place so that you can, in fact, hit more returns into the court. Wow! How is that for a mouthful?

Of course, there are always exceptions to every rule. When I play against my doubles partner and he hits his serve to my forehand when I am in the deuce court, I do not hit my return to his forehand if I can help it. That is because he can hit his forehand so well down the line that I can't get to it.

Against another player I used to play, I would not hit any of my returns, if I could help it, to his forehand because his forehand was such a weapon that he would hurt me bigtime with it. Likewise, if I were playing Roger Federer, I would never choose to hit to his forehand as he has probably the best forehand in the game.

My final point is that if hitting cross-court is good enough for the best players in the world, it should be good enough for us. In the 2005 U.S. Open Finals, I observed both Agassi and Federer hitting their return of serves cross-court more than 95 percent of the time. They must have learned it from me (ha ha).

The Return Of Serve When Playing Doubles

In doubles, obviously you will want to hit your return of serves cross-court most of the time.

The thing to remember here is that if your opponents are poaching a lot, it becomes a cat and mouse game as to where you hit your return.

Remember, however, what I said earlier. It is the team that hits the most returns that wins, so just because your opponent is moving a lot at net, keep your focus and make sure you don't let him or her take your focus away from seeing the ball so that you miss. I know, this is easier said than done, but you can begin to guard against this situation if you are aware of it.

If you decide to hit the ball down the line in doubles, and this applies to singles also, program where you are going to hit it before the ball is served and then let your body hit it. If you do hit the return at the net person, one of the big things to remember is that your opponent still has to hit the winner. How many times have you hit a ball right to the net person and he or she has missed the volley? Please don't let the net person screw up your focus so that you miss the ball. Just make it okay for the ball to go where it goes

One last thought about your doubles return of serve. If you are having difficulty getting the return back or if your opponent is moving a lot and hitting a lot of winners, have your partner stand back on the base line. This will take the pressure off of you because now the net person cannot hit winners so easily with both of you in the back court.

Playing Zen-Sational Tennis

Here is one more last thought. I see so many players stand inside the base line to return the serve in doubles so that they can hit the return and get to the net. I also see these same players missing return after return. My question is, "What good is it to get to the net quickly if they don't get the return back in the first place?" And, on the serves they do return, they don't win that many points anyway because they're returns many times are weak.

That brings up another last point when you are playing doubles. I sure have a lot of last points here, don't I?

All of these points I am making up to now relate to making sure that you get the return back. This final last point not only addresses that but also addresses what happens after you get the return back. First of all, if you will stand further back than normal, which means standing back behind the baseline to return serve, it helps in a number of ways.

First of all, it not only gives you more time to hit the ball, but it gives you more distance to the back line so your ball won't have the tendency to go long. But, you say, "The server is going to get to the net before I do." I say, "So what?" Think about what happens. You hit a good return and then begin to move into the net. At best you can only get to the service line before the ball comes back to you. Where is the ball when you go to hit it? The ball is just above the net or it is lower than the net. Sometimes it is even at your feet. Given that the distance to the back line is much shorter and given that the ball is not higher than the net when you hit it, you cannot hit the ball very hard so that you can force an error, etc. And many times you are forced to hit the ball easy enough so that your opponent can hit the winner.

Here is what I do when I play doubles. I stand back behind the baseline so that on a first serve I have more time to react and on a second serve I can return much more aggressively. I still stay back and wait for the server to return the ball to my side. I don't have to worry about him hitting it out of my reach because I only have my side to cover. If the ball comes back anywhere short, I can now hit my second ball with power and placement which is usually down the middle.

Ever heard that the best shot in doubles is down the middle? It is amazing how many points I get doing this even against much better players than I am.

Another plus for our side is this. When I can power the return of serve, it gives my partner, who is at net, a better chance to move in and cut off the return of my return and therefore win the point.

Sorry to get into so much doubles strategy, but so much of doubles is dictated by the return of serve. Obviously, there is so much more to doubles, and I won't be getting into it too much in these lessons.

Lesson No. 59: How To Hit The Return Of Serve Into The Court

First of all, I will bet that 99% of tennis players don't practice the return of serve. Is this true of you? So, why don't you? I believe that one of the reasons is that it is not convenient. Before I get into how to hit returns more consistently, let me give you two terrific ways to practice your returns.

Practice Your Returns: Method No. 1

If you warm up your serve the way most players do when you are playing a practice match, you most likely will serve three balls, which your opponent catches and then they serve them back to you which you then catch. You do this back and forth until you feel that you have had enough serves.

If you are playing with a friend and it is not a tournament match, here is what you can do instead.

One of you will choose to warm up the serve. The other player will practice their return of serve. You will do this until the person serving has had enough serves. Then you change and the other person serves while you practice returning.

When you are practicing returning, you are to practice hitting your best return. You are not to hit the ball just back to the server.

When I started to do this, I noticed that I would serve more balls than when I warmed up the other way. I could really work on my focus on the serve so much better. It was like I was out serving a mini bucket of balls.

This way you will be able to practice your return even if it is only for a short period of time. It also really helped my return of serve from the moment the game started.

After warming up your serve and return of serve this way, you will be surprised how much better your serve and returns will be in a very short time.

You will also have a benchmark when you begin to play the points. You can ask yourself, "Am I returning serve as well, now that we are keeping score, or am I tensing up and trying too hard to hit the serve back?"

You can also warm up this way when you play doubles, but you will have to have the cooperation of all four of you. It is much easier to do this in singles. And, of course, if you are really working on improving, you need to play mostly singles.

Doubles is a lot of fun, but not as helpful in improving your tennis game as singles, unless your goal is just to improve your serve, volley and your returns.

Practice Your Returns: Method No. 2

Here is another way to practice your returns. This one you can do when you are actually playing a practice match. And again, you must have a willing opponent and obviously you can't do it in a tournament match.

- The point cannot start until the return of serve has been returned into the court.
- If you missed the return on your backhand side, your practice partner must then serve all serves to your backhand until you get it back into the court.

- If you missed the return on their first serve, then your practice partner will serve another first serve.
- If that first serve is missed, then your practice partner will serve a second serve, but it still must be hit to the backhand side until you get it back.
- If your practice partner misses the second serve, he or she will keep serving second serves until the ball is in play. This means that he or she cannot double fault and this way both of you get to practice until you get it right.
- If your practice partner serves an ace, then the challenge for him or her is to hit another ace.
- If you miss the return on the first serve, then the challenge for the server is to hit two first serves in a row.
- If the server double faults, he or she will have a chance to practice a second serve. That way the server gets to practice also.

This drill will allow you to do the return of serve over and over without worrying about losing the point and you get to hit the same return until you get it in the court. It also takes the advantage away from the server, as the server doesn't get a free point just because he or she hit a good serve. It is a terrific way to work on one of the most important shots in tennis.

Hitting A More Consistent Return

Now that you will be practicing your return from now on, let's talk about how you should be hitting it so that you can return it much more consistently.

Playing Zen-Sational Tennis

As you know, hitting the return of serve is a little different from hitting a normal ball. One reason is because you have the chance to get yourself ready before you have to hit the ball. Once the point has started, you cannot stop and say you are not ready.

Another reason is because the serve is usually hit harder than a regular shot – and sometimes a lot harder – so you must also prepare yourself to be able to react quickly.

If you find yourself not returning very well, here are some issues you may want to address. As you may have gathered, one of the best tools that I use for learning and becoming aware of what is going on, is to ask questions.

Here are some you can ask yourself about your return of serve while you are practicing or playing.

- Am I truly **consciously** seeing the ball come off the racquet as my opponent hits the ball? As you see the ball hit your opponent's racquet, be sure to look for the direction and the speed of the ball as soon as possible .
- Is my exhale starting before my opponent serves the ball and continuing through my hit?
- Am I **consciously** seeing the ball spinning after the ball bounces and keeping my eyes at the contact point for a moment, even if I miss?
- Is my body and especially my grip relaxed enough as I am waiting to hit the return and as I am hitting the ball?
- Am I relaxing my arm enough to make a full finish?
- Did I program (visualize) the ball going where I wanted to?
-

Playing Zen-Sational Tennis

If you answer "no" to any of the above, then you will have to let go of whatever it is that may be interfering with your ability to stay focused. You should also use the reprogramming method to help you focus properly.

Here are 2 more questions that you may need to know the answers to.

- Am I hitting the ball long?
- Do I feel really rushed when hitting my returns?

If your answer to either of these questions is "yes," try hitting the ball just a little easier. This means relaxing your grip and wrist a little (maybe a lot) as you hit the ball as well as swinging a little slower from the shoulder. Do you remember that when I said to you earlier that hitting easier is a code word for being more relaxed?

Also, try standing back three to six feet if you are continuously hitting the ball long or you are feeling rushed. This will give you much more distance for your ball to drop in. If you still are feeling rushed try standing back even further. If you have watched some of the pros return, you will see some of them standing 8 to 15 feet behind the baseline, so let's do what they do if you find yourself missing too many returns.

To further your education on the return of serve, be sure to read Ron Waite's article "Many Happy Returns." You will find these if you go to my website **www.maxtennis.com** and click on Articles.

Lesson No. 60: How To Warm Up For A Match

Do you have a set method for warming yourself up? Does it work for you?

Here I will present a method that I believe is as good as any for warming up. Please work on it and use it as it will really get you ready for when the real points start.

I will address the warmup for only the following two situations: one situation is when you are just playing a match for fun, and the other will be when you are warming up for a tournament match. Let's take the friendly match first, since you will most likely be playing more of these.

If you are going to play a friendly game, your warmup time will be the foundation that you will build upon when the game actually starts. When the game does start, you will want to be able to continue playing as well as or better than you did when warming up.

If you are very comfortable with both the breathing and seeing the ball, then I would suggest that you start out on the very first ball doing both seeing the ball, keeping your focus on the contact point for a short time, and the breathing. Otherwise, you should start by focusing only on the ball, making sure that you can really see it the way I have presented in Lesson No. 6. Once you have gotten comfortable with seeing the ball, add the breathing component and then work toward doing both.

Playing Zen-Sational Tennis

If you need work on your strokes so that they can become more consistent, start out with also doing the Mother of All Tips. This exercise is found in Lesson No. 20. This is especially important if your strokes are feeling a little out of sorts.

After you get comfortable with seeing the ball and breathing, add some relaxation awareness. Start with feeling the grip and the wrist at impact to make sure they are very relaxed. By now you should know the signs that tell you if the grip needs to be relaxed a little more. Be sure to also feel the arm at the shoulder to make sure you aren't tensing up somewhere there during your swing and are taking a full finish on every ball.

All of these things should also be done with volleys, overheads and serves, and shouldn't take much time. When warming up your overhead, if you are playing with a friend who is willing, use the lob and overhead exercise found in Drill No. 10 in the Drills section in the back of this book.

When you warm up your serve, depending on how much time you have, use the following pattern:

1. Hit a minimum of three first serves in a row to the backhand or the right corner.
2. Hit a minimum of three first serves in a row to the forehand or the left corner.
3. Hit a minimum of three second serves in a row to the backhand or the right side.
4. Hit a minimum of three second serves in a row to the forehand or the left side.
5. In your next three practice serves, hit one first serve to the right side, hit another first serve to the left side, and then hit

Playing Zen-Sational Tennis

a second serve to the right side. Do the opposite if you are playing against a left-hander.

6. If you have enough time, repeat this in the ad court.

And, of course, while you are serving, you are seeing the ball to the blur of the racquet, keeping a relaxed grip, and exhaling properly.

When your opponent is practicing serving, you can practice seeing the ball spinning after the bounce as you catch it. This way you will be used to seeing the ball when the match starts. You can also use the serve and warm up method I will talk about in Lesson No. 63 that is coming up.

When warming up for a tournament, there will be little difference from warming up for a practice match.

You can do everything described in warming up for a practice match, except for two things. One of these is that you will do the warm up as described above for a practice match, only you will do it one to three hours earlier than your actual match. The second is that you may want to do a few easy placement drills like hitting cross-court, down-the-line drills, and you will want to serve a few more balls. You may even want to play a few points. Other than these additional items, this warm-up will be the same as the practice match warm-up. This practice should be only for 20 to 30 minutes.

When you actually get on the court to play your match, you usually get 5 to 10 minutes to warm up.

During this short warm-up time, you will just be watching the ball, keeping your focus on the contact point for a short time, keeping a relaxed grip, and working with your breathing as if you were playing the match. You will have no thought of the stroke, except to relax it

230

and make a complete follow-through, and you will have the Core Principles in mind. This way, when the match starts, you will be ready.

Lesson No. 61: How To Aim The Serve

In this lesson I will be talking more than just about how to aim.

This lesson is really more about not missing your serve and/or about hitting a much higher percentage of your first serves into the court.

How many double faults do you hit in a set or in a match? And, what about your first serve? What is your percentage? Do you know how to hit your serve in the court other than just going out and hitting bucket after bucket of balls?

You should be practicing your serve anyway by going out with a bucket of balls, but here I will give you a terrific technique not only for aiming your serve but also for improving your serving percentages.

You won't have to worry or think about double-faulting because if you take the time to visualize properly, you will not double-fault, or if you do, you will do it very rarely. And you will find that you will be hitting many more first serves in, and with better accuracy.

There are going to be three parts to this section on the serve. I will first tell you about how to do the full visualization, then how you can visualize very quickly which is what you will be doing most of the time anyway, and then what to do if your visualization is not working and you are still missing serves.

The Full Visualization

The first thing to do is to pick out the exact spot, on the court where you want your ball to bounce. Again, I am not talking about a general area. I am talking about a very precise spot. Use a road cone or tennis ball can to mark your spot if you are just hitting a bucket of balls. Then visualize and consciously see with your eyes the trajectory back to where the ball would cross the net.

When you look at the net, you will notice that it is made up of little squares. **Consciously** look at the square where your serve must pass over. Then visualize and **consciously** see with your eyes the ball passing over this square.

Do you know how high over the net your serve should pass on a first serve? So many people say about two feet and sometimes even higher. On most first serves you will need to hit the ball two to six inches and about a foot to a foot and a half for a second serve.

After seeing how high over the net your ball must go, then visualize and **consciously** see with your eyes the trajectory back to the place over your head where you are going to make contact with the ball.

Then starting from the beginning, visualize yourself starting your serve, seeing the ball on the toss, imagining or visualizing seeing the

232

ball to the blur of the racquet, keeping a relaxed grip, and with a perfect exhalation. Be sure you start the exhale just as you release the ball on your toss to make sure you are exhaling before making contact with the ball and make sure you are continuing your exhale until your ball bounces on the other side.

The general concept of the full visualization method is starting your visualizing and see where you want your ball to hit, moving your imaginary ball back to the start of the serve and then following the trajectory of the ball back to where you want it to hit.

When you go to actually serve, just **"know"** where you want the ball to go, see the ball all the way to the blur of the racquet, and keeping a very relaxed arm and grip as we talked about earlier. Remember to start your breathing using a very relaxed exhale as you release the ball on your toss and continue to exhale long after.

Trust your body to hit it to your target or let your body learn how. If you feel like you are doing everything right and the ball is not going where you want it to, or you notice that your body is not learning how to hit your target, then you may need to relax some part of your body more. Remember that on the serve, the arm, grip, and wrist are usually the place to relax first.

One of the biggest "errors" you may be making when doing this technique, is that you may not be taking enough time before each serve to do justice to the process of visualizing. Remember, when you are serving, you have control of when you start the point.

Another error you may be making is to forget to do any visualizing at all when you are playing. You have to become aware of the fact that your first serve is not going in enough or you

233

are double-faulting a lot, and then have the presence of mind to stop and use this visualizing technique.

This is a very powerful technique and as you work with this visualizing process, you will see your serve become more and more consistent and accurate.

You will begin to hit more first serves in, even during a match, but you have to remember to use this process. Don't forget to go out and hit some buckets of balls, as the more you practice, the faster the improvement.

The Quick Visualization

You will use this quick visualization most of the time because you have served so many times and your body will already know how to serve accurately and consistently. You can use this all the time when you are serving, but you will go to the full visualization technique if your serve breaks down.

The quick version of aiming the serve is to just pick the exact spot on the court where you want the ball to hit, and where and how high the ball must be over the net. This means actually looking with your eyes at these two spots. This is all you do.

When you go to serve, just **"know"** where you want the ball to go. Then just see the ball all the way to the blur of the racquet, starting your breathing using a very relaxed long exhale before you make contact with the ball, and continue to exhale long after. Trust that your body will hit it where you want it to go, or let your body learn how.

Playing Zen-Sational Tennis

Are you getting tired of hearing me tell you to see the ball and breathe? Hopefully, you know the reason by now. These concepts are the absolute key to allowing your body to play its very best.

If you miss the ball long or into the net, you may want to take a moment to more formally visualize seeing the ball going two to six inches over the net. If you feel like you are doing everything right and the ball is still not going where you want it to, or you notice that your body is not learning how to hit your target, then you will need to determine what part of your body is too tense or where your focus is off.

Use the following checklist to determine what is going on:

- Am I **consciously** seeing the ball to the blur of the racquet?
- Am I following the ball as it goes to my opponent's racquet? You won't be able to see it spin, but you can focus on it.
- Have I visualized the serve, including seeing the ball, as well as the speed, the stroke, and the exact path of the ball going two to six inches over the net immediately before I serve? Part of this visualizing is that you will **consciously** look at the spot where you want the ball to go and **consciously** look at the point where you want your ball to cross the net.
- Am I allowing a long and relaxed exhalation starting when I release the toss and after I hit the ball?
- Am I relaxing my grip and/or my wrist enough as I make contact with the ball?
- Am I relaxing my elbow enough as it goes through the swing? Remember, your arm should be like a wet noodle.
- Am I relaxing my wrist enough so that my racquet drops down behind my back all the way?

Playing Zen-Sational Tennis

A "no" answer to any of these questions means that you need to pay attention to that aspect, knowing that it needs to change and improve.

I want to put on my professor hat for a moment and give you a short lesson in physics. Some of you may know the answer to this, but for those who don't it will be good to know as it will illustrate the importance of relaxation.

Here is the question.

Most, if not all of you, have seen a Zorro movie and know that he uses a whip as one of his weapons. Do you know why his whip makes a snapping sound when he wields his whip? If you answered that the tip of his whip actually breaks the sound barrier, you would be correct. Did you know that?

So what does this have to do with tennis and the serve? There are actually two things. One is: Do you think Zorro's whip would be breaking the sound barrier if it were stiff?

The second point is that if you really relax your arm at the elbow, not only will you get more power with less effort, but by letting your arm be like a wet noodle, you will be turning over to your Other-Than-Conscious Mind any control of your stroke and thereby allowing your body to hit a more consistent and accurate serve.

There have been many times once I have my student relax his arm like a wet noodle he or she would hit the target cone within 5 serves. Sometimes even on the first one.

Using this technique when you serve is a very powerful one and it is that much more effective because you are always standing in the same place when you serve and you don't have the variability of having to run and chase the ball like on a ground stroke.

Let me tell you a couple of fun stories that show how powerful this technique is.

I was playing in a 24-hour tennis event for charity one year at my club and one of the events was to serve and try to hit a cone. Everyone was trying so hard to hit the cone and there were so many balls that came very close. I, on the other hand, was doing the opposite. I was visualizing and just letting go. Guess who won the contest? If you guessed that I did, you would be correct. This technique works bigtime, so please put it into your toolkit.

Here is the other fun story for you. When I am teaching this technique on how to aim the serve, at some point I will demonstrate to my student what this technique actually looks like. At this point I have not hit any serves so when I serve, I am pretty cold. On one occasion of demonstrating this, I hit the cone twice in a row on the first two serves.

I don't tell you this to brag, but to show you how powerful this technique is and how unbelievably accurate the body can become. I also don't have a clue on how I did it, but my body knows. I will admit that this has only happened once, but I have hit the cone a few times after only one or two tries. Guess what? When you work with this technique, you and your body can do it also.

I have one last thought about aiming your first serve that you may want to do once you see how accurate your first serve can be using this technique. In the past when I chose the exact spot I wanted my first serve to go, I chose a spot about a foot inside the lines. I felt that extra foot would give me a margin of error. I found that I could hit the cone at least one out of 10 times and sometimes more than that. I had the thought that if my serve was that accurate (thanks to my body), I would change my exact spot to right on the lines.

My serve became much more effective because I was now able to hit ever so much closer to the lines. Even if your serve is not that fast, that extra distance closer to the lines really makes a difference. Not having a very hard serve, I got tired of having players return my serve, and this way they have to work just a little bit harder.

Lesson No. 62: A Checklist If You Are Missing Your Serve

If you have been known to miss a first serve, then this checklist is very important.

As I have said before, you should use the process in the previous lesson (Lesson No. 61) to work on any of these issues.

- See the ball spinning as it is tossed into the air, and see the blur of the racquet as it hits the ball.
- See the ball as it goes to the opponent's racquet.
- Bend your knees a little when serving.
- Rotate shoulders on the serve.
- Always hit a slight amount of side-spin on the first serve. This helps keep the ball in.

Playing Zen-Sational Tennis

- Exhale through the mouth in a relaxed way, using a sigh, just starting just as you release the ball on the toss and allow the exhale to continue until your ball bounces on the ground.
- Keep a very relaxed grip as you contact the ball
- Keep a very relaxed arm, especially at the elbow and at the wrist
- If you miss a first serve, take time to visualize the ball going into the court before your next first serve.
- If you miss a second serve which means, of course, you double faulted, take time to visualize the ball going into the court before your next second serve.

Below are some questions you may want to ask yourself if you are missing your first serve a lot. I believe that you should be hitting 75 to 80 percent or higher of your first serves in. If you are not, then by asking yourself these questions and actively adjusting what you are doing, you will see your first-serve consistency improve.

The same applies for your second serve. If you serve more than one double fault a set, then you need to take a look at what is going on and make some adjustments.

As you will notice, many of these questions are the same as the checklist that I gave you earlier. The difference, of course, is that you will be asking them during a match if you find yourself missing more than normally.

The other checklist contains things you are to do when you are practicing your serve. I am hoping that you are taking the time to actually hit a bucket of balls from time to time and not just using the matches you play for practice.

Here are the questions.

- Am I seeing the ball to the blur of the racquet?
- Am I seeing the ball to the opponent's racquet?
- Have I visualized the serve, including seeing the ball, the speed, the stroke, and the exact path of the ball going two to six inches over the net immediately before I serve?
- Am I taking enough time before I serve to truly do a complete and thorough visualization?
- Am I gently exhaling starting just as I release the ball on the toss and allow the exhale to continue until my ball bounces on the ground?
- Am I relaxing my grip and/or my wrist enough as I make contact with the ball?
- Am I relaxing my arm enough as it goes through the swing? Remember it should be like a wet noodle.
- Am I relaxing my wrist enough so that my racquet drops down behind my back all the way.

Lesson No. 63: Warm Up Your Serve and Return Of Serve This Way

Serves and return of serves are a very important part of your game, which is why I am re-visiting this idea again. I am hoping that by repeating these techniques of practicing your serve and return of serves, you will spend more time doing it. Of course, you must have a cooperative playing partner and you won't be doing this if you are playing in a tournament.

If you warm up your serve the way most players do when you are playing a practice match, you most likely will serve three balls, which your opponent catches and then they serve them back to you which you then catch. You do this back and forth until you feel that you have had enough serves. Please re-read Lesson No. 60 for more details on how to warm up.

So, do you warm up your return of serve? You warm up everything else. Well, here is a really good way to warm up and practice both serves and return of serves.

One of you will choose to warm up and practice serving. The other player will practice their return of serve. You will do this until the person serving has had enough serves. Then you change and the other person serves while his/her opponent practices returning.

When you are practicing returning, you are to practice hitting your best return. You are not to hit the ball just back to the server.

When I started to do this, I noticed that I would serve more balls than when I warmed up the other way and I found I could really begin to focus so much better on my serve. It was like I was out hitting a mini bucket of balls.

And when was the last time you really practiced your return of serve? This way you will be able to practice it even if it is only for a short period of time. After warming up your serve and return of serve this way, you will be surprised how much better your serve and returns will be in a very short time. It also really helped my return of serve from the moment the game started.

You will now have a benchmark when you begin to play the points. You can ask yourself, "Am I returning serve as well, now that we are keeping score or am I tensing up and trying too hard to hit the serve back?"

I guess you can warm up this way when you play doubles but you will have to have the cooperation of all four of you. It is much easier to do this in singles.

And, of course, if you are really working on improving, you need to play mostly singles. Doubles is a lot of fun, but not as helpful in improving your tennis game as singles, unless your goal is just to improve your doubles.

Hopefully, you know that you would not and cannot do this in a real tournament match. You would be warming up earlier in the day where you would be hitting some return of serves and serving.

Lesson No. 64: Do Not Hit Winners

What? You don't think I should ever hit a winner?

Do you try hard to hit winners? Do you get frustrated when you either miss the ball or you couldn't hit the ball good enough so that it was a winner? When you understand about winners, you may just find yourself hitting more of them.

Playing Zen-Sational Tennis

The concept of hitting winners is like the concept of winning. You are not to try to win. You are to find a way to play your very best and let winning take care of itself. Likewise, you are not to try to hit winners. You are to just hit the ball where you want it to go using the appropriate power, and if it is a winner, so much the better.

When you try to hit winners, you should know by now that most likely you will not be watching the ball very well, nor will your breathing be relaxed, and I will bet that your grip is a lot tighter than it should be.

I also hope that you know by now that I am not talking about never hitting the ball hard. I am talking about just knowing when you need to hit the ball hard. This is the same as knowing where you want the ball to go. If you place it well and your opponent can't get to it, then by its very nature it will be a winner. You don't have to try to do it.

And after you hit this great shot, do you pump your fist and say "Yes!"? I hope not.

Here is a much better way. Just pat yourself on the back, thank your body for hitting the great shot and say to your body. "Body, that was a great shot, please keep those great shots coming."

If you are playing doubles and your partner does not understand about who hits the ball like you do, then when you "high five" and he/she says "great shot," "come on," or "lets go," "let's get this

point", or any other comment that encourages you to try harder, you need to translate this.

Just know that you want to keep letting your body keep playing without the control of your Conscious Mind. And, of course, you do this by staying focused on the ball, your breathing, and hitting with a relaxed grip.

Please resist the thought that you did it, as this will lead to trying. Remember, the you I am talking about here is your Conscious Mind.

Also, please resist the urge to start trying to hit more and more winners or more and more good shots. Just keep your Conscious Mind out of the way and know that your body will do it for you. Believe me, it can and it will.

Read on as I will give you some more "goodies" about hitting winners.

As you may know, it is pretty hard to hit a normal winner without hitting the ball hard. The only exceptions will be dropshot winners, lob winners, or very sharp angle winners like on the volley.

So how do you hit the ball hard?

When you know it is time to hit the ball hard, you must learn to swing hard but still with proper relaxation. You don't need to tense up any other parts of your body. But you will be using more muscle energy so that the racquet swings faster.

And you can still do this with a relaxed grip, a relaxed arm and a relaxed face. Just in case you didn't know, if you are exhaling properly, even during a hard hit ball, your face will be automatically relaxed. Just watch Roger Federer's face when he hits a hard forehand.

The main point to understand is that a hard hit ball is done just by using the muscles you need to swing the racquet so that the racquet moves faster through the air.

One way to practice what it feels like to swing fast but relaxed is to take some practice swings very fast without the ball. This way you can easily check out your grip, wrist, arm, and your breathing to make

sure they are relaxed. See if you can identify which part of your body needs to work harder to make the racquet mover faster.

Now, once you have hit the ball hard and it is a great shot and/or a winner, just pat yourself on the back, thank your body for hitting the great shot by saying to your body, "Body, that was a great shot, please keep those great shots coming." Then don't try to hit any more winners.

Lesson No. 65: Why You Should Hit Your Overheads As Hard As You Can

Do you want to win the point every time you hit an overhead? Well, maybe not every time but 95% of the time? If your answer is yes, then you must do what I am going to tell you now about how to hit your overhead.

Let me tell you a story. Quite a few years ago, I was playing in a tournament on a slow court against a steady player who was fast on his feet. I felt I needed to go to the net because I couldn't win the points from the baseline as he was tiring me out. But when I went to the net, he lobbed a lot and I just tried to angle my overhead off. I quickly found out that didn't work. He just ran it down and hit an even better lob or hit a passing shot. Not only did I get very tired, I lost the match.

After the match, I got to thinking that if I hit my overhead as hard as I could, I could end the point then and there, and I wouldn't get so tired.

I also thought that all I had to do was to hit my overhead five or six feet away from him and because my ball was going so fast he, most likely, would not have time to get to it, and if he was able to get his racquet on it, his shot would be weaker, and I would be able to really put the ball away on the next shot.

So, here is what happened. I started hitting my overheads as hard as I could and I found from then on that I almost never missed my overhead and I almost always won the point on the first hit. Because I was ending the point sooner I was less tired.

Obviously, you must use some common sense when hitting your overhead as hard as you can. That means that if you can just barely reach the ball, you cannot and should not try to hit it hard. To do so may hurt your arm or shoulder because of the awkward way you must hit the ball. But if you are in position, you must hit it very hard.

I can't tell you how many times I have seen players who just hit the overhead easy just to get it back and end up losing the point. Why not hit the ball hard so that the point is over right then. I do believe you will find yourself winning that many more points. And besides, have you ever seen the pros hit easy overheads?

So, you need to treat the overhead as a point ending shot. Either you will win the point or you will lose the point. There is no in between and the only exception is if you can barely reach the ball as it goes over your head and you physically can't hit it hard.

Lesson No. 66: How To Hit Running Balls

I admit that I have not ever done charting on where people miss the ball when they are running. What have you observed as to where other people miss the ball when they are running hard for a ball? And when you miss a ball when you are running, do you know whether you miss the ball wide, long or in the net?

If you have observed yourself or other players when running hard for a ball, you may have seen a pattern as to where the ball is missed. I have observed in myself and others that most players miss the ball long. The next time you watch a game or when you play, take a look and see if this is true.

Anyway, the point is that when you run, you have the tendency to run hard with the lower body, and as a result the upper body follows suit. This fast-moving upper body makes you swing at the ball faster, and/or more tense. Therefore you may be hitting the ball long if you miss because you have hit the ball too hard.

What must be learned is to run relaxed but fast with your legs, but allow the upper body to be as relaxed and swing at the ball as if you were standing still.

Playing Zen-Sational Tennis

Easier said than done, you say? The way you can work on this is to really pay attention to your breathing when you are running fast for a ball, and make sure that you are not holding your breath and that your exhalation is as relaxed as possible before and after you hit the ball. You can also work on paying attention to your swing thereby allowing your swing to be slower, more relaxed, and to be independent of your legs.

When I work on my running and hitting, I really work on relaxing my breathing. And, seeing the ball to the blur of your racquet, keeping your focus on the contact point for a short time, and keeping a relaxed grip is also very helpful in allowing the upper body to be relaxed. Did you know that if you are able to breathe properly on a running ball, your face will be as relaxed as Roger Federer's? Just think. You can then say that you play just like he does.

When you are working on slowing down the swing when running hard, just feel your swing and let your arm at your shoulder and your grip be that much more relaxed. It just takes awareness and practice. You can practice running and hitting by playing two points or rallies paying attention to your breathing, two points seeing the ball, and then two points combining.

Another good way to practice running and hitting is to start with an easy run to the ball to see if you can still keep your breathing and grip relaxed and swing speed relaxed through the hit. Then see if you can still do this on faster and faster runs to the ball. Pretty soon it will be easier. If you have access to a ball machine, you can set it up so that you can work on running faster and faster for balls.

As critical as breathing is when running and hitting, so is the skill of seeing the ball to the blur of the racquet and keeping your eyes on the contact point for a short time, and it must be worked on until you have it mastered even on a ball that you must run very fast for.

If you really analyze why you have missed a ball when you have had to run hard for it, you will find out that you have made one or all of these classic errors.

- Holding your breath
- Not seeing the ball to the racquet
- Not keeping your eyes on the contact point for a short time
- Having some part of your body being too tense, especially your grip at contact

In the next lesson, I will give you some drills for practicing running and hitting. In the meantime, work with paying attention to your upper and lower body and see if you can begin to isolate them.

Lesson No. 67: Two Running Drills

Hopefully, you have done or at least read about Drills No. 1 through No. 4 which are in my book and CDs. Now do these drills again, but this time you will hit your balls to alternate sides while your practice partner will hit to one side only. When the person running gets tired, switch so that you get to run.

Drill No. 6: Running Drill No. 1

The purpose of this drill is two-fold.

The one hitting from side to side gets to practice seeing the ball, breathing, and keeping a relaxed grip while hitting a change-of-direction ball.

The runner gets to practice seeing the ball, feeling his or her breathing, and keeping a relaxed grip while running and hitting. You may find that your focus will not be as good as when you were just standing and hitting so here are some variations if you are having problems with your focus.

- Spend some time just **consciously** watching the ball spinning, keeping your focus on the contact point for a short time and forget about your breathing.
- Spend some time just **consciously** feeling your breathing and forget about focusing on the ball.
- Spend some time just **consciously** feeling your grip and forget about focusing on the ball or your breathing.
- Start combining seeing the ball, breathing and relaxing the grip.
- Pretend that someone will pay you $1 million for every time you can see the ball, breathe and relax properly. This is just about how important you must make your focus.

When you are doing this running drill, again awareness is very important and again you will need to have these following questions handy so that you can ask yourself these awareness questions:

- On the balls that I have to run hard for, am I still able to see the ball spinning to the blur of my racquet and keep my focus on the contact point for a short period of time? If your answer is no, you need to let go more and to make this more important.

- Am I still able to feel my breathing and do a long exhale just before and through hitting the ball? If your answer is no, you need to let go more and again make this more important.

- When I am aiming my ball, am I trying so hard to aim that I have not watched the ball and kept my focus on the contact point for a short period of time? If your answer is yes, you need to learn to let go more and let your body do the aiming while you are busy seeing the ball.

- Was I able to keep my awareness on my breathing while I was thinking about aiming? If your answer is no, you need to learn to let go more and let your body do the aiming while you are busy breathing.

- Am I able to keep my arm relaxed at the elbow and at the grip as I am hitting the running balls?

Here is another running drill:

Drill No. 7: Running Drill No. 2

This drill is a variation to the previous one (Drill No. 6), so I just call it "Another Running Drill."

Do Drill No. 6 again, but this time one of you will hit your balls anywhere while the other will hit to one side only. When the person running gets tired, switch so the other person gets to run.

The purpose of this drill is again twofold.

The one hitting anywhere gets to practice seeing the ball spinning, keeping their focus on the contact point for a short time, breathing, and keeping a relaxed grip while deciding where to hit the ball for maximum effect.

The runner gets to practice seeing the ball spinning, keeping their focus on the contact point for a short time, feeling his or her breathing and keeping a relaxed grip while running and hitting.

The real value of this drill is to find out what state of mind you must be in to choose where you want the ball to go. You do it by making sure that the thought of where you want the ball to go is just a **knowing**, and it must follow in fourth place behind seeing the ball spinning, keeping your focus on the contact point for a short time, and being aware of your exhaling. And when you know where you want the ball to go, let your Other-Than-Conscious Mind direct your body.

Here are the awareness questions to ask yourself to make sure you are getting the most from this drill:

- When I miss the ball, am I really seeing the ball properly or am I putting aiming the ball first?
- When I miss the ball, am I feeling my breathing first, or am I putting aiming the ball first?
- When I miss the ball, am I keeping my focus on the contact point for a short time, or am I putting aiming the ball first?

- Am I trying too hard to hit the ball to where I want it to go? If your answer is yes, you need to relax more, starting with your grip, wrist, and arm at the shoulder when you make contact with the ball.

- On the balls that I have to run hard for, am I still seeing the ball spinning to my racquet keeping my focus on the contact point for a short period of time?

- Am I still feeling my breathing and exhaling just before hitting the ball on the hard running balls?

- Am I able to keep my arm relaxed at the elbow and at the grip as I am hitting the running balls?

- Am I able to still do a full finish even though I am running hard?

I do hope that you are spending some time drilling and not just playing. Yes, I know that drilling may not be as much fun, but it is critical to improvement.

Lesson No. 68: How To Think About And Deal With Your Weaknesses

Do you acknowledge your weaknesses and spend time working on them? Or, do you try hard to sweep them under the rug or just don't care that you have any?

Playing Zen-Sational Tennis

When you can embrace your weaknesses, you will begin to see them diminish or even disappear. And guess what? Even the best players have weaknesses.

How you deal with them is always an interesting issue. I see a lot of people trying very hard to avoid their weaknesses. For example, the most obvious one is when I see players running around their backhands just for the sake of avoiding them. Or I see players practicing their forehands by the hour with no thought of hitting backhands.

From my way of thinking, if your backhand is weaker, you should be wishing that your opponent hit all the balls to your backhand. Likewise, if you have difficulty hitting down the line, you should be hitting down the line even if you miss and lose the point.

Sometimes I even hit my weak shot when it is not the best time to do it from a strategy point of view just so I can hit more of them.

I heard of an interesting phrase the other day. It was "practice the impossible." What a concept. The point is that if there is something or some shot you can't do very well, work on it until you can do it.

In the above discussion, I am not suggesting that you practice your weakness if you are playing for money, playing in a tournament, or playing in any match where it is critical to win. But when you change the way you feel about your weaknesses and deal with them head on, this approach will lead to a much faster strengthening of those weaknesses.

Lesson No. 69: How To Determine If Your Opponent's Forehand Or Backhand Is Weaker

What if you start warming up and you can't tell if your opponent's forehand or backhand is weaker?

What about once you have started playing, can you tell then? Here is how you can decide.

When you are warming up, you should be able to get a pretty good picture of which stroke is stronger or weaker. Be sure to hit enough balls to each side so that you have enough information to make a determination.

If your opponent's forehand and backhand look the same, you will need to do some more investigating. When the game starts, assume that the backhand is weaker.

If you find you are getting hurt by the backhand, change and begin hitting most of your balls to the forehand and see what happens.

Use the same plan for determining weaknesses when your opponent is warming up volleys and overheads.

Lesson No. 70: How To Play At The Top Of Your Game Every Time

Do you play your very best every time you go on the court? Why not? You now have all the tools so that you can get into the zone.

Obviously, it is not that easy to get into the zone and play your best every time, but there are many things you can do to turn things around for the better. If you find yourself not playing very well, do you know what some of them are?

There are some things, however, that are out of your control that just happen and you must be aware of them.

For example, there will be times when your body just doesn't work very well. This can happen if you are tired, sick or if your body is just out of sorts.

Have you ever heard of biorhythms which used to be the rage in the old days. It measured your physical, mental, and emotional state on each day? Well, I believe that there are some days your body and your brain just work better than others and you just can't do anything about it.

But what you can expect is that whatever condition your body and your brain are in, you can play the very best in that moment. Even if you start at a lower than normal level of play, you can and should be able to improve as the match continues.

Playing Zen-Sational Tennis

Here are some specific things to be aware of that can creep into your mind and will need to be addressed.

The first one is judgment of your play. Here is a really good way to know if you are judging something – if at any time you react verbally, mentally or physically to a missed shot, then that is the sign that you are judging your shots and trying too hard.

Once you are aware of these judgments, just let go of them and get back to using the Core Principles. You may find yourself playing really well again and very quickly.

There also may be times that no matter how hard you try to let go of judgments, or even focus as well as you have in the past, that your Conscious Mind just won't cooperate. When that happens, one really good way to get back into the here and now is to do a meditation on deep breathing.

In between points and when you are changing sides, sit down, focus on deep breathing, slow it down and just let go of all other thoughts. During the point, however, just continue to work on letting go. You may find that your Conscious Mind will begin to release its grip on you.

You might even try to have a longer dialogue with your Conscious Mind and see if you can get it to cooperate and release control.

You can use these ideas anytime and not just when your body is out of sorts. So, work with them and you will see that the more you use them the better and more powerful these ideas become.

Lesson No. 71: A Basic Doubles Strategy, Version No. 1

Doubles is a fascinating game as there are an unlimited number of things to do strategy-wise. And most of them are pretty hard to do because so much depends on what your opponents do with the ball and what you and your partner do with the ball.

However, in my lessons on doubles strategy, I have tried very hard to make it as easy as possible for you to follow, but when you do read it, your eyes may glass over if you have tried to follow and remember and do everything in the lesson all at once.

With that in mind, here is what I want you to do for the next two weeks (or maybe for the next 6 months). I have divided up the strategy into little sub headings to make it easy for you to understand and work on. I want you to break these strategies down into sections and work on them one part at a time. Read through it all once and then spend time on only one part at a time and don't move on to the next part until you are comfortable doing that part.

Doing these basic strategies will absolutely make you a better doubles player. Here is a good example of how powerful these doubles concepts are. When I was living in Victoria, B.C., one year I coached

a local high school team. There were no boys teams or girls teams, as they combined both girls and boys together.

I had these two girls on the team who were literally beginners. They were, however, terrific athletes and they learned very fast how to hit the ball into the court. Because they didn't know any other way, they

258

were able to execute the basic doubles strategy that I am going to present to you here.

It was amazing to watch because they beat some teams that were better players and came within a point of beating a team that was much, much better. The only reason they didn't win was because the other team had enough experience to change their play to neutralize my girls' strategy, and my girls didn't know how to change what they were doing.

Most, if not all, of the following doubles strategy I learned from Dick Leach, who was one of the most successful coaches at the University of Southern California (USC) for a number of years. When I was in college, doubles was my best game and my partner Horst Ritter and I were undefeated. I thought I was this big mucky-muck doubles player and that I knew a lot about how to play it.

After I started my career as a teaching pro, Dick invited me up to his tennis camp in Big Bear, Calif., to play and enjoy some time off. It was here that I observed what Dick was teaching about doubles strategy in a clinic. I was shocked and amazed at how little I really knew. I didn't know any of the things he was teaching. What he taught made so much sense, and I, of course, stole his ideas and began to teach my students the same strategy.

Years ago Dick put together a more complete booklet of his doubles strategy and he has made it available to me to give to you. If you purchased a book from my website you received this doubles booklet as a bonus. If you didn't get it and you want it, go to **www.maxtennis.com/download.php** so you can download it.

As the name of this lesson indicates, there are more than one version of my doubles strategy. In the next lesson, I will give you another version of the same doubles strategy I am giving to you now. I do this because this strategy is not easy to understand or to put into your play and I felt that if I went over the strategy in a little different format, it may begin to make more sense and make it easier for you to implement.

In Lesson No. 73, I will give you some ideas on how to breathe when playing doubles. This will help you to execute these strategies as well play your best.

So, take your time going through all this doubles stuff and really focus on it one segment at a time. That way you should be able to implement these ideas a lot easier.

When You Are At Net

Always hit your volley at the opposite net person (this includes the overhead). This shot is most effective when aimed at knee level of your opponent. If you, by chance, actually hit your opponent, just say you are sorry, but do not change your strategy.

If you find that your balls are not being hit at your opponent who is at net, you need to do some reprogramming. Before the next point is started, you must imagine, visualize, and see where you want your volley to be hit.

When and how to change this strategy:

If your opponent has great reactions and is returning most of your shots, then hit your volley three feet to the outside part (toward the doubles line) of that person.

Where To Stand And What To Do When You Are At Net And Your Partner Is Serving.

Stand in the exact center of the service box, and when the ball hits the court, move in a straight line directly toward the center strap, stopping when you get three feet from the net. Remember to hit the ball at the opposite net person if you are able to hit the ball. If you cannot or do not hit the ball, you must back up, all the way to the "T" if possible.

If you are playing at a high level, then these movements are shortened because the speed of the ball going back and forth will not give you much time to move very far. This does not mean that you don't make an effort to move some with always moving in as the most important thing to do.

When and how to change this strategy

When you have lost two points on the deuce side from having your opponent hit a ball down the line, you must change your strategy.

Likewise, when you have lost two points in the ad court, this also means you must change your strategy. Now you will move in toward the net, following a path parallel to the ball again getting as close to the net as possible.

If your opponent lobs the return a lot, then you cannot move in toward the net and be ready to move back so you can hit an overhead.

261

Notice that these changes in strategy are independent of each other. So, when one of these situations occurs, you will move straight in, or if the serve is hit wide, you will move in at an angle parallel to it.

If your opponent returns most balls high over the net or hits a lot of lobs, then you must adjust and maybe not move forward at all every time. You will then still move in from time to time depending on where your opponents return the ball.

Where To Stand And What To Do When You Are At Net And Your Partner Is Receiving The Serve

Stand on the serviceline in the middle. When your partner returns the ball and **IT GOES PAST THE NET PERSON**, then you will move in toward the center strap. Again, remember to hit your volley at the net person.

If you cannot or do not hit the next ball, you must back up to the T, if possible.

If you are playing at a high level, then these movements are shortened because the speed of the ball going back and forth will not give you much time to move very far. This does not mean that you don't make an effort to move some.

When and how to change this strategy

When you have lost two points on the deuce side from having your opponent hit a ball down the line, you must change your strategy.

262

Likewise, when you have lost two points in the ad court, this also means you must change your strategy. Now you will move in toward the net, following a path parallel to the ball.

If your opponent lobs the return a lot, then you cannot move in toward the net and be ready to move back so you can hit an overhead.

Where To Stand And What To Do When You Are Serving In The Deuce Court

When you are serving in the deuce court, it is absolutely critical that you serve the ball most of the time to your opponent's backhand (assuming that he or she is right-handed). Most of the time means 98 percent of first serves and 100 percent of second serves.

How far you stand from the centerline depends on how well you are able to serve to the backhand.

If you are having trouble serving to the backhand when standing over from the middle, you must move toward the center to assure that your serve goes down the middle to the backhand.

If by chance you are standing in the middle and you serve to the forehand, you must be ready to move over to the right to protect an angled return of serve that is hit wide to your forehand.

If you are an advanced player, serving into the body of your opponent is also very effective.

263

Where To Stand And What To Do When You Are Serving In The Ad Court

When you are serving in the ad court, you must also serve the ball to the backhand side most of the time. Although it is not as critical as in the deuce court, the percentages stay the same as when serving in the deuce court.

You should stand over about eight to 10 feet from the center so that it is easier to serve to the backhand.

If you are an advanced player, serving into the body of your opponent is also very effective.

For help on serving more accurately, see Lessons No. 59 and No. 60.

Where To Stand And What To Do When You Are Receiving The Serve In The Deuce Court

If you are receiving in the deuce court, you want to stand far enough to the left so that you can hit as many forehands as possible (assuming that your forehand is your best shot), but not so far over that the server can hurt you with a wide serve. Most of the time you will want to return the serve cross-court and back to the server.

One of the dirty little secrets of doubles is that most of the time the team that returns the most balls wins the match. In order to do this you must figure out a way to return the serve into the court **NO MATTER WHAT**.

For more on the return of serve, see Lesson No. 58 & No. 59.

Where To Stand And What To Do When You Are Receiving In The Ad Court

If you are receiving in the ad court, again, stand far enough to the left so that you can use your forehand (assuming that it is your best shot) but not so far that you get into trouble if the ball is hit down the middle.

The Basic Rule On Where To Be Positioned When At Net

When your partner is hitting the ball and he or she is at the baseline, then you should be back on the service line so you can play defensive should the ball be hit to you.

If your opponent is at the baseline and he or she is hitting the ball, then you should be moving in toward the net so you can play offensive should the ball be hit to you. Be sure to hit your volleys at the opposite net person.

However, if your partner has a pattern of never hitting the ball to the net person, you can be moving in before the ball has passed the net person.

The Three Basic Rules

If for some reason, you still are not (or don't want to) able to do these strategies, let me give you three simple ideas that you absolutely need to do. I won't go into the reasons here so you will just need to trust me and follow these instructions like good little boys and girls. ☺

Rule No. 1: Serve to the backhand 98% of the time on the first serve and 100% on your second serve. This is absolutely critical when serving in the deuce court (assuming a right handed player).

Rule No. 2: When you are at net and your partner is serving or receiving, you absolutely must move in toward the net getting within 3 feet of the net. The only time you will not do this is if your opponents lob over you every time. Even if they lob over you a lot, you still must move in but now you will be trying to guess about whether a lob is coming or not.

Rule No. 3: When you are at net and the ball comes to you, you must hit your volley at your opponent who is at net. Do not hit it back to the player who is in the back court.

As the title says, these are just basic strategy rules. Doubles is a very complex game, and there are many variations to the above strategies such as poaching, signaling, playing Australian doubles, serving and going to the net, returning serve and going to the net, hitting your return down the line, playing the angles, how to defend against poachers, and when to lob, to name more than a few. However, when you master these basic strategies, your value as a doubles

partner will be measurably enhanced and you will be winning more points.

As I said in the last paragraph, there are variations and exceptions to every rule and you must be flexible and be able to change should the situation change. However, before you worry about changing what you do, it is important for you to master these basics.

Spend as much time as you need to on all these ideas, but do them one at a time. Even though I call these ideas Basic Strategies, they are the backbone of all doubles play and they are very powerful.

And above all, have fun doing them as this is what make doubles so interesting.

Lesson No. 72: A Basic Doubles Strategy, Version No. 2

I have also talked about some doubles strategy in Lesson No. 58 which is about the return of serve. And in the last lesson I gave you a more formal description of doubles strategy. If you haven't read these lessons yet, you really need to.

267

Playing Zen-Sational Tennis

The strategies in this lesson were given to you in the previous lesson, but I wanted to give them to you again in a different format. I am hoping that by doing this you will be able to more easily understand them and use them when you play.

Just reading this doubles strategy can be a little hard to follow, so you may want to read it all the way through and then go back and read one part at a time while you implement it the next time you play. Then go on to the next part.

Strategy No. 1: When you are at the net, always hit your volley at the opposite net person. This includes the overhead. This shot is most effective when aimed at knee level of your opponent. If you, by chance, actually hit your opponent, just say you are sorry, but do not change your strategy.

Here is when and how to change this strategy. If your opponent has great reactions and is returning most of your shots, you will then want to hit your volley three feet to the outside part or towards the doubles line of that person.

Strategy No. 2: When you are at net and your partner is serving, you will want to stand in the exact center of the service box. As soon as your partner's serve bounces in the service court, move in at a straight line directly toward the center strap, stopping when you get three feet from the net. The purpose is to get close to the net (within three feet) where your volley is so much more effective and you cut off the angle of the return.

If you are able to hit the ball, remember to hit the ball at the opposite net person. If you do hit the ball, you will stay in your position in case the ball is returned to you. Hopefully, you have hit a winner.

268

If you cannot or do not hit the ball, you must back up, all the way to the "T" if possible. Sometimes the ball is going back and forth so quickly that you won't have time to get all the way to the "T", but you need to move in that direction.

You will need to change this strategy, when you have lost two points on the deuce side from having your opponent hit a return of serve down the line. Likewise, when you have lost two points in the ad court, you must also change your strategy. Notice that these changes in strategy are independent of each other.

When you do need to make a change, instead of moving toward the center strap, you will move straight in, or if the serve is hit wide, you will move in at an angle parallel to it. You will always move in close to the net no matter whether you are moving toward the center strap, moving straight in or at an angle if the ball is served wide.

If your opponent returns most balls high over the net or hits a lot of lobs, then you must adjust and maybe not move forward at all. After you determine that your opponent can hit down the line, you will then play a cat and mouse game. You will still want to move in towards the center strap, but from now on you will see if you can out guess your opponent as to where he will hit the ball and move accordingly. You will still want to move to the center strap from time to time just to keep your opponents guessing.

Strategy No. 3: When you are at net and your partner is receiving, you will want to stand on the serviceline in the middle of your half. Please don't stand off center towards the alley. If you want to stand off center, stand closer to the center serviceline.

When your partner returns the ball and **IT GOES PAST THE NET PERSON**, then you will move in toward the center strap.

Playing Zen-Sational Tennis

Again, remember to hit your volley at the net person. If your partner is hitting great returns and your opponent who is at net never hits the ball, you can then begin to move in a little sooner. The purpose is to get close (within three feet) to the net where your volley is so much more effective and you cut off the angle of the return.

If you cannot or do not hit the next ball, you must back up to the T, if possible. If you are playing at a high level, then these movements are shortened because the speed of the ball going back and forth will not give you much time to move very far. This does not mean that you don't make an effort to move some but with moving in close to the net being the most important thing to do.

You will need to change this strategy when you have lost two points on the deuce side from having your opponent hit a ball down the line. You must also change your strategy when you have lost two points in the ad court. Now you will move in toward the net, following a path parallel to the ball. If your opponent lobs his ball a lot, then you cannot move in toward the net and you must be ready to move back so you can hit the ball using an overhead.

Again, and after you determine that your opponent can hit down the line, you will then play a cat and mouse game. You will still want to move in towards the center strap, but from now on you will see if you can out guess your opponent as to where he will hit the ball.

What is important here is that you are moving around. This will keep your opponents guessing and many times it will throw them off so that they will miss balls they would normally be able to hit.

General Rules For When You Are At Net

To help you understand a little easier the concepts of where you need to be when you are playing at net, here are the general rules.

General Rule No. 1: When your partner is hitting the ball and he or she is at the baseline, then you should be back on the serviceline so you can play defensive and have more time to react should the ball be hit to you from the opposite net person.

General Rule No. 2: If your opponent is at the baseline and he or she is hitting the ball, then you should be moving in toward the net so you can play offensive should the ball be hit to you. However, you should not be moving in until the ball has passed the net person. And if you do hit the ball, you will want to stay close to the net in the event the ball comes back to you.

Serving and receiving strategies

This next strategy deals with when you are serving or when your partner is serving. If you are playing with someone who does not know this strategy, it will be up to you to tell them what to do. That is, of course, if you think they would be open to improving their doubles. Please don't be telling your spouse these things. I don't want to be responsible for any divorces.

Strategy No. 1: When you are serving in the deuce court, and assuming that your opponent is right-handed, it is absolutely critical that you serve the ball most of the time to your opponent's backhand which is, of course, down the middle. Most of the time means 98 percent of first serves and 100 percent of second serves.

271

Playing Zen-Sational Tennis

How far away you stand from the center to serve depends on how well you are able to serve to the backhand. If you are having trouble serving to the backhand when standing over from the middle and close to the doubles alley, you must move closer to the center to assure that your serve goes down the middle to the backhand. If by chance you are standing close to the middle and you serve wide to the forehand, you must be ready to move to the right to protect an angled return of serve that is hit wide to your forehand.

Again, serving to the backhand when serving in the deuce court is extremely important and if you are not able to serve to the backhand, you may want to read Lesson No. 61 on aiming the serve, get out with a bucket of balls, and practice doing so. I can't tell you how many points you will win doing this if you can effectively serve to the backhand.

Strategy No. 2: When you are serving in the ad court, you must also serve the ball to the backhand side most of the time. Although it is not as critical as in the deuce court, the percentages stay the same. You should stand over about eight to 10 feet from the center so that it is easier to serve to the backhand. Here it is OK to stand closer to the doubles alley if you want.

Strategy No. 3: When you are receiving in the deuce court, and assuming that your forehand is your best shot, you want to stand far enough to the left so that you can hit as many forehands as possible, but not so far over that the server can hurt you with a wide serve. Most of the time you will want to return the serve cross-court which means hitting the ball back to the server.

One of the dirty little secrets of doubles is that with few exceptions, the team that returns the most serves wins the match. In order to do this you must figure out a way to return the serve into the court **NO**

MATTER WHAT. And **NO MATTER WHAT** means even if you hit your return to the net person. If you haven't read Lesson No. 56 on the return of serve yet, you may want to do that as I talk more about doubles and the return of serve.

Strategy No. 4: If you are receiving in the ad court, assuming that your forehand is your best shot, again stand far enough to the left so that you can use your forehand more often but not so far that you get into trouble if the ball is hit down the middle.

In case you think that I have unknowingly made a mistake and am repeating myself here, you would be wrong. I have repeated myself on purpose in order to help you understand what you need to do and in case you only read just one version of the Doubles Strategy Lessons.

As I said before, these are just basic strategy rules. Doubles is a very complex game, and there are many variations to the above strategy such as poaching, signaling, playing Australian doubles, serving and going to the net, returning serve and going to the net, hitting your return down the line, playing the angles, how to defend against poachers, and when to lob, to name more than a few. However, when you master this basic strategy, your value as a doubles partner will be measurably enhanced. Then you can begin to play around with the other variations and strategies.

As I said in the last paragraph, there are variations and exceptions to every rule and you must be flexible and be able to change should the situation change. However, before you worry about changing what you do, it is important for you to master these basics.

Spend as much time as you need to on all these ideas. Even though I call these ideas Basic Strategies, they are the backbone of all doubles play. They are very powerful.

And above all, have fun doing them as this is what makes doubles so interesting.

Lesson No. 73: Breathing Patterns When You Play Doubles

Since I had you working on or at least thinking about your doubles play in the last two lessons, I thought I would add information on breathing when you play doubles. You may even want to re-read the

lesson on breathing (Lesson No. 8) even though you already should have read it a few times.

Have you found that breathing in doubles is a little trickier than in singles? I am not sure there is any really good answer in how to do it the best way, but certainly working with the rhythm of breathing in singles is a very good place to start. Here is what I do when I play doubles and I am working on my breathing.

When I am serving or returning serve, I start my breathing as I normally do which means starting my exhalation as I release the ball on my toss when serving and starting my exhalation when my opponent hits the ball on the serve. When my partner is serving I start my exhale just before my opponent, who is returning, hits the ball. That way I will be exhaling if the ball comes to me.

Then I will attempt to start my exhale every time and just before my opponent hits the ball. This helps to keep me in the here and now during the point and it helps my body know when the ball is being hit.

I do the same when my partner is returning serve. I will exhale just before my opponent serves the ball and then continue exhaling every time my opponent hits the ball so that I will be exhaling if my opponent who is at net hits the ball to me.

When I exhale just before my opponents hit the ball it helps relax my body so that many times when I need to hit a reflex volley, my body just does it. It also helps bigtime if I am able to keep my grip extremely relaxed.

Have you listened to or read the info on the second generation Bounce-Hit technique? I am going to assume that you are familiar with it. If not, you will need to refer to it to get the most of this next part. See Lesson No. 7 to review.

Personally, I will not ever play again without using this technique. It has helped me so much with my reaction volleys and, of course, with all my other shots. The only time I may not do the Bounce-Hit is when I am serving or returning serve. But I still do it then from time to time.

So, when my partner is serving, I start the Bounce-Hit when the serve bounces in the service box. When my partner is receiving, I start the Bounce-Hit when the serve is hit.

The key to making this work, as in all cases, is that I really need to see the ball to my racquet as I say hit and that I say hit with a relaxed tone. This is very hard for me to do in doubles but to the extent I can do it, I play extremely well. I have been able to hit more reaction volleys back in the court since I have been doing this than I have in my whole life. Even my regular volley has improved bigtime.

Make sure that you keep saying the Bounce-Hit until the ball makes its final bounce when the point is over. Again, for me, this is hard to do, but the rewards are great even if I can't do it very well.

Let's get back to working on just breathing on the volleys. It may be a good idea to work on just the breathing before going to the Bounce-Hit technique. Or, work on both at different times.

When volleying, I make my exhales a little shorter while still making sure the exhale starts before contact. I will work on starting the exhale when my opponent hits the ball and keep exhaling until the ball goes over the net after I hit it. I do this every time my opponent hits the ball.

If I am doing any reaction volley drills, I will just work on doing a very short exhale always starting just as my opponent makes contact with the ball.

In case you didn't notice, both breathing and seeing the ball in doubles is so much more of a challenge than in singles. And again, that is not a good reason to not practice and master it.

These ideas on how to breathe while playing doubles are not hard and fast.

Experiment with them and see what combination works best. Even when you think you have the best combination, don't be rigid. Tomorrow, some other combination may just work better. That being said, I have done a whole lot of experimenting with my breathing and found the way I have described in this lesson to be the best for me and when my students can do it, they also report that it works extremely well.

The really important thing is that you keep working on your breathing even if it is difficult.

Lesson No. 74: Playing In Front Of Crowds

It is fun to play in front of crowds, don't you think?

But what if you don't like it? What if you let the crowd affect your play? How do you deal with it?

The bottom line is that if you are bothered by crowds, then you are not focusing very well. Your focus needs to be on the ball and on your breathing. Sounds easy, doesn't? But when you are in that situation, everything changes and an audience can keep you from doing what you normally do.

Some people have a specific issue of wanting to look good in front of a crowd. Here are some ideas and things to think about.

Do you think wanting to play well for the crowd is going to actually help you play well? I don't think so, because as we have talked about, trying to do anything doesn't work very well. However, I do believe that if the crowd is on your side, the energy from them will help you focus – but you can't always depend on the crowd being on your side.

I remember one time when I was in high school, one of the players on the team was practicing with me. He had a very hard serve but almost never got it in. Then along came his girlfriend who stopped to watch for a while. The next time he served, he hit two aces in a row. He couldn't keep that up, but you can see how even a crowd of one can affect your play.

When you have the feeling that you want to play well for the crowd, family, girlfriend, spouse, team, or country, or anyone else you must keep in mind what it is that you must do in order to actually play well. And, you now know that staying focused on the ball and breathing with proper relaxation is the key.

When you let any other thoughts of wanting to play well for anyone into your thoughts, it leads to trying which leads to being too tense and judgments which in turn keeps you from focusing and playing as well as you could.

So, here is what you can do. The moment you have these thoughts, you need to say to yourself, "Cancel, Cancel," or you can yell as loud as you can to yourself silently "Stop!"and replace the thoughts with more productive ones.

And one of these thoughts, which you will say to yourself a million times is, "I am staying focused on the ball and I am focusing on the contact point for a short time. I am exhaling properly, keeping a very relaxed grip, finishing my stroke and letting my body play."

As long as we are talking about crowds, I might as well talk a little about other distractions. These ideas will help you deal with them.

Playing Zen-Sational Tennis

The first thing to do is to really focus on your breathing in between points. Almost like meditating on it. This means doing slow, deep inhales and exhales with the emphasis on relaxing when you exhale.

What this does is keep you in the here and now and helps to let go of "other thoughts" that may be distracting to you like the crowd, etc. However, it could be an airplane going overhead or cars honking, or a player in the next court grunting. All of these and more will come into your universe at some time.

The other part to dealing with any of these distractions is to do what I learned in a yoga class many years ago. At the end of the class, the instructor always had us do the corpse posture. If you have ever taken yoga, you know what this is. You just lie down on your back and completely relax every muscle in your body. It really feels good.

As we were just starting to relax, the instructor would have us listen and pay attention to any noise that we heard. Since the class was near an airport and you could always hear planes, and cars go by etc. There was always something making noise.

The instructor then said to hear this noise and understand that this noise is just part of life and to make it truly OK for it to be there because you have no control over it. Then the instructor said to just

let this noise be in the background and now to focus on letting every muscle go and relax.

It really made a difference just to make these distractions a natural part of life.

Likewise, make the crowd and what it is doing a natural part of your world and make it OK. Then, like I said earlier, just let it be there and continue to focus on your breathing in between points and, of course, seeing the ball and breathing when you are playing the point.

I hope this helps and in any case as you play in front of crowds more often, you will get used to it. However, once you get used to crowds, there will always be something else. This is why it would be a good idea to work on and practice the concepts I have just told you about.

Lesson No. 75: The Difference Between Those Who Play The Mental Game And Those Who Don't?

I talked about playing at the top of your game in Lesson No. 72. This lesson will address another related issue but with a little different slant.

Ok, you are starting to play the match and you become aware that you are not playing as well as you would like. What do you do?

What is going on in your mind is very interesting. When you begin to pay attention to it, as you are doing now that you are playing the Mental Game, you will be able to direct it to the place where it belongs so that you can begin to play better immediately.

I have been playing the Mental Game for over 25 years and still my mind tries to take control and won't let my body play without interfering. Sometimes, I still have to struggle to let go. Sometimes, even my body rebels and doesn't function very well.

However, there are two important differences between those who do not play the Mental Game and those of us who do play it.

The first difference is that you now know why you miss the ball. Most other players do not have a clue as to why they missed the ball and the only way they know how to do better is to try harder, yell at their body to hit the ball into the court or to blame something like the wind, or the other player, etc.

The second difference is that because you know why you miss, you can begin to make the changes in your mind, which in turn helps your body play better. You don't need to go practice for hours and hours before you can improve like the non-Mental Game players. Practicing for hours and hours is a good thing, but in the middle of a match it is not possible.

But what happens if you know what to do, you "try" to do them, and as a result of your trying either your mind or your body just won't cooperate? This happens to me a lot if I haven't been playing much. Here is the answer. You just keep relaxing and letting go of that part that you think is interfering.

You keep making your play less and less important and just stay with the Core Principles. At some point, the mind will give up and let your body play. And nobody knows how long this will take. I will talk about going to your "foundational place" in Lesson No. 77 so that is something that I do bigtime to help me let go.

I will repeat what I said earlier. I said that there may also be times that no matter how hard you try to let go of judgments or even try to focus as well as you have done in the past that your Conscious Mind just won't cooperate.

When that happens, one really good way to get back into the here and now is to do a meditation on deep breathing. Just pay attention to your breathing in between points and see if you can make it slow way down and make it deep.

When you are changing sides, you can also focus more on deep breathing. It should be easier while you are sitting to slow it down and just let go of all other thoughts.

While you are hitting the ball, however, just continue to work on letting go. You may find that your Conscious Mind will begin to release its grip on you.

I know what some of you are going to say: "That letting go and making it less important doesn't make sense. If I make it less important, I won't run for the ball, I won't move my feet, or hit the ball hard or I will only hit the ball down the middle."

All I can say is that if you do it properly, it works, and here is how you can tell. No matter how well you play when you start the match, if your play doesn't get better as the match progresses, then you need to change something.

And, if it is working, you must continue to do it more and better.

That doesn't mean that you will always win, but you should be improving during the match. When this does happen, no matter how slightly, you can be sure you are playing and winning the Mental Game. See, I do want you to win.

After having read all these lessons on the Mental Game, you now know in more complete detail what I am talking about. In fact, all of the lessons on the Mental Game is about letting go and how to do it.

However, the most important thing is to study, know and use the Core Principles. You are probably sick of hearing me say it, but these principles are where it is at if you really want to play the Mental Game.

Lesson No. 76: What Is EFT ?

Ever heard of EFT?

The other information that you get with this book is the Emotional Freedom Technique (EFT) that I customized for tennis. Have you downloaded the EFT Scripts and used them?

If you have not yet downloaded them, you will need to go here to download the scripts.

www.maxtennis.com/Download files/Tapping For Tennis.zip

I knew about EFT for a long time but it was being used for non-sports issues. Then I found a person who was using it for sports with a section on using it for tennis. I purchased the e-book for $40 to see what it was all about and found it lacking so I wrote my own "scripts" just for tennis. These you get free with this book.

I Paid $197 So You Wouldn't Have To.

I also ran across another person who had some EFT techniques for tennis (and some other sports) and it cost $197. I went ahead and purchased it because I figured if they were charging this much it must be really good.

It turned out this e-book encompasses a lot more than just the EFT techniques for tennis. I also felt the scripts on tennis were still missing some important parts but in general this book was pretty good. They just were not as good as my scripts. At least according to my way of thinking.

Please don't think these scripts are not valuable just because you get them for free.

The 9 EFT scripts can be used very effectively with a little study and you get them free without spending the $197.

You can also use the basic EFT for just about anything.

I want to help you play your very best and by giving you these extra tools, it will speed up your improvement. I also believe that by learning about EFT it can help you in other areas of your life.

If you want to explore EFT (or Tapping) and how to use it in other areas of your life, please go to this website for The Tapping Solution.

www.thetappingsolution.com

Here you can get DVDs etc and learn how to use this incredible tool in any area of your life. It is a very powerful tool as you will see when you look into it.

Below are a couple more places to go to get information on this tapping technique.

284

www.bradyates.net - go here for Brad Yate's website.

Go to **www.emofree.com** to learn more about tapping.

There is a bigtime baseball coach that uses this technique as the centerpiece of his coaching and I have personally seen a video of a big league professional baseball player using this technique. The announcers did not have a clue what he was doing, but I doubt that he would be doing it if he thought it wasn't helpful.

Now that you know a little bit about EFT, please start using my scripts for your tennis.

Lesson No. 77: What Is A Foundational Place Anyway?

What is a foundational place anyway, and why would you want to go there? The foundational place is a new term I started to use a while back to describe the ultimate mental environment you need to be in to play at the top of your game.

When I was playing tournaments a few summers ago, I found myself missing balls that I thought I should not miss. And, of course, when I start missing balls, it usually means that I am getting behind in the score.

As I always do, I begin to wonder what I can do to "fix" the errors I am making.

Playing Zen-Sational Tennis

Eventually, I get to what I am now calling my foundational place. When I am able to get there, my game improves, sometimes dramatically.

Here is what I say to myself to help me get there. I say, "I am going to let the ball go anywhere it wants to go. I am going to let go of any strategy that I am doing and I am not even going to try to hit the ball in the court. If all the balls go down the middle, I don't care. I am just going to see the ball spinning to the blur of my racquet, breathe very relaxed, let my grip be very relaxed, finish all my strokes and let go of any judgments."

Of course, my balls do not go down the middle, my strategy is as good or better than when I was thinking about it and I begin make fewer errors.

Being in my foundational place is an amazing place to be!

This brings me to another concept that, in the past, I have had a hard time describing. This is the concept of how you hit the ball to where you want it to go without trying so hard that you miss it. This is the concept that you read about in Lesson No. 57 about **"knowing."**

I have become a little clearer on what **"knowing"** where you want the ball to go means, and how it works. I will try to explain it to you here.

When we are hitting the ball to a particular place, our Conscious Mind is involved with deciding where we want the ball to go. Hopefully, you know by now, that you need to let your Other-Than-Conscious Mind actually execute the shot.

Playing Zen-Sational Tennis

Well, the Conscious Mind has a lot of trouble not getting involved so it then tries to control the body. Maybe you have experienced this and when the Conscious Mind tries to do the controlling, it does not work very well, especially on important points.

The better way is what happens when you get to your foundational place. The analogy is like when you lose your car keys. Because you have to go somewhere in your car and can't find her keys, you use your extra set of keys and then let go of thinking about where your other keys are for the time being. Then, when you are not thinking about it, your mind tells you, "Your keys are on your desk."

The concept is that the thought of where to hit the ball comes **TO your Conscious Mind** rather than **FROM your Conscious Mind.**

This way, it is so much easier to let your body hit the ball to where your Other-Than-Conscious Mind directs it to go, and many times the choice of where to hit the ball is better than if you were consciously trying to think about it.

I hope this is making some sense to you. In any case, the next time you play, see if you can get to your foundational place and let the thoughts of where to hit the ball come to you.

It takes a lot of letting go so that your body and Other-Than-Conscious Mind can, in fact, play better than with your Conscious Mind in control. When you get there, you will see a big difference in your play. Guaranteed.

Lesson No. 78: Why Losing Is Good

When I'm working with a new student, their reaction to a loss is often comments like "I played terrible," or "I should have won." Have you ever heard yourself say either of these two statements or something similar?

My first response to "I played terrible" is to ask, "What did you do when you were on the court to turn your play around?" Did you re-program or visualize your shots going in?

In my opinion, this is the difference between playing the Mental Game the way I see it and playing tennis the traditional way. 95% (or maybe more) of the players do not have a clue as to why they miss balls or how to fix their shots on the spot. No wonder these players get angry or frustrated.

So, let's say that you did play terrible. You need to ask yourself, "What part of my game was not working?" Usually, it was only one shot that was off that day or they played one "bad" game and the person translated that into "everything was terrible."

Once you have isolated where your game went wrong, I then ask, "Were you aware of this while you were playing?" and then, "What should you have done about it?" And finally, I will ask, "What can you do about it now that the match is over?"

I am hoping that you can see what I am doing with my questions. I am helping to isolate the problem so that you can do something about it the next time you are playing as well as go out and practice the shot or shots that were weak or not working very well. But to just say, "I played terrible" is not helpful.

Sometimes my students will say, "I should have won," I ask them why. They may say that, "I was ahead and lost (choked)," or "I am a better player" or "they got lucky," or "they were just a dinker," or "I just didn't play well" or any number of things about the match. I tell them, "No, you should not have won because, for whatever reason, your opponent played better than you did and you need to figure out how you lost the points and how you can do better the next time."

If you have ever said these things, once you figure out how you were losing the points, you can then go and practice these shots.

Also, once you understand that your opponent was actually better than you were, I tell them, "If you don't like the fact that your opponent was better than you, then you need to hit 50 million more balls so that you improve." Of course, I believe that while you are hitting these 50 million balls, you will improve that much faster if you focus on the Core Principles of the Mental Game.

The whole point of losing is that you get to find out where your weaknesses are. If you played a 2-year-old, you could just about do anything and you would win.

When you lose, it should be an incentive for you to go out and hit those 50 million more balls so that the next time you will play better.

Most of the time when I play tournaments, I put myself into a situation where I will not win. For example, I don't play in my age division (except when I play in National tournaments) because I need to be pushed and I need to find out where my weaknesses are so that I can improve and fix them. And, just for the record, as soon as you think that you have fixed your weakness, another one is presented to you the next time you lose.

So really take the time to find out why you lost and then go and practice using the Mental Game Principles. You will find that your game will continue to improve and maybe you won't have to actually hit 50 million more balls.

Lesson No. 79: What To Do When You Have A Question And Don't Know The Answer

Have you ever lost something and then after you gave up looking for it, the answer just came to you as to where it was. What about when you forgot someone's name and later in the day when you were doing something else, the name came into your mind? This same power of the mind is what we tap into when we use the "Wondering Technique."

This is one of the terrific concepts I learned from Dave Dobson who was an absolute master of Neural Linguistic Programming commonly known as NLP. Here is one of many many ways you can use this technique.

If you are behind in the score and you can't figure out what strategy change you need, you would say to your Other-Than-Conscious Mind, "I wonder how I can change my strategy so that I will be more effective." Or you could say, "I wonder what I could do to play better." Then you just relax and let the answer come to you.

Here is the reasoning behind this technique. Back in the old days when we were on the phone and someone tried to call us, they got a busy signal because we didn't have "call waiting" then. There was no way that the person calling you could get through, and you didn't even know that someone was trying to call you.

Trying hard to think about what different strategy to use is like being on the phone, and when the answer does come, your answer will get a busy signal and not get through because your mind is too active. So just relax your Conscious Mind and let the answer come to you.

With practice, this can be a very powerful tool. And you don't have to limit it to tennis. You can use this technique for any issue in your life that you need answers for.

Lesson No. 80: Where To Hit Your Lob And How To Practice It

Where To Hit Your Lob

Always hit your lob cross-court. This will give you the longest distance to hit, thereby giving you a greater margin of error. If you think back to when you have had to hit an overhead that has been hit cross-court, you will know how much harder it is for you to hit.

Yes, your opponent has more time to get to your lob because your lob has longer to travel, but they will have to run that much farther. Obviously, this idea as to where you hit your lob applies to singles only. In doubles, lobbing over the net player is usually the place to lob.

How To Practice Your Lob

Most of the time when you are warming up your opponent's overhead, you just try to feed the lob to him/her, so they can hit an easy overhead.

When you are warming up with a partner who not only is a friend but is also into practicing a little, do the following drill when you are warming up his/her overhead.

Hit the first ball to make your opponent hit a volley, then hit a lob on the return of that shot. When you hit your lob, do not try to just feed it to him/her. Go for the perfect lob cross-court. If your opponent hits an overhead back to you, hit your opponent another volley (not a lob), and then hit another lob if he/she returns your shot.

Here is my reasoning. This way you can practice your lob every time you warm up, assuming you are playing with someone you know who wants to warm up this way.

By only hitting a lob from a volley, you will be practicing hitting a lob like you would in a match.

When you hit your lob make sure you see the ball spinning all the way to your racquet and with a relaxed grip. This is a common focus error when lobbing.

When your opponent is hitting their overhead, he/she should hit all their overheads for winners. This way you can warm up practicing what you would do in an actual match.

One last thought. You and your opponent may want to hit a few easy overheads in the beginning to warm up your arms. So just feed a few easy lobs and then do this overhead and lob drill.

And remember from Lesson No. 65 about why you want to hit your overhead as hard as you can.

Lesson No. 81: If You Get A Short Ball

There are some inherent problems with short balls. Do you know what they are? Are you aware of what you do when you get a short ball? Do you ever hit a drop shot or do you only go for the approach shot?

Here is one of the problems with short balls. I am not talking about short high balls. I am talking about short low balls. Short high balls should be hit hard.

Because the ball is low and because the ball is short, the distance to the back line is shorter. Therefore you must hit the ball easier than normal, otherwise the ball will go out. Because you are hitting the ball easier, your opponent will have more time to get to the ball thereby making a passing shot more likely.

Playing Zen-Sational Tennis

When you do get a short ball, I recommend that you hit a drop shot and then move close to the net to cut off any angle. Even if your drop shot is not really good, there are still a lot of advantages.

In order for your opponent to hit his or her ball into the court, he or she must hit the ball easier because again, the distance to the baseline is shorter, and he or she must hit up on the ball in order to get it over the net. This will give you more time to react and hit a winner, but many times your opponent will just miss the ball or not even get to it.

If your opponent tries to lob, the same principle applies. Because the distance is shorter to the base line, your opponent must hit the lob more up and down and with good touch. If he or she doesn't miss the ball long, you will have more time to run it down because the ball has to go at a much more vertical angle while you are running straight back.

After your opponent has figured out that you will drop shot on a short ball, he or she will start moving in toward the net. This is the time to hit your normal approach shot.

Because your opponent is moving toward the net to get your drop shot, your normal approach shot will be that much more effective. Then keep mixing them up and your opponent will never know what you are going to do.

One point on your focus:

If you are like me when I hit a drop shot, I have a tendency to not stay focused on the ball after I hit it. My focus gets sidetracked by my thinking whether he or she will get to the ball in time or I will be thinking about where the ball will be hit. As a result, so many times I don't move well for the ball.

When I just watch the ball and not my opponent running for the ball, I win that many more points – unless, of course, my opponent hits a really great shot.

Lesson No. 82: Three Special Additions To The Core Principles

As you should know by now from doing the Core Principles, the most important things to do are the seeing of the ball, breathing, and relaxing properly (especially the grip). Of course, the others are important, but these are the driving force for all the rest.

If you have spent any time reading this book, listening to my CDs, or taking lessons, you would have heard me say that playing the Mental Game is a process and that you will be discovering things about yourself and your game until you retire from playing.

The same is true for me. I am always discovering things that help me play better which I then pass on to you. Here are three of them. Two are just a variation of the relaxation part and the other is an alternative to the breathing part.

In another of my Lessons (Lesson No. 21), I talk about the importance of finishing the follow-through **NO MATTER WHAT**.

This is really a relaxation issue because if your arm is relaxed the way it should be, guess what, you will finish the follow-through. The important thing is that we may not be aware of the fact that on certain shots, the follow-through doesn't finish completely because there is too much tension.

I've found that when I focus on letting the stroke finish completely, **NO MATTER WHAT**, my shots are harder, more accurate and more consistent. Because of this I have added it to my set of Core Principles.

The second addition to my Core Principles is the relaxation of the grip and the wrist. I talk about this in detail in Lesson No. 13.

The last addition to the Core Principles concerns the breathing. Since I have begun working on saying Bounce-Hit when I play (and I will not ever play again without doing this some of the time), I can't also do the breathing the way I talk about in the lesson on breathing and in the Core Principles.

But, here is what I have found. The Conscious Mind just doesn't want to let go of control. I will then spend some time doing the relaxed breathing and sometimes doing the Bounce-Hit . Even within the same match. By doing both from time to time, you will be encouraging the ego mind to let go and this process will be a lot faster if you do both the breathing thing and the Bounce-Hit thing at different times, of course.

Please play with these new ideas and see how you can use them effectively and add them to your list of Core Principles. They work. I know because I use them and my students use them.

Lesson No. 83: The Final Bounce

I am wondering how many of you are really working on doing the second generation Bounce-Hit method. (See Lesson No. 7)

Are you working on it when you actually play sets or matches? I hope you are because I believe that it is one of the best methods there is. Tim Gallwey really hit the jackpot on this exercise.

I now tell people that I will never again play without doing this second generation Bounce-Hit method. It has done more for my game than any other method. Playing the short game the way I describe to you in Lessons No. 11 and 12 comes a close 2nd. There are several reasons why this works so well and why you need to do it also.

The most obvious reason is that when you are saying Bounce-Hit, your Conscious Mind is so occupied that it can't take control of your body, at least, not very easily. So when you do this, you are experiencing what truly letting your body play means.

Another benefit you will get from doing this method is you will be shown exactly where your focus goes off. For example, if you find that you lose saying bounce when you think your ball is going long,

then you know that you are judging your ball or worrying that your ball is going out. This is one issue I am still dealing with.

Another area where I also lose my focus is if a ball comes very deep or very fast to me. It would be very hard for me to know this if I wasn't saying the Bounce-Hit. Now that I am aware of these areas I can begin to deal with them.

Playing Zen-Sational Tennis

One other big area that I tend to lose my focus is on the "final" bounce. This means that I have difficulty saying "bounce" when the ball hits the ground if I hit my ball out or hit a winner.

My intention is to also say "bounce" as the ball hits the ground after it goes into the net. For some reason, my focus goes haywire at the end of the point. When I can do it, though, my game really improves because then I have truly let go of my judgments.

Another area that I believe people may have difficulties on is the serve and return of serve. At least I do. These are very important times to stay focused because of the fact that the ball is usually going faster than normal and sometimes much faster. On these shots also check to see if you are still saying hit softly and not tensely.

Playing doubles is another possible area of difficulty. Because the points are short and sometimes fast, you may have difficulty keeping your focus on saying Bounce-Hit.

It may be difficult because you must say hit even when your partner is hitting the ball. Your Conscious Mind may just have a harder time letting go of control. And when you can do it, you know that you are letting go properly.

Maybe this is because doubles is such a more complex game that your mind says that it can't play doubles well unless it (your Conscious Mind) directs the play.

For me, some part knows that this is not true because when I can stay with the Bounce-Hit all the way up to the final bounce, my doubles as well as my singles play improves a lot.

Ok. How do you work on this difficulty of letting go? What you want to do is to say to yourself that you are not going to worry about even hitting the ball. You are just going to say Bounce-Hit.

Pretend as if you were standing on the sideline watching the play. If you were doing this, you would have no problem saying Bounce-Hit. The idea is to imagine what that would be like and just trick your mind into that same mindset. When you do this, you will feel so much calmer and in control and, of course, you will be playing better.

Please use this method of playing often if you aren't already. Be aware of where you miss saying either the bounce or hit and then work on those areas. Also, be aware of whether you can say the final bounce. You won't regret it.

Lesson No. 84: Relaxing Between Hits

Ok, in this book and on my CD's I talk a lot about relaxing when you hit the ball.

There is another place that you will need to check to see if you are relaxed. If you haven't guessed from the title, you need to relax between hits as well.

If you are anything like me, you just might be too tense even after you hit. I know I am. I can tell when I get really tired after a long point where I really haven't run that much. That is my sign that maybe I need to do a little relaxing after each time I hit the ball.

To do this sounds simple, but it may be hard to do because you are in the heat of the battle. Anyway, just after you hit the ball and you are getting ready for the next hit, let your grip open up on your racquet so that it almost falls out of your hand. Of course, you don't want to drop your racquet but it should feel very loose.

This can be fairly easy to do when you are in a rally from the backcourt, but what if you are at net or you are playing doubles and the ball is going back and forth when all of you are at net? Then it can be pretty challenging.

So in order to do this you have to practice it when you are not playing a match. Go to the net and hit some volleys and consciously relax your grip after every volley.

It shouldn't take too much time to start relaxing after you hit the ball, whether you are at net or in the backcourt hitting ground strokes. And pretty soon, it will be happening automatically.

Like all the rest of the concepts, this is an easy one to understand. Please spend some time working with your awareness after you hit to see if you are tensing up too much.

Then deal with it even when you play a match. I know that you will find it helpful.

Lesson No. 85: Help! My Conscious Mind Won't Stop Interfering

If your Conscious Mind works anything like mine, it is always trying to find a way to interfere with my play and control my body.

Just when I think that I am seeing the ball really well or when I am really using the Bounce-Hit method well, I find myself sometimes missing balls that I think I should be able to hit.

When this happens, I go through my checklist of places where my focus might be going off. Eventually I do find where my focus got sidetracked. And, invariably, I find that I thought I was focusing correctly but really wasn't.

My Conscious Mind had found a way to "trick" me into thinking that I was letting go and focusing properly.

Here is what I've found that I need to do about this. As long as I am playing really well, obviously, I don't need to do anything. But the moment I begin to miss balls that I was making before, I just change my focus to another pattern. I will even change this pattern during a match.

Here are the combinations I have found work for me and hopefully you can make them work for you:

Combination No. 1: Focus on **consciously** seeing the ball to the blur of the racquet while exhaling with a sigh. This is the main way of focusing that I've talked about for years.

301

Combination No. 2: Focus on saying "Hit-Bounce" while **consciously** seeing the ball and making sure that you are saying "Hit" with a soft sound. Saying the Hit-Bounce with a relaxed sound takes the place of exhaling with a sigh.

Combination No. 3: Focus on **consciously** seeing the ball to the blur of the racquet while exhaling with a sigh while feeling and relaxing the follow-through so that it makes a complete finish every time, **NO MATTER WHAT!**

Combination No. 4: Focus on **consciously** seeing the ball spinning after the bounce, keeping your focus on the contact point for a short time (like Federer does).

Combination No. 5: Focus on saying Hit-Bounce while **consciously** seeing the ball and making sure that you are saying "Hit" with a soft sound while you are feeling and relaxing the follow-through so that it makes a complete finish, **NO MATTER WHAT!**

Combination No. 6: Focus on your breathing while feeling and relaxing the follow-through so that it makes a complete finish, **NO MATTER WHAT!**

Combination No. 7: Focus on your breathing while feeling and relaxing the grip bigtime, **NO MATTER WHAT!**

Combination No. 8: Focus on any combination of seeing the ball, breathing, feeling and relaxing the follow-through, or saying Hit-Bounce that you feel helps you.

By continuing to mix up these combinations, you will be keeping your Conscious Mind from interfering so much because as soon as the Conscious Mind starts interfering, you change your focus, which then derails the Conscious Mind. At least for a little while.

There are some other benefits from doing this other than just playing better. I'm finding that by going back and forth with my focus, each time I go to another combination I am able to focus on that combination that much better. My mind is calmer and I see things and feel things that much easier.

You can also work with the EFT Scripts that I gave you in Lesson No. 76.

I'm just hoping that someday, my Conscious Mind will get tired trying to control my body and just give up.

My biggest wish is that you don't have this same issue. But if you do, I know this mixing up of where you place your focus will help.

Lesson No. 86: When You Serve A Let Ball On Your First Serve

One day when I was playing and I served a let on my first serve, I got to thinking about where I would hit my next serve. I asked myself, "What would my opponent be thinking about as to where I might hit the next serve

This conversation with myself came to the conclusion that I would most often be thinking about the serve coming to the same side, so I made a rule that I would serve to the other side if I served a let on my first serve.

When I do this, I discovered that many times my opponent would miss the return. This doesn't work every time, but it has worked enough for me to use it.

When I am watching Roger Federer play, I always look to see what he does and although I have not charted it, it is my belief that he does this more times than not. Anyway, try it out for yourself and see if it works. It is as good a strategy as any.

Of course, if your opponents know that you have read my book, he or she will know where you will hit your next serve should you have hit a let on your last ball. And, of course, if you ever play against me, you will know where I will be hitting.

Lesson No. 87: Watch Out For Your Ego Mind

From the lessons you now have read and put into practice, I am hoping you have experienced how powerful seeing the ball correctly is, how breathing helps, and how it helps when relaxing the muscles that you don't need while using the proper tension of the muscles.

Have you noticed that maybe you are not making doing these Core Principles as important anymore? Or have you forgotten to work on these concepts altogether?

This seems to be a natural progression for most of us because the "ego mind" does not want to be so far out of the picture. It will constantly sneak in and tell you that it knows better than you do about how to play well.

If you have used these three concepts in your play and saw the immediate improvement, then you know this thought is not true.

My point is that if you found that you played better when you used these concepts, then using them more and more and getting better and better at letting your body learn and figuring out how to hit the ball the way you want to are the issues you need to address.

So, how do you deal with this Ego Mind? First of all, you need to just not believe the Ego Mind when it says that it needs to control your body in order to hit the ball into the court or that this stuff doesn't work.

Then you need some strategies that will help you keep letting go and letting your body play and learn.

One of these strategies is that you just keep on focusing on the five concepts given to you no matter what your Ego Mind says. In case you don't remember what these five things are, here they are again.

- Seeing The Ball
- Breathing
- Having A Very Loose Grip
- Making A Relaxed And Full Finish
- Reprogram All Missed Shots (if you don't remember how to reprogram, look up the lessons in my book)

However, I find that most people who have taken lessons need some additional help, and this is why I created my books, course and CDs. If you get my course, you get a reminder every week or when you read another lesson each week you get to think about and work on some aspect of your Mental Game. Doing this you will be overriding the Ego Mind. Maybe just buying my book or CDs is enough for you to keep working on these ideas and keeping your ego mind at bay.

Either way should help you stay focused on the things that allow you to play well every time.

And please, always keep in mind that this way of playing is a process and you will not one day "just do it" perfectly. You will be constantly learning more and more about yourself and how you can play better and better no matter your age. At the time of writing this, I am 67 years old and I am still learning things, and although I can't move as well, I am still getting better in a lot of areas.

So, please keep reading these lessons over and over so you can make sure you stay on the road to playing what I believe to be the only way to play. A way that is fun and exciting because you will always be improving, and of course, you will be winning more matches, more close matches – and feeling good about it all.

Just don't let your Ego Mind tell you otherwise.

Lesson No. 88: Books And Articles To Read

Do you ever read other articles or books on tennis? In my opinion, you will learn an unbelievable amount about all aspects of the game if you read Ron Waite's articles and David Smith's Books.

While Ron has written so many terrific articles and an e-book, David has written two terrific books. **If you read just these two people's books and articles, you won't have to read any others.** They are always so right on the money.

About Ron Waite

Ron Waite is a certified USPTA tennis instructor who took up the game of tennis at the age of 39. Frustrated with conventional tennis methods of instruction and the confusing data available on how to learn the game, Ron has sought to sift fact from fiction.

In his many years of tennis, Ron has received USTA sectional ranking for four years, has successfully coached several NCAA Division III men's and women's tennis teams to post season competition, and has competed in USTA National singles tournaments. Ron has trained at a number of tennis academies and with many of the game's leading instructors.

In addition to his full-time work as a professor at Albertus Magnus College, Ron photographs ATP tour events for a variety of organizations and publications. The name of his column, TurboTennis, stems from his methods to decrease the amount of time it takes to learn and master the game of tennis.

Ron has written some terrific articles on just about all aspects of tennis. If you are really serious about your Mental Game, as well as learning about a wide variety of subjects, go here on my web page **www.maxtennis.com/articles.php**, and you can find the links to all his articles. I have not read any articles by anyone that are better.

About David Smith

David Smith has written two very impressive books. His first book is called *Tennis Mastery, Advance Beyond the 3.5 Level.* It is probably the most complete guide to learning, developing and mastering the sport of tennis out there.

His second book is called *Coaching Mastery, The Ultimate Blueprint for Tennis Coaches, Tennis Parents, and Tennis Teaching Professionals.* If you are a coach, you will learn how to attract players to your programs, develop sustainable programs, and build championship teams. If you are a parent, you also will find this book indispensable.

Even if you are not a coach, this book will give you a great deal of terrific info on the game and how to play it. Who is David Smith? Go to his websites **www.coaching-mastery.com** and **www.tnt-tennis.com** to find out or order his books.

To make it easy for you, I have both links to Ron and David's website if you go to this page on my website. **www.maxtennis.com/articles.php.**

So, please do your homework. Be sure to read my book all the way through again and again and read all of Ron's articles as well as David's books that I have listed on my website.

I will be giving you a surprise test next week on the information in these articles and books and if you don't pass, you will have to go hit 10,000 backhands down the line until they all go in. ☺

Lesson No. 89: A Before and After Match Analysis

I developed these questions for you so that there would be no doubt in your mind as what you should be thinking and doing before and after you play a match. I don't believe that you will find a more complete questionnaire anywhere that will not only keep you on track when you play matches, but will help you determine where you need the most work.

Playing Zen-Sational Tennis

This information is extremely valuable to you so please print out these questions and do a de-briefing after every match. And, be sure to read the first part before each match so that you have the best chance to be in the "right" state of mind for your match.

Before The Match

Did you read the Core Principles 10-15 minutes before you played? _____

Did you read the Summary of What to Do When You Play Points, Games, or a Match (Lesson No. 17) before you played? _____

Did you do any mind calming or meditation before you played? _____

Did you pre-program any strategies before the match? _____

Did you warm up before the match using the ideas found in Lesson No. 60 of my book? _____

On Seeing the Ball During the Match

Did you **consciously** see at least one ball spinning, before the ball bounced as it came to you and then saw the ball spinning with topspin after the bounce? _____

Did you **consciously** see at least one ball spinning after you hit it as it went over to the other side? _____

Playing Zen-Sational Tennis

Did you **consciously** see at least one ball make contact with your opponent's racquet? _____

Did you **consciously** see at least one ball all the way to your racquet and consciously see the blur of the racquet as you made contact with the ball? _____

If you saw at least one ball, did you make seeing the ball over and over again a priority? _____.

What % of the time were you able to see the ball the way you know it should be seen? _____

Did you reprogram seeing the ball after you missed a shot?

_____

When you miss a shot, you need to find out if there were any patterns as to why you missed. Do you think that maybe you were missing shots because you didn't see the ball properly? _____

When you hit a volley, were you able to **consciously** see at least one ball spinning to the blur of your racquet? _____

Did you work on focusing on a ball even in between points?

_____

On a scale of 1 to 10, how important is **consciously** seeing the ball to you? _____

If seeing the ball is important to you, what is keeping you from making it more important and focusing on doing it more?

_____

If you just forgot to work on seeing the ball when you played and especially when you missed a shot, what strategies can you use to help you remember the next time you play a match?

_____

If you really desired to see the ball well, and it was your intention to see the ball well, but just couldn't do it during the point, what is going on with you mentally that keeps you from doing it the way you want?

_____

On Breathing During the Match

Were you able to exhale before you hit the ball and then allow it to continue until the ball bounced on the other side at least once?

_____

If you were able to breathe on more than one ball, what % of the time were you able to exhale properly? _____

When you miss a shot, you need to find out if there were any patterns as to why you missed. Do you think that maybe you were missing shots because you didn't breathe properly or that you held your breath? _____

If you were playing singles, were you able to exhale properly on at least one volley? _____

If you were playing doubles, were you able to start your exhale when your opponent hit the ball and continue your exhale as you hit it or as it went to your partner for at least one point? _____

Did you work on being aware of your inhales and exhales even in between points? _____

On a scale of 1 to 10, how important is breathing to you? _____

If breathing is important to you, what is keeping you from making it more important and focusing on doing it more?

_____

If you just forgot to work on your breathing when you played and especially when you missed a shot, what strategies can you use to help you remember the next time you play a match?

_____

If you really desired to breathe properly, and it was your intention to breathe properly but just couldn't do it during the point, what is going on with you mentally that keeps you from doing it the way you want?

_____

On Relaxing The Grip And Wrist During The Match

Do you think that you were able to **consciously** feel, during your play, the five fingers around your racquet or your 10 fingers if you hit a two-handed backhand? _____

Did you ever take a practice swing just keeping your grip and wrist extremely relaxed? _____

On the return of serve, were you able to keep a very relaxed grip as you made contact with the ball? _____

When you are serving, were you able to keep your grip and wrist very loose when you made contact with the ball? _____

When you hit your volleys, were you able to keep a very relaxed grip as you made contact with the ball? _____

If you found that your grip and wrist was very tight and you were having difficulty relaxing it, did you not only take practice swings feeling the grip of wrist but did you make it really important? _____

On Reprogramming Your Shots

Did you take at least one practice swing after you missed a shot? _____

If you did take a practice swing, did you reprogram seeing the ball go where you wanted it to as well as take a very relaxed swing with a relaxed grip? _____

Are you absolutely certain you know how to re-program a ball that goes long, wide, or into the net? _____ (See Lesson No. 51)

If you were missing a lot of first serves, did you spend more time before you started serving to visualize as you learned in Lessons No. 59 & 60? _____

On a scale of 1 to 10, how important to you is reprogramming your shots when you miss? _____

If reprogramming your shots works and is important to you, what is keeping you from making it more important and focusing on doing it more? _____

If you just forgot to reprogram your shots and/or your serve when you missed, what strategies can you use to help you remember to reprogram and visualize the next time you play a match? _____

Other Things To Consider

If you ever found yourself thinking about winning or losing or any other unproductive thoughts, did you use the "Cancel, Cancel" or the "STOP" technique to stop these thoughts in their tracks? _____ (See Lesson No. 38)

If you found yourself missing shots, did you go back to your Foundational Place? (See Lesson No. 77) _____

If or when the match got close or if you were playing in a tiebreaker, did you do the things I suggested in Lessons No. 31, No. 34, & No. 44? _____

Did you spend any time focusing on seeing a ball and paying attention to your inhales and exhales AT ALL TIMES, even in between points? _____ (This is what leads you to the playing in the Zone)

Did you sit down when you changed sides and take a very relaxing exhale to calm and clear your mind and body and then re-focused on doing the Core Principles? _____

315

Did you let your opponent's attitude or behavior get to you? _____ (Remember, you are only playing the ball, not your opponent)

Did you let any other distractions get to you? _____ (See Lesson No. 74)

About Strategy

Did you know how you were losing points? _____

Was it because your opponent was more consistent? _____

Was it because your opponent was hitting winners or hitting balls that forced you into an error? _____

When they hit winners, were they hitting forehand winners mostly or a combination of backhand and forehand winners? _____

If you were behind in the score or struggling, did you think to hit the first three balls in a row to the backhand (assuming that was the weak side)? _____ (You would do this even if it was the wrong strategy and would start the three balls to the backhand after you hit your serve or after you hit your return of serve.)

If you were behind in the score, did you use the Wondering Technique found in Lesson No. 79? _____

If you were playing singles, did you come to the net on the appropriate ball? _____ Did it work? _____

Did you hit easy balls hard, medium balls medium and hard balls more defensively? _____

If you were playing doubles, were you aware of how you were losing points? _____

If you were playing doubles, were you moving up and back properly when at net? _____

If you were playing doubles, were you returning serve cross-court enough so that your opponent at net couldn't hit your return? _____

If you were playing doubles, did your opponent who was at net hit too many shots? _____ (This means that you were hitting too many balls to the net person at the wrong time)

If you were playing doubles, did you try signaling and/or playing Australian? _____

If you were playing doubles, did you try changing strategies? This, of course, assumes that what you are doing wasn't working question. _____

Lesson No. 90: Five Things You Absolutely Have To Work On When You Drill

1.   Seeing The Ball

2. Breathing
3. Having A Very Loose Grip
4. Making A Relaxed And Full Finish
5. Reprogram All Missed Shots (if you don't remember how to reprogram, look up the lessons in my book)

The best way to do all of this is in the short game. You start out by doing one at a time then work on combining.

After the short game, do the same when you are hitting from the backcourt.

If you're just rallying, hit all balls to the backhand.

If you're having difficulty doing one of the things you can choose to work on it only for the entire practice session. You can also always choose to work on two things for an entire practice session or any combination of the above for an entire practice session.

However, the main issue is that you must work on all of these things, as doing these things easily is what is going to help you learn the fastest – and play your best.

Here is some additional information for when you drill.

I am going to use as my example the basic forehand cross-court drill. It doesn't really matter which drill you are doing, but this is the general process to use as you do any drill.

Always start out with the basic concepts which, as you know, is seeing the ball, keeping your focus on the contact point for a short time, allowing your breathing to be exhaling properly, keeping a relaxed grip, and making a full follow-through. Then, as you are hitting fore hand cross-courts, begin to notice what is going on with your ball. For example, if you see that your ball is going long, start paying attention to your grip and wrist so that you can relax it a little more (maybe a lot more). You can do this while you are still seeing the ball and/or breathing. For a reminder on how to deal with missed balls, please read again to Lesson No. 51.

How long you will pay attention to your grip and wrist will depend on how soon you are able to stop hitting your balls long. As you continue hitting cross-court, maybe you see that the pattern of your balls is going too much down the middle. You will stop for a few seconds and re-visualize the path of the ball, then begin to work on letting your body hit the ball to your target.

If you see a pattern of your balls going into the net, then you will spend some time working with relaxing your backswing.

If your whole stroke feels out of sorts, you will want to do the Mother of all Tips I talked about in Lesson No. 20 for a few minutes.

So, you will change what you practice on depending on what is happening.

Each day you practice, there will be something different. It won't always be that you are hitting your balls into the net, so you will have to change what you work on, as it may be different from your last practice session. All the while you still work on seeing the ball, keeping your focus on the contact point for a short time, keeping the grip relaxed, breathing, and making a full follow-through.

Then there are the times when you will work on the things on your checklist. If you see that you are missing a lot of balls, you may want to re-program the ball going into the court, but because you are practicing some other physical issue that is on your checklist this is the time where you don't really want to make it too important if you are missing a lot of balls.

For example, if you are working on your split step, it doesn't matter where your ball goes. You are playing a different game. You will still work on your seeing the ball and breathing, etc. but even this doesn't matter. What you are doing is making the item on your checklist the important thing.

You will do this process while doing all the drills I will give at the end of this book. All these drills will help you develop your physical game, but more importantly they will help you discover what state of focus and relaxation your body needs to be in for you to play at the top of your game. Another important part of each drill is what I call "mind awareness." When you continuously ask yourself questions it will be the key to improving this mind awareness.

If you find that you are not getting better as you drill, then you are not doing the Mental Game correctly. Most likely, you are trying too hard and therefore are too tight in some part of your body. So, just do the opposite of what you have been taught in the past. Try less, relax some part of your body more (especially your grip), let go of judging your shots, and stop thinking about the drill. Really work on getting your Conscious Mind out of the way and letting your Other-Than-Conscious Mind direct your body. In other words, revisit the Core Principles.

Lesson No. 91: This Lesson Is The Last One That You Will Get

Please congratulate yourself for all your hard work and persistence in getting all the way to the end of this book. You get an A+++.

Since this whole Mental Game is a process and since you will have progressed a great deal if you have chosen to work on your game from this mental perspective, you may want to start the lessons all over again. If you do, I believe that you will progress on the mental path as much or more than the first time around.

So, start today, go back to Lesson No. 1 and work through all the lessons again. Trust me, you will find a lot of techniques, concepts, ideas that you missed the first, second, or even the third time around. And, at the very least, you will get a deeper understanding to playing this great game of tennis.

Mental Game Core Principles Drills

The next 4 drills are the absolutely critical drills to help you play the Mental Game the way it needs to be played. These 4 drills will help you learn what it really means to see the ball, breathe and relax. These drills are where you can begin to be aware of what kind of balls you are having difficulty with staying focused on.

You may want to print out these drills and/or take this book with you when you play.

Until you can really do these drills really well, you need to spend some serious time with them. Please don't forget using the short game to drill. By using the short game it can speed up your improvement immensely.

Drill No. 1: Seeing The Ball

Spend five minutes or any period of time you want just seeing the ball. Seeing the ball means focusing on the ball and being able to tell yourself at all times what direction the ball is spinning. Seeing the ball means **consciously** seeing what direction the ball is spinning as the ball comes over the net, after the ball bounces, all the way to the blur of your racquet, keeping your focus on the contact point for a short time and as your ball bounces to your opponent's racquet. It also means **consciously** seeing the ball spinning when you miss the shot long, wide, or into the net. You may want to read Lesson No. 7 on seeing the ball again.

In order to see the ball completely, keep thoughts about your stroke or hitting the ball into the court out of your head. Just focus on seeing the ball spinning. In addition, make seeing the ball easy. Relax your eyes. Just think about when you read. You don't try hard to see the words, you just do.

As you do this drill, pay attention to the different balls that you are hitting. Are there any balls that "make" you lose your focus? These will be the balls you really need to work on as you get beyond seeing

322

a normal ball. For example, you might have difficulty seeing a really deep ball to the blur of your racquet, or maybe you have trouble seeing the ball when you hit the ball out.

Anyway, once you get good at seeing the ball, you will constantly need to refine it. If you are anything like me, there will be times when you think you are seeing the ball, but you just really aren't.

Here are some more questions to ask yourself after a point or rally is over so that you can make sure you are seeing the ball correctly:

- Am I seeing the ball spinning all the way to my racquet?
- Am I seeing the blur of the racquet as the ball hits the strings, in other words, am I seeing the ball to the presence of the racquet?
- Am I seeing the ball spinning after the bounce?

- Am I keeping my eyes on the contact point after I see the ball to the blur?
- Am I seeing the ball spinning after it crosses the net and to the other side of the court?
- Am I seeing the ball spinning, even when I hit the ball long, wide, or into the net?

Any "no" answer means that you have some more practicing and letting go to do.

Here are a few more questions.

- Am I worrying about hitting the ball into the court?
- Am I trying to hit the ball into the court?
- Am I worrying about stroking the ball correctly?

- Am I trying to stroke the ball correctly?
- Am I trying to direct the ball to a certain spot on the court?

Any "yes" answer means that you have some more practicing and letting go to do.

Let's move on to a drill to practice your breathing.

Drill No. 2: Paying Attention To Your Breathing

In this drill, you will be working primarily on your breathing. Many of my students tell me that the breathing part is the hardest. Please don't let this keep you from working on it. Even if you are not able to do it very well, it will still have huge benefits and will lead you to the next level.

You may want to read Lesson No. 8 again on the breathing.

Here is how you can practice it.

Spend five minutes or any period of time you want paying attention to your breathing.

The ideal breathing pattern is to allow your breathing to be very relaxed, to use a long exhale with a sigh before you make contact with the ball and to continue exhaling through the hit. Use the ball bouncing on your side as a place to start your exhale. That way you will be certain you are starting your exhale before you strike the ball.

Playing Zen-Sational Tennis

Paying attention to your breathing means **consciously** feeling your breathing, even after the point or rally is over. The idea is to be able to do this over an extended period of time.

To do this exercise properly, you will have to keep thoughts about your stroke or about hitting the ball into the court out of your head. Focus only on your breathing.

You also need to know that you may or may not hit the ball very well, and you need to let go of this. This exercise is not designed to maximize hitting the ball into the court. It is an exercise of relaxing and letting go. However, you just may find yourself hitting better. My point is that you are not to worry or even pay attention to this aspect.

Here are some questions to ask yourself after a point or rally is over:

- Am I **consciously** feeling myself exhaling?
- Is my breathing very relaxed?
- Am I starting sighing when the ball bounces and continuing it until my ball bounces on the other side?
- Am I **consciously** and continuously aware of my breathing even in between points and into the next point or rally?
- Am I able to stay focused on my breathing, even when I hit the ball long, wide, or into the net?

Any "no" answer means that you have some more practicing and letting go to do.

Here are some more questions for you to ask yourself.

- Am I worrying about hitting the ball into the court?
- Am I worrying about stroking the ball correctly?
- Am I trying to direct the ball to a certain spot on the court?

A "yes" answer means that you have some more practicing and letting go to do.

Drill No. 3: Combining Seeing The Ball And Breathing

After spending some time just watching the ball and then working on just your breathing, now you need to do the ultimate. Here is what you want to do.

Spend five minutes or any period of time you want working on **consciously** seeing the ball and **consciously** feeling your breathing at the same time.

Again, you must keep your mind free of thoughts about hitting the ball into the court or about your stroke or you won't be able to do this. Focus only on the ball spinning and your breathing. Refer to the questions to ask yourself in Drills No. 1 and No. 2.

Drill No. 4: Feeling And Relaxing Your Strokes

This next drill helps you develop the proper amount of relaxation when you hit the ball and works on really grooving your strokes. Actually, this is a bunch of small drills because you will be doing this drill with every stroke and paying attention to different parts of your stroke.

326

Playing Zen-Sational Tennis

If you feel like your strokes are not consistent, then you will want to spend more time with this drill.

Have you heard me say that the follow-through is the most important part of the stroke? When you work on the follow-through, many things happen and some of them you won't even know about. The main component of this drill is doing the Mother of all Tips that I talked about in Lesson No. 20. Hopefully, you have already spent some time doing it and here I give you some additional ideas to work on while you do this Mother of all Tips.

You will want to spend five minutes holding the follow-through until it comes to a complete stop. This means stopping and holding the footwork also. Spend some time combining holding the follow-through with consciously seeing the ball spinning or consciously feeling your breathing. When you do this, it becomes an extremely powerful exercise.

Spend five minutes on each stroke doing the following. Without controlling or judging, **consciously** feel your complete forehand stroke from the time you are in the ready position to the time you recover back to the ready position. Then spend five minutes with the backhand, five minutes with the forehand volley, and five minutes with the backhand volley or any other stroke you want.

While you are consciously feeling the stroke, keep thoughts about hitting the ball in the court out of your head. In case you were wondering, feeling the stroke means that you are able to absolutely describe the exact movement of your arm, wrist and the racquet as you are moving it through the stroke.

For example, do you know if your racquet is going up, down, or straight back when you are taking the racquet back on your forehand?

327

Playing Zen-Sational Tennis

Since so many of my students have difficulty with being accurately aware of their swings, you may want to take some videos of your swing so that you can be really sure you are swinging the way you think you are. When you get comfortable with feeling your stroke, add either seeing the ball spinning or your breathing, but not both.

Here are some specific mini drills that you may want to work on. If you know that you are having difficulty with a stroke, by paying attention to and feeling the different parts of the stroke it will help a lot.

If you have not done these awareness exercises, then it will be very helpful in improving your strokes. Even if you don't know how to fix a particular stroke, it won't matter. By paying attention and feeling your strokes, changes happen for the better even if you are not aware of any changes.

Mini Drill No. 1: Spend some time **consciously** feeling the direction the arm and racquet travels on the backswing from the ready position?

Mini Drill No. 2: Spend some time **consciously** feeling the direction the arm and racquet travels as the racquet starts forward?

Mini Drill No. 3: Spend some time **consciously** feeling the direction the arm and racquet travels as the racquet goes forward and makes contact with the ball?

Mini Drill No. 4: Spend some time **consciously** feeling the path of the arm and racquet after the racquet makes contact with the ball?

Mini Drill No. 5: Spend some time **consciously** feeling and knowing exactly where your follow-through ends? Remember that the follow-through is the most important part of the swing.

The key to doing these drills is to absolutely know what is going on with your stroke during these specific parts of the stroke. In order to do this, you must be letting go of where your ball goes and even trying to make your stroke "right." Your only job is to just feel what the arm and racquet are doing.

When you get really good at this drill, you can begin to feel the entire stroke all at once.

Drill No. 5: A Consistency Drill

After you are comfortable focusing on the ball and feeling your breathing, you are ready to work on maximizing the number of balls going into the court. So, how do you make the ball go into the court over and over again? You should know the answer to this by now. Did you say just focus on the ball, focus on your breathing, and keeping your body relaxed? Very good. You get an A.

Using the drills explained previously and spending as much time as needed on each drill, do the following:

Every time you miss the ball, take the time to take a practice stroke as you visualize or talk to yourself about exactly where you wanted the ball to go. If your stroke doesn't feel right, take a practice stroke without the ball and make it more relaxed so that it is more relaxed the next time you hit the ball. If after re-visualizing and/or talking to yourself your balls don't get more consistent, then you are too tight somewhere in your body and you must relax more. Start with relaxing your grip and/or your wrist to the extreme.

See if you can hit 10 balls in a row. Then see if you can hit 15, then 20 in a row. Doing this will help you discover what state of mind you need to be in to hit consistently. It will also help you learn to stay focused for longer and longer periods of time.

After working on hitting 10 or more in a row, play a game of up to five points as I explained in Lesson No. 4. Look to see how, if at all, your focus and concentration are affected.

If your shots change once you start the game of five, then you know that you have some more letting go to do. Also pay attention to the way you hit the ball. Did it change? Do you all of a sudden hit the ball easier so that you don't miss it? Ideally, you should be hitting the ball the same as you did before the game of five starts. So, if you aren't hitting the same, you need to "just do it," to use a popular saying.

This game of five that you do when hitting forehands cross-court, backhands cross-court and down the line shots are really consistency drills. When you hit to only one place, you will not be able to really hurt your drill partner as you can't make them run and likewise, they can't make you run, so it is the person who can hit the most number of balls in the court that is going to win.

If you have trouble focusing or you find that you are missing shots you were making before playing the points, ask yourself these questions:

- Am I trying to win? If yes, you must know by now that trying doesn't work. Only seeing the ball, keeping your focus on the contact point for a short time, breathing, and relaxing properly does. Remember: if you play better than your opponent, winning will take care of itself. Your job is to find what state of mind you need to be in to maximize the consistency of your play.

- Am I trying to stroke the ball correctly? Am I thinking about my stroke? If you answer yes, you will need to let go and trust that your body will do this for you.

- Am I making **consciously** seeing the ball spinning, keeping my focus on the contact point for a short time, and **consciously** feeling my breathing the most important thing in my life when I am playing? Here is one of the little tricks that might help you stay focused. If I told you that every time you see the ball correctly and breathe correctly when you hit the ball that I would pay you $1,000,000, do you think you would make doing these things more important? Most people would say yes. I think the only person who would maybe say no would be Bill Gates. Even if you do make it important, you don't need to try hard to do it. You just need to do it.

Drill No. 6: Running Drill No. 1

Now do drills No. 1 through 4 again, but this time you will hit your balls to alternate sides while your practice partner will hit to one side only. When the person running gets tired, switch.

Playing Zen-Sational Tennis

The purpose of this drill is two-fold. The one hitting from side to side gets to practice seeing the ball and breathing while hitting a change-of-direction ball. The runner gets to practice seeing the ball and feeling his or her breathing while running and hitting. You may find that your focus will not be as good as when you were just standing and hitting so here are some variations if you are having problems with your focus.

- Spend some time just **consciously** watching the ball spinning, keeping your focus on the contact point for a short time and forget about your breathing.
- Spend some time just **consciously** feeling your breathing and forget about focusing on the ball.
- Combine seeing the ball and breathing.
- Pretend that someone will pay you $1 million for every time you can see the ball and breathe properly. That is just about how important you must make your focus.

When you are doing this running drill, again awareness is very important and again you will need to have these following questions handy so that you can ask yourself these awareness questions:

- On the balls that I have to run hard for, am I still able to see the ball spinning to the blur of my racquet and keep my focus on the contact point for a short period of time? If your answer is no, you need to let go more and to make this more important.
- Am I still able to feel my breathing and do a long exhale just before and through hitting the ball? If your answer is no, you need to let go more and again make this more important.

- When I am aiming my ball, am I trying so hard to aim that I have not watched the ball and kept my focus on the contact point for a short period of time? If your answer is yes, you need to learn to let go more and let your body do the aiming while you are busy seeing the ball.

- Was I able to keep my awareness on my breathing while I was thinking about aiming? If your answer is no, you need to learn to let go more and let your body do the aiming while you are busy breathing.

- Was I able to keep my grip very relaxed when I had to run hard for a ball?

- Was I able to make a full follow-through even though I had to run for the ball?

Drill No. 7: Running Drill No. 2

Do Drill No. 6 again, but this time one of you will hit your balls anywhere while the other will hit to one side only. When the person running gets tired, switch.

The purpose of this drill is again twofold. The one hitting anywhere gets to practice seeing the ball spinning, keeping their focus on the contact point for a short time, and breathing while deciding where to hit the ball for maximum effect. The runner gets to practice seeing the ball spinning, keeping their focus on the contact point for a short time, and feeling his or her breathing while running. Don't forget about keeping a very relaxed grip and making a full follow-through, **NO MATTER WHAT.**

Playing Zen-Sational Tennis

The real value of this drill is to find out what state of mind you must be in to choose where you want the ball to go. You do it by making sure that the thought of where you want the ball to go is just a **knowing**, and it must follow in fourth place behind seeing the ball spinning, keeping your focus on the contact point for a short time, and being aware of your exhaling. And when you know where you want the ball to go, let your Other-Than-Conscious Mind direct your body.

Here are the awareness questions to ask yourself to make sure you are getting the most from this drill:

- When I miss the ball, am I really seeing the ball properly or am I putting aiming the ball first?
- When I miss the ball, am I feeling my breathing first, or am I putting aiming the ball first?
- When I miss the ball, am I keeping my focus on the contact point for a short time, or am I putting aiming the ball first?
- Am I trying too hard to hit the ball to where I want it to go? If your answer is yes, you need to relax more, starting with your grip, wrist, and arm at the shoulder when you make contact with the ball.
- On the balls that I have to run hard for, am I still seeing the ball spinning to my racquet keeping my focus on the contact point for a short period of time?
- Am I still feeling my breathing and exhaling just before hitting the ball on the hard running balls?

Drill No. 8: Volley Drills

You can use all of the above drills to practice volleys as well, while keeping the following ideas in mind.

In my opinion, breathing properly and keeping a relaxed grip are the most important things to do while volleying. If you are serving and volleying, see if you can feel your breathing as you are moving to the net. If you are just standing at the net, practice feeling your breathing first using a relaxed exhale before and continuing after you hit the ball and at the same time, but secondarily, work on seeing the ball. Then see if you can hit your volleys with a very relaxed grip.

Also, work on keeping your focus on the contact point for a short period of time. When you volley, you will have to make this focus on the contact point a lot shorter than when you are hitting a groundstroke.

Obviously, if the other player is at net and you are hitting groundstrokes, again you will have to keep your focus on the contact point just as short. But, you can do it and it works bigtime.

In the next set of drills, I will give you some terrific drills for the return of serve, the lob and overhead. Also, I will give you one drill that you absolutely will want to do as it not only is a good drill to do, but you may want to use it in a match. In case you are wondering which drill that is, it is what I call the Second Generation Bounce-Hit drill.

Drills for Specific Shots and Other Little Games

Drill No. 9: The Return Of Serve Drill

I am willing to bet that you don't spend much time practicing your return of serve. Am I right? I also wonder, why not? The return of serve is so important because breaking serve is very hard and is impossible if you don't get the serve back. And, just getting it back is not always enough. You need to get it back so that you have a chance to win the point.

So, when you are playing a willing opponent who is a friend, here are two ways to practice your return of serve. You can only do this in practice matches and not in tournaments. You can even do it in doubles if all four of you agree to practice it.

Here is the first way.

The main idea is that the point cannot start until the return of serve has been hit into the court.

If you missed the return on your backhand side, your practice partner must then serve all serves to your backhand until you get it back into the court. If you missed the return on the first serve, then your practice partner will serve another first serve. If that first serve is missed, then your practice partner will serve a second serve, but it still must be to the backhand side until you get it back.

Playing Zen-Sational Tennis

If your practice partner misses the second serve, he or she will keep serving second serves until the ball is in play. This means that he or she cannot double fault. This way you get to practice your backhand return until you get it right.

If your practice partner serves an ace, then the challenge for him or her is to hit another ace. If you miss the return on the first serve, then the challenge for the server is to hit two first serves in a row. If the server double faults, he or she will have a chance to practice a second serve. That way the server gets to practice also.

This drill will allow you to do the return of serve over and over without worrying about losing the point. It also takes the advantage away from the server, as the server doesn't get a free point just because he or she hit a good serve. It is a terrific way to work on one of the most important shots in tennis.

Here is another way.

This time it is a way to practice the return of serve every time you are warming up in a non-tournament match. In case it sounds familiar, it is the same way that I have already explained in Lesson No. 63.

If you warm up your serve the way most players do when you are playing a practice match, you most likely will serve three balls, which your practice partner catches and then he or she will serve them back to you which you then catch. You do this back and forth until you feel that you have had enough serves.

If you are playing with a friend and it is not a tournament match, here is what you can do instead.

Playing Zen-Sational Tennis

One of you will choose to warm up the serve. The other player will practice their return of serve. You will do this until the person serving has had enough serves. Then you change and the other person serves while you practice returning.

When you are practicing returning, you are to practice hitting your return as if you were actually playing. You are not to hit the ball just back to the server.

When I started to do this, I noticed that I would serve more balls than when I warmed up the other way. I could really work on my focus so much better. It was like I was out hitting a mini bucket of balls. It also really helped my return of serve from the moment the game started.

This way you will be able to practice your return even if it is only for a short period of time. After warming up your serve and return of

serve this way, you will be surprised how much better your serve and returns will be in a very short time.

You will also have a benchmark when you begin to play the points. You can ask yourself, "Am I returning serve as well, now that we are keeping score or am I tensing up and trying too hard to hit the serve back?"

Drill No. 10: The Lob And Overhead Drill

Here is a terrific way to practice both the lob and overhead. You can also do this one every time you warm up in a practice match if you want to take just a little more time warming up and if you have a willing partner who will do this drill with you.

Here is what you do.

Hit the first ball to make your hitting partner hit a volley, then hit a lob on the return of that shot. When you hit your lob, do not try to just feed it to him or her. Go for the perfect lob cross-court. If your hitting partner hits an overhead back to you, hit your hitting partner another volley and not a lob. Then hit another lob if he or she returns your shot.

Your hitting partner should be hitting overheads as hard as possible and for winners. This way you both can warm up practicing what you would do in an actual match. See Lesson No. 65 again if you have forgotten why you want to hit your overhead as hard as you can.

Here is my reasoning. Using this drill, you can practice your lob every time you warm up, assuming you are playing with someone who wants to warm up this way. By only hitting a lob from a volley, you will be practicing hitting a lob like you would in a match. When you hit your lob, make sure your breathing is relaxed, and you see the ball spinning all the way to the blur of your racquet, still keeping your focus on the contact point. Since I consider the lob to be a "touch shot," relaxing more as you hit the ball is a must.

If you are doing this drill to just practice your lob and overheads, try playing a game of up to five to add a little pressure like you would have in a match. Check to see if you still hit your lobs and overheads the same as you were before you kept score.

Drill No. 11: The Second Generation Bounce-Hit Game

Caution: This Exercise may be hazardous to your Conscious Mind.

This is the most advanced of the "letting go" exercises. Use at your own risk. When you do this exercise, your Conscious Mind will not be able to try, think, judge or do.

At least, not very much.

You should be familiar with the normal Bounce-Hit exercise, as I talked about in Lesson No. 7 on Seeing the Ball. If you are not already familiar with this Bounce-Hit drill, this second Generation Bounce-Hit drill may not make complete sense to you. If you haven't worked with the Bounce-Hit exercise yet you may just want to do the original one first in practice until it is familiar before trying to do this advanced one.

Many years ago, when I learned from Tim Gallwey about the Bounce-Hit exercise for seeing the ball, I used it when I was rallying or practicing. However, when I used it during a game, I found I couldn't do it. I then proceeded to give it up and forgot about doing it in a match for all these years.

I had been struggling with my Conscious Mind for a while because it kept interfering with my game. It wanted to get involved with hitting the ball in the court. I had visualized letting go many times. I had reprogrammed letting go over and over again and still my Conscious Mind just kept interfering. When I say interfering, it means that I was choking.

Playing Zen-Sational Tennis

So, over the few months that I was finding myself choking, I was searching for ways to keep my focus on the ball and my breathing for the entire point, especially when the point and the match got tight. I was really good at seeing the ball and breathing during a match, except when it came to the "crunch" time when all I had to do was hit the ball in to win the point. I would then try too hard to hit the ball how and where I wanted to and ended up missing the ball.

As it happens, when I work on a problem, the answer comes. This time it took months. For some reason, I thought about and started to do the Bounce-Hit during my practice. The thought came to me that I should try it when I played a match, as I had not done it for years and years. I wanted to see if I could do it now that I was so good at seeing the ball and breathing. I felt that I was now sufficiently "mentally developed," that I would be able to actually do it right.

It was amazing. Not only was I able to do it – even though it was not perfect at first –but I found I did not miss the balls I was missing before. When I played three days later, I did the Bounce-Hit method when I served and volleyed. I found that for the first time in my tennis life, I did not panic on a hard half-volley and my other volleys were so much more relaxed. I still missed some balls, but they were ones that I was still too tight on.

But, here are the "kickers" I discovered while practicing this exercise and why I call it the "second generation."

When you say the word "hit" it is a hard sound. I noticed that when I was saying it, my voice was at a higher octave than normal and it was a tense sound. I began to soften the saying of "hit" and it made a lot of difference.

Playing Zen-Sational Tennis

I also noticed that I was doing the same thing when my opponent was hitting the ball, especially when he was serving and when I was serving. Again I began to soften the word "hit" when my opponent was hitting the ball as well as on my serve. I saw a big difference in the way I felt and how well I hit. Lo and behold, my Conscious Mind could not get control of my body. At least not very easily.

By the way, I would say the Bounce-Hit out loud, but very softly so only I could hear myself saying it. You would not be able to hear me say it from the other side but you could hear me say it if you were standing close to me. I suggest doing this as it helps you be aware of how you are saying the Bounce-Hit and whether or not you are relaxed when you say it.

Here is the other "kicker." At the same time as I was saying "Bounce-Hit ," I started to **consciously** see the ball to my racquet

like I normally would do when not doing the Bounce-Hit and that added the icing on the cake.

To sum up, make sure that you say the word "hit" softly with a very relaxed voice as the ball travels to both sides. This, of course, includes when you serve and when your opponent serves. At the same time you are doing this Bounce-Hit exercise, **consciously** see the ball all the way until you say "hit." Make sure you are still keeping your focus on the contact point for a short time and keeping a relaxed grip. And, again, see the ball and say "Bounce-Hit" as the ball is going to the other side of the net.

If you can't do this very well at first, all it means is that you have some more "letting go" to do. You may need to work on what I call the "foundational place" of the Mental Game, which is truly letting go of everything. I talked about this in Lesson No. 77. This means

342

letting go of hitting the ball into the court, letting go of any strategy, letting go of aiming, and letting go of trying to do anything else that you may be thinking of when you are playing. Thinking about these things is your Conscious Mind getting involved. Once you get to this place, you will find doing the Bounce-Hit exercise, seeing the ball and breathing much easier.

And, the dirty little secret is that this is the place you are searching for. This is where you need to be when you play. It is the ultimate place to be so that you play your very best every time you play.

Don't believe me on how amazing this second generation Bounce-Hit is. Do it and see for yourself.

Drill No. 12: The Spinning Game

Another game to play is to say out loud or to yourself what direction the ball is spinning. When you hit the ball, say what direction it is spinning as it is going over the net and again when the ball is coming back toward you. Don't forget to **consciously** see the spin after the bounce. And you know what direction that is, right? If you don't then you have not done your homework in Lesson No. 7.

Drill No. 13: The Trajectory Drill

Here is another game to play. Watch the trajectory of the ball as it comes to you and as it goes back to the other side. Ask yourself whether the ball is still rising, has reached its peak, or is dropping when you hit it. Do the same when your opponent is hitting the ball. You can also look to see how high over the net the ball goes and see if it has reached its peak before, as, or after the ball crosses the net.

This drill can be an eye opener when you do this when you are volleying. Did you know that probably 99% of balls you hit when you volley are dropping before you hit it? The other 1% is at the peak. If you hit a ball that is rising, then you need to know that the ball would be going long if you didn't hit it. So, let all rising balls go so you will win the point.

Drill No. 14: The Listening Game

If you have done the Bounce-Hit game that I explained in Drill No. 11, then this concept of listening is very similar except that you are hearing the ball instead of saying "bounce" or "hit." Of course, you will want to see the ball at the same time.

Just hear the ball bounce on the ground and hear the sound that the ball makes when it makes contact with the racquet. Hear these sounds on both sides of the court. Try this in a practice game situation and see what happens.

Two Fun Quizzes If You Are Feeling Smart

A Little Quiz

Take this quiz (if you are feeling a little smart).

If you are a coach and want to test your students, print the test without the answers and give the test. Otherwise, have someone ask you the questions and see how much you know.

1. What is the most important part of the stroke?
2. How do you know if you are executing the stroke properly?
3. What is a good way to practice the forehand and backhand?
4. What should you do when you start the rally but you are not playing a match?
5. If you find you are not stroking a particular stroke properly, how can you fix it?
6. When you are practicing your strokes, what should you refrain from doing?
7. If you want the ball to go into the court, what should you refrain from doing?
8. If you want the ball to go into the court, what should you be doing?
9. When you miss a ball, how can you practice hitting it into the court using a perfect stroke without actually hitting more balls?
10. When you are serving, where should your front foot be placed?

11. When you are serving, how can you practice your toss?
12. Where do you want to aim most of your serves and why?
13. What is the most important strategy to use when you are playing a match, if you want to win?
14. How do you win?
15. Where do you want to aim most of your shots and why?
16. What is important to know about your grip, wrist, and arm?
17. How can you find out if your grip, wrist, or arm is too tight?
18. How do you make sure you are using the correct grip?
19. Are you checking once in a while to make sure that the "trigger finger" is spread out away from the other fingers? How do you do this?
20. What is a good way to warm up your serve and practice your swing at the same time?
21. Where do you want your balls to go when hitting forehands and backhands?
22. How do you maximize your performance?
23. How can you practice your tennis when you are off the court or cannot play?

Answers to the Little Quiz

1. **What is the most important part of the stroke?** The follow-through

2. **How do you know if you are executing the stroke properly?** With body awareness. Feel your arm stroking the ball.

3. **What is a good way to practice the forehand and backhand?** Hold your follow-through until you see the ball bounce. If the follow-through is not correct, then relax and fix it before you recover.

4. **What should you do when you start the rally but you are not playing a match?** Take a perfect stroke every time you start the ball. Make sure to start some rallies with a backhand.

5. **If you find you are not stroking a particular stroke properly, how can you fix it?** Take a practice stroke without the ball. Visualize a perfect stroke. Hold the follow-through and fix it before you recover.

6. **When you are practicing your strokes, what should you refrain from doing?** You should refrain from thinking about where the ball is going.

7. **If you want the ball to go into the court, what should you refrain from doing?** You should refrain from thinking about your strokes.

8. **If you want the ball to go into the court, what should you be doing?** You should be watching the ball, breathing, relaxing the grip, and making a full follow-through.

9. **When you miss a ball, how can you practice hitting it into the court using a perfect stroke without actually hitting more balls?** Visualize or talk to yourself about exactly how you would like the ball to go, with a perfect stroke.

10. **On the serve, where should your front foot be placed?** Two to six inches behind the baseline.

11. **When you are serving, how can you practice your toss?** By tossing the ball into the air, keeping your arm up in the air, and seeing if the ball falls into your hand.

12. **Where do you want to aim most of your serves and why?** To the backhand, because that is usually your opponent's weaker side.

13. **What is the most important strategy to use when you are playing a match if you want to win?** Keeping the ball in play by hitting it easy, aiming three to ten feet over the net and right down the middle.

14. **How do you win?** If you maximize your performance, and play better than your opponent, winning will take care of itself. Maximizing your performance is a better goal than worrying about beating your opponent.

15. **Where do you want to aim most of your shots and why?** If you are a beginner, you should hit the ball three to six feet over the net, right down the middle. As you get better, hit your balls to the backhand of your opponent.

16. **What is important to know about your grip, wrist, and arm?** That they must be relaxed.

17. **How can you find out if your grip, wrist, or arm is too tight?** By paying attention to or feeling your grip, wrist, or arm as you hit the ball.

18. **How do you make sure you are using the correct grip?** By paying attention to, or feeling, all five fingers on the racquet.

19. **Are you checking once in a while to make sure that the trigger finger is spread out away from the other fingers?** How do you do this? By paying attention to your trigger finger as you hit the ball.

20. **What is a good way to warm up your serve and practice your swing at the same time?** Take a series of continuous swings, making sure you are loose, allowing the arm to bend completely behind your back, and making sure that your follow-through is on the left side (if you are right-handed).

21. **Where do you want your balls to go when hitting forehands and backhands?** If you are a beginner, you should hit the ball three to ten feet over the net, right down the middle. As you get better, hit your balls to the backhand of your opponent.

22. **How do you maximize your performance?** See My Mental Game Core Principles.

23. **How can you practice your tennis when you are off the court or cannot play?** By practicing mentally using visualization, talking to yourself, or fantasizing about playing perfect tennis.

A Big Quiz

Take this big quiz (if you are feeling really smart).

If you are a coach and want to test your kids, print the test without the answers and give the test. Otherwise, have someone ask you the questions and see how much you know.

Once you think you are ready, here is a quiz to check if you are really able to see the ball.

1. What direction is the ball spinning after the bounce?

2. What are the patterns of the spin (how your ball spins most of the time) on your forehand?

3. What are the patterns of the spin (how your ball spins most of the time) on your backhand?

4. Can you tell yourself on any given ball whether it is spinning fast, slow, or medium?

5. Have you ever seen the ball traveling through the air when it had no spin?

6. Have you ever really seen the ball spinning after the bounce on the return of serve? Is it any different from the answer to question No. 1?

7. Have you ever spent a great deal of time seeing the ball and breathing for more than one point?

Answers to the Big Quiz

1. **What direction is the ball spinning after the bounce?** The ball always has top spin on it after the bounce. The only exception is when someone serves a ball fairly hard with side spin. Then the ball will begin to have top spin but will still be spinning sideways. Don't take my word for it. See the ball for yourself.

2. **What are the patterns of the spin (how your ball spins most of the time) on your backhand?** There is no way that I can answer this question. However, do you ever see side spin or under spin, or do you just assume you know what kind of spin you are putting on the ball? The key to this answer is that you must see for yourself.

3. **What are the patterns of the spin (how your ball spins most of the time) on your backhand?** See No. 2 for this answer, as it is the same.

4. **Can you tell yourself on any given ball whether it is spinning fast, slow, or medium?** Again, the key to this answer is whether you ever notice the difference in how fast the ball is spinning and with enough awareness to tell someone else about what you have observed.

5. **Have you ever seen the ball traveling through the air when it had no spin?** The thing about a ball that has no spin is that it should stand out like a sore thumb because it is so rare. If you can't answer yes to this question, then you need to become more aware of the ball.

6. **Have you ever really seen the ball spinning after the bounce on the return of serve?** Is it any different from the answer to questions No. 1? See the answer to No. 1.

7. **Have you ever spent a great deal of time seeing the ball and breathing for more than one point?** If you ever can do this, it is the way to getting into a trance state that will allow you to truly play out of your mind.

Made in the USA
San Bernardino, CA
19 October 2013